Three Stoic Classics:

Meditations
by Marcus Aurelius

The Shortness of Life
by Seneca

Selected Discourses
by Epictetus

BENEDICTION CLASSICS

ISBN: 978-1-78943-231-2.
© 2020 Benediction Classics, Oxford.

CONTENTS

MEDITATIONS

by

Marcus Aurelius

The Meditations of Marcus Aurelius

His First Book - Concerning Himself

Wherein Antoninus recordeth, What and of whom, whether Parents, Friends, or Masters; by their good examples, or good advice and counsel, he had learned:

Divided into Numbers or Sections.

ANTONINUS Book vi. Num. xlviii. Whensoever thou wilt rejoice thyself, think and meditate upon those good parts and especial gifts, which thou hast observed in any of them that live with thee:

as industry in one, in another modesty, in another bountifulness, in another some other thing. For nothing can so much rejoice thee, as the resemblances and parallels of several virtues, eminent in the dispositions of them that live with thee, especially when all at once, as it were, they represent themselves unto thee. See therefore, that thou have them always in a readiness.

The First Book

I. Of my grandfather Verus I have learned to be gentle and meek, and to refrain from all anger and passion. From the fame and memory of him that begot me I have learned both shamefastness and manlike behaviour. Of my mother I have learned to be religious, and bountiful; and to forbear, not only to do, but to intend any evil; to content myself with a spare diet, and to fly all such excess as is incidental to great wealth. Of my great-grandfather, both to frequent public schools and auditories, and to get me good and able teachers at home; and that I ought not to think much, if upon such occasions, I were at excessive charges.

II. Of him that brought me up, not to be fondly addicted to either of the two great factions of the coursers in the circus, called Prasini, and Veneti: nor in the amphitheatre partially to favour any of the gladiators, or fencers, as either the Parmularii, or the Secutores. Moreover, to endure labour; nor to need many things; when I have anything to do, to do it myself rather than by others; not to meddle with many businesses; and not easily to admit of any slander.

III. Of Diognetus, not to busy myself about vain things, and not easily to believe those things, which are commonly spoken, by such as take upon them to work wonders, and by sorcerers, or prestidigitators, and impostors; concerning the power of charms, and their driving out of demons, or evil spirits; and the like. Not to keep quails for the game; nor to be mad after such things. Not to be offended with other men's liberty of speech, and to apply myself unto philosophy. Him also I must thank, that ever I heard first Bacchius, then Tandasis and Marcianus, and that I did write dialogues in my youth; and that I took liking to the philosophers' little couch and skins, and such other things, which by the Grecian discipline are proper to those who profess philosophy.

IV. To Rusticus I am beholding, that I first entered into the conceit that my life wanted some redress and cure. And then, that I did not fall into the ambition of ordinary sophists, either to write tracts concerning the common theorems, or to exhort men unto virtue and the study of philosophy by public orations; as also that I never by way of ostentation did affect to show myself an active able man, for any kind of bodily exercises. And that I gave over the study of rhetoric and poetry, and of elegant neat language. That I did not use to walk about the house in my long robe, nor to do any such things. Moreover I learned of him to write letters without any affectation, or curiosity; such as that was, which by him was written to my mother from Sinuessa: and to be easy and ready to be reconciled, and well pleased again with them that had offended me, as soon as any of them would be content to seek unto me again. To read with diligence; not to rest satisfied with a light and superficial knowledge, nor quickly to assent to things commonly spoken of: whom also I must thank that ever I lighted upon Epictetus his Hypomnemata, or moral commentaries and common-factions: which also he gave me of his own.

V. From Apollonius, true liberty, and unvariable steadfastness, and not to regard anything at all, though never so little, but right and reason: and always, whether in the sharpest pains, or after the loss of a child, or in long diseases, to be still the same man; who also was a present and visible example unto me, that it was possible for the same man to be both vehement and remiss: a man not subject to be vexed, and offended with the incapacity of his scholars and auditors in his lectures and expositions; and a true pattern of a man who of all his good gifts and faculties, least esteemed in himself, that his excellent skill and ability to teach and persuade others the common theorems and maxims of the Stoic philosophy. Of him also I learned how to receive favours and kindnesses (as commonly they are accounted:) from friends, so that I might not become obnoxious unto them, for them, nor more yielding upon occasion, than in right I ought; and yet so that I should not pass them neither, as an unsensible and unthankful man.

VI. Of Sextus, mildness and the pattern of a family governed with paternal affection; and a purpose to live according to nature: to be grave without affectation: to observe carefully the several dispositions of my friends, not to be offended with idiots, nor unseasonably to set upon those that are carried with the vulgar opinions, with the theorems, and tenets of philosophers: his conversation being an example how a man might accommodate himself to all men and companies; so that though his company were sweeter and more pleasing than any flatterer's cogging and fawning; yet was it at the same time most respected and reverenced: who also had a proper happiness and faculty, rationally and methodically to find out, and set in order all necessary determinations and instructions for a man's life. A man without ever the least appearance of anger, or any other passion; able at the same time most exactly to observe the Stoic Apathia, or unpassionateness, and yet to be most tender-hearted: ever of good credit; and yet almost without any noise, or rumour: very learned, and yet making little show.

VII. From Alexander the Grammarian, to be un-reprovable myself, and not reproachfully to reprehend any man for a barbarism, or a solecism, or any false pronunciation, but dextrously by way of answer, or testimony, or confirmation of the same matter (taking no notice of the word) to utter it as it should have been spoken; or by some other such close and indirect admonition, handsomely and civilly to tell him of it.

VIII. Of Fronto, to how much envy and fraud and hypocrisy the state of a tyrannous king is subject unto, and how they who are commonly called Eupatridas , i.e. nobly born, are in some sort incapable, or void of natural affection.

IX. Of Alexander the Platonic, not often nor without great necessity to say, or to write to any man in a letter, 'I am not at leisure'; nor in this manner still to put off those duties, which we owe to our friends and acquaintances (to every one in his kind) under pretence of urgent affairs.

X. Of Catulus, not to contemn any friend's expostulation, though unjust, but to strive to reduce him to his former disposition: freely and heartily to speak well of all my masters upon any occasion, as it is reported of Domitius, and Athenodotus: and to love my children with true affection.

XI. From my brother Severus, to be kind and loving to all them of my house and family; by whom also I came to the knowledge of Thrasea and Helvidius, and Cato, and Dio, and Brutus. He it was also that did put me in the first conceit and desire of an equal commonwealth, administered by justice and equality; and of a kingdom wherein should be regarded nothing more than the good and welfare of the subjects. Of him also, to observe a constant tenor, (not interrupted, with any other cares and distractions,) in the study and esteem of philosophy: to be bountiful and liberal in the largest measure; always to hope the best; and to be confident that my friends love me. In whom I moreover observed open dealing towards those whom he reproved at any time, and that his friends might without all doubt or much observation know what he would, or would not, so open and plain was he.

XII. From Claudius Maximus, in all things to endeavour to have power of myself, and in nothing to be carried about; to be cheerful and courageous in all sudden chances and accidents, as in sicknesses: to love mildness, and moderation, and gravity: and to do my business, whatsoever it be, thoroughly, and without querulousness. Whatsoever he said, all men believed him that as he spake, so he thought, and whatsoever he did, that he did it with a good intent. His manner was, never to wonder at anything; never to be in haste, and yet never slow: nor to be perplexed, or dejected, or at any time unseemly, or excessively to laugh: nor to be angry, or suspicious, but ever ready to do good, and to forgive, and to speak truth; and all this, as one that seemed rather of himself to have been straight and right, than ever to have been rectified or redressed; neither was there any man that ever thought himself undervalued by him, or that could find in his heart, to think himself a better man than he. He would also be very pleasant and gracious.

XIII. In my father, I observed his meekness; his constancy without wavering in those things, which after a due examination and deliberation, he had determined. How free from all vanity he carried himself in matter of honour and dignity, (as they are esteemed:) his laboriousness and assiduity, his readiness to hear any man, that had aught to say tending to any common good: how generally and impartially he would give every man his due; his skill and knowledge, when rigour or extremity, or when remissness or moderation was in season; how he did abstain from all unchaste love of youths; his moderate condescending to other men's occasions as an ordinary man, neither absolutely requiring of his friends, that they should wait upon him at his ordinary meals, nor that they should of necessity accompany him in his journeys; and that whensoever any business upon some necessary occasions was to be put off and omitted before it could be ended, he was ever found when he went about it again, the same man that he was before. His accurate examination of things in consultations, and patient hearing of others. He would not hastily give over the search of the matter, as one easy to be satisfied with sudden notions and apprehensions. His care to preserve his friends; how neither at any time he would carry himself towards them with disdainful neglect, and grow weary of them; nor yet at any time be madly fond of them. His contented mind in all things, his cheerful countenance, his care to foresee things afar off, and to take order for the least, without any noise or clamour. Moreover how all acclamations and flattery were repressed by him: how carefully he observed all things necessary to the government, and kept an account of the common expenses, and how patiently he did abide that he was reprehended by some for this his strict and rigid kind of dealing. How he was neither a superstitious worshipper of the gods, nor an ambitious pleaser of men, or studious of popular applause; but sober in all things, and everywhere observant of that which was fitting; no affecter of novelties: in those things which conduced to his ease and convenience, (plenty whereof his fortune did afford him,) without pride and bragging, yet with all freedom and liberty: so that as he did freely enjoy them without any anxiety or affectation when they were present; so when absent, he found no want of them. Moreover, that he was never commended by any man, as either a learned acute man, or an obsequious officious man, or a fine orator; but as a ripe mature man, a perfect sound man; one that could not endure to be flattered; able to govern both himself and others. Moreover, how much he did honour all true philosophers, without upbraiding those that were not so; his sociableness, his gracious and delightful conversation, but never unto satiety; his care of his body within bounds and measure, not as one that desired to live long, or over-studious of neatness, and elegancy; and yet not as one that did not regard it: so that through his own care and providence, he seldom needed any inward physic, or outward applications: but especially how ingeniously he would yield to any that had obtained any peculiar faculty, as either eloquence, or the knowledge of the laws, or of ancient customs, or the like; and how he concurred with them, in his best care and endeavour that every one of them might in his kind, for that wherein he excelled, be regarded and esteemed: and although he did all things carefully after the ancient customs of his forefathers, yet even of this was he not desirous that men should take notice, that he did imitate ancient customs. Again, how he was not easily moved and tossed up and down, but loved to be constant, both in the same places and businesses; and how after his great fits of headache he would return fresh and vigorous to his wonted affairs. Again, that secrets he neither had many, nor often, and such only as concerned public matters: his discretion and moderation, in exhibiting of the public sights and shows for the pleasure and pastime of the people: in public buildings. congiaries, and the like. In all these things, having a respect unto men only as men, and to the equity of the things themselves, and not unto the glory that might follow. Never wont to use the baths at unseasonable hours; no builder; never curious, or solicitous, either about his meat, or about the workmanship, or colour of his clothes, or about anything that belonged to external beauty. In all his conversation, far from all inhumanity, all boldness, and incivility, all greediness and impetuosity; never doing anything with such earnestness, and intention, that a man could say of him, that he did sweat about it: but contrariwise, all things distinctly, as at leisure; without trouble; orderly, soundly, and agreeably. A man might have applied that to him, which is recorded of Socrates, that he knew how to want, and to enjoy those things, in the want whereof, most men show themselves weak; and in the fruition, intemperate: but to hold out firm and constant, and to keep within the compass of true moderation and sobriety in either estate, is proper to a man, who hath a perfect and invincible soul; such as he showed himself in the sickness of Maximus.

XIV. From the gods I received that I had good grandfathers, and parents, a good sister, good masters, good domestics, loving kinsmen, almost all that I have; and that I never through haste and rashness transgressed against any of them, notwithstanding that my disposition was such, as that such a thing (if occasion had been) might very well have been committed by me, but that it was the mercy of the gods, to prevent such a concurring of matters and occasions, as might make me to incur this blame. That I was not long brought up by the concubine of my father; that I preserved the flower of my youth. That I took not upon me to be a man before my time, but rather put it off longer than I needed. That I lived under the government of my lord and father, who would take away from me all pride and vainglory, and reduce me to that conceit and opinion that it was not impossible for a prince to live in the court without a troop of guards and followers, extraordinary apparel, such and such torches and statues, and other like particulars of state and magnificence; but that a man may reduce and contract himself almost to the state of a private man, and yet for all that not to become the more base and remiss in those public matters and affairs, wherein power and authority is requisite. That I have had such a brother, who by his own example might stir me up to think of myself; and by his respect and love, delight and please me. That I have got ingenuous children, and that they were not born distorted, nor with any other natural deformity. That I was no great proficient in the study of rhetoric and poetry, and of other faculties, which perchance I might have dwelt upon, if I had found myself to go on in them with success. That I did by times prefer those, by whom I was brought up, to such places and dignities, which they seemed unto me most to desire; and that I did not put them off with hope and expectation, that (since that they were yet but young) I would do the same hereafter. That I ever knew Apollonius and Rusticus, and Maximus. That I have had occasion often and effectually to consider and meditate with myself, concerning that life which is according to nature, what the nature and manner of it is: so that as for the gods and such suggestions, helps and inspirations, as might be expected from them, nothing did hinder, but that I might have begun long before to live according to nature; or that even now that I was not yet partaker and in present possession of that life, that I myself (in that I did not observe those inward motions, and suggestions, yea and almost plain and apparent instructions and admonitions of the gods,) was the only cause of it. That my body in such a life, hath been able to hold out so long. That I never had to do with Benedicta and Theodotus, yea and afterwards when I fell into some fits of love, I was soon cured. That having been often displeased with Rusticus, I never did him anything for which afterwards I had occasion to repent. That it being so that my mother was to die young, yet she lived with me all her latter years. That as often as I had a purpose to help and succour any that either were poor, or fallen into some present necessity, I never was answered by my officers that there was not ready money enough to do it; and that I myself never had occasion to require the like succour from any other. That I have such a wife, so obedient, so loving, so ingenuous. That I had choice of fit and able men, to whom I might commit the bringing up of my children. That by dreams I have received help, as for other things, so in particular, how I might stay my casting of blood, and cure my dizziness, as that also that happened to thee in Cajeta, as unto Chryses when he prayed by the seashore. And when I did first apply myself to philosophy, that I did not fall into the hands of some sophists, or spent my time either in reading the manifold volumes of ordinary philosophers, nor in practising myself in the solution of arguments and fallacies, nor dwelt upon the studies of the meteors, and other natural curiosities. All these things without the assistance of the gods, and fortune, could not have been.

XV. In the country of the Quadi at Granua, these. Betimes in the morning say to thyself, This day I shalt have to do with an idle curious man, with an unthankful man, a railer, a crafty, false, or an envious man; an unsociable uncharitable man. All these ill qualities have happened unto them, through ignorance of that which is truly good and truly bad. But I that understand the nature of that which is good, that it only is to be desired, and of that which is bad, that it only is truly odious and shameful: who know moreover, that this transgressor, whosoever he be, is my kinsman, not by the same blood and seed, but by participation of the same reason, and of the same divine particle; How can I either be hurt by any of those, since it is not in their power to make me incur anything that is truly reproachful? or angry, and ill affected towards him, who by nature is so near unto me? for we are all born to be fellow-workers, as the feet, the hands, and the eyelids; as the rows of the upper and under teeth: for such therefore to be in opposition, is against nature; and what is it to chafe at, and to be averse from, but to be in opposition?

XVI. Whatsoever I am, is either flesh, or life, or that which we commonly call the mistress and overruling part of man; reason. Away with thy books, suffer not thy mind any more to be distracted, and carried to and fro; for it will not be; but as even now ready to die, think little of thy flesh: blood, bones, and a skin; a pretty piece of knit and twisted work, consisting of nerves, veins and arteries; think no more of it, than so. And as for thy life, consider what it is; a wind; not one constant wind neither, but every moment of an hour let out, and sucked in again. The third, is thy ruling part; and here consider; Thou art an old man; suffer not that excellent part to be brought in subjection, and to become slavish: suffer it not to be drawn up and down with unreasonable and unsociable lusts and motions, as it were with wires and nerves; suffer it not any more, either to repine at anything now present, or to fear and fly anything to come, which the destiny hath appointed thee.

XVII. Whatsoever proceeds from the gods immediately, that any man will grant totally depends from their divine providence. As for those things that are commonly said to happen by fortune, even those must be conceived to have dependence from nature, or from that first and general connection, and concatenation of all those things, which more apparently by the divine providence are administered and brought to pass. All things flow from thence: and whatsoever it is that is, is both necessary, and conducing to the whole (part of which thou art), and whatsoever it is that is requisite and necessary for the preservation of the general, must of necessity for every particular nature, be good and behoveful. And as for the whole, it is preserved, as by the perpetual mutation and conversion of the simple elements one into another, so also by the mutation, and alteration of things mixed and compounded. Let these things suffice thee; let them be always unto thee, as thy general rules and precepts. As for thy thirst after books, away with it with all speed, that thou die not murmuring and complaining, but truly meek and well satisfied, and from thy heart thankful unto the gods.

The Second Book

I. Remember how long thou hast already put off these things, and how often a certain day and hour as it were, having been set unto thee by the gods, thou hast neglected it. It is high time for thee to understand the true nature both of the world, whereof thou art a part; and of that Lord and Governor of the world, from whom, as a channel from the spring, thou thyself didst flow: and that there is but a certain limit of time appointed unto thee, which if thou shalt not make use of to calm and allay the many distempers of thy soul, it will pass away and thou with it, and never after return.

II. Let it be thy earnest and incessant care as a Roman and a man to perform whatsoever it is that thou art about, with true and unfeigned gravity, natural affection, freedom and justice: and as for all other cares, and imaginations, how thou mayest ease thy mind of them. Which thou shalt do; if thou shalt go about every action as thy last action, free from all vanity, all passionate and wilful aberration from reason, and from all hypocrisy, and self-love, and dislike of those things, which by the fates or appointment of God have happened unto thee. Thou seest that those things, which for a man to hold on in a prosperous course, and to live a divine life, are requisite and necessary, are not many, for the gods will require no more of any man, that shall but keep and observe these things.

III. Do, soul, do; abuse and contemn thyself; yet a while and the time for thee to respect thyself, will be at an end. Every man's happiness depends from himself, but behold thy life is almost at an end, whiles affording thyself no respect, thou dost make thy happiness to consist in the souls, and conceits of other men.

IV. Why should any of these things that happen externally, so much distract thee? Give thyself leisure to learn some good thing, and cease roving and wandering to and fro. Thou must also take heed of another kind of wandering, for they are idle in their actions, who toil and labour in this life, and have no certain scope to which to direct all their motions, and desires.

V. For not observing the state of another man's soul, scarce was ever any man known to be unhappy. Tell whosoever they be that intend not, and guide not by reason and discretion the motions of their own souls, they must of necessity be unhappy.

VI. These things thou must always have in mind: What is the nature of the universe, and what is mine—in particular: This unto that what relation it hath: what kind of part, of what kind of universe it is: And that there is nobody that can hinder thee, but that thou mayest always both do and speak those things which are agreeable to that nature, whereof thou art a part.

VII. Theophrastus, where he compares sin with sin (as after a vulgar sense such things I grant may be compared:) says well and like a philosopher, that those sins are greater which are committed through lust, than those which are committed through anger. For he that is angry seems with a kind of grief and close contraction of himself, to turn away from reason; but he that sins through lust, being overcome by pleasure, doth in his very sin bewray a more impotent, and unmanlike disposition. Well then and like a philosopher doth he say, that he of the two is the more to be condemned, that sins with pleasure, than he that sins with grief. For indeed this latter may seem first to have been wronged, and so in some manner through grief thereof to have been forced to be angry, whereas he who through lust doth commit anything, did of himself merely resolve upon that action.

VIII. Whatsoever thou dost affect, whatsoever thou dost project, so do, and so project all, as one who, for aught thou knowest, may at this very present depart out of this life. And as for death, if there be any gods, it is no grievous thing to leave the society of men. The gods will do thee no hurt, thou mayest be sure. But if it be so that there be no gods, or that they take no care of the world, why should I desire to live in a world void of gods, and of all divine providence? But gods there be certainly, and they take care for the world; and as for those things which be truly evil, as vice and wickedness, such things they have put in a man's own power, that he might avoid them if he would: and had there been anything besides that had been truly bad and evil, they would have had a care of that also, that a man might have avoided it. But why should that be thought to hurt and prejudice a man's life in this world, which cannot any ways make man himself the better, or the worse in his own person? Neither must we think that the nature of the universe did either through ignorance pass these things, or if not as ignorant of them, yet as unable either to prevent, or better to order and dispose them. It cannot be that she through want either of power or skill, should have committed such a thing, so as to suffer all things both good and bad, equally and promiscuously, to happen unto all both good and bad. As for life therefore, and death, honour and dishonour, labour and pleasure, riches and poverty, all these things happen unto men indeed, both good and bad, equally; but as things which of themselves are neither good nor bad; because of themselves, neither shameful nor praiseworthy.

IX. Consider how quickly all things are dissolved and resolved: the bodies and substances themselves, into the matter and substance of the world: and their memories into the general age and time of the world. Consider the nature of all worldly sensible things; of those especially, which either ensnare by pleasure, or for their irksomeness are dreadful, or for their outward lustre and show are in great esteem and request, how vile and contemptible, how base and corruptible, how destitute of all true life and being they are.

X. It is the part of a man endowed with a good understanding faculty, to consider what they themselves are in very deed, from whose bare conceits and voices, honour and credit do proceed: as also what it is to die, and how if a man shall consider this by itself alone, to die, and separate from it in his mind all those things which with it usually represent themselves unto us, he can conceive of it no otherwise, than as of a work of nature, and he that fears any work of nature, is a very child. Now death, it is not only a work of nature, but also conducing to nature.

XI. Consider with thyself how man, and by what part of his, is joined unto God, and how that part of man is affected, when it is said to be diffused. There is nothing more wretched than that soul, which in a kind of circuit compasseth all things, searching (as he saith) even the very depths of the earth; and by all signs and conjectures prying into the very thoughts of other men's souls; and yet of this, is not sensible, that it is sufficient for a man to apply himself wholly, and to confine all his thoughts and cares to the tendance of that spirit which is within him, and truly and really to serve him. His service doth consist in this, that a man keep himself pure from all violent passion and evil affection, from all rashness and vanity, and from all manner of discontent, either in regard of the gods or men. For indeed whatsoever proceeds from the gods, deserves respect for their worth and excellency; and whatsoever proceeds from men, as they are our kinsmen, should by us be entertained, with love, always; sometimes, as proceeding from their ignorance, of that which is truly good and bad, (a blindness no less, than that by which we are not able to discern between white and black:) with a kind of pity and compassion also.

XII. If thou shouldst live three thousand, or as many as ten thousands of years, yet remember this, that man can part with no life properly, save with that little part of life, which he now lives: and that which he lives, is no other, than that which at every instant he parts with. That then which is longest of duration, and that which is shortest, come both to one effect. For although in regard of that which is already past there may be some inequality, yet that time which is now present and in being, is equal unto all men. And that being it which we part with whensoever we die, it doth manifestly appear, that it can be but a moment of time, that we then part with. For as for that which is either past or to come, a man cannot be said properly to part with it. For how should a man part with that which he hath not? These two things therefore thou must remember. First, that all things in the world from all eternity, by a perpetual revolution of the same times and things ever continued and renewed, are of one kind and nature; so that whether for a hundred or two hundred years only, or for an infinite space of time, a man see those things which are still the same, it can be no matter of great moment. And secondly, that that life which any the longest liver, or the shortest liver parts with, is for length and duration the very same, for that only which is present, is that, which either of them can lose, as being that only which they have; for that which he hath not, no man can truly be said to lose.

XIII. Remember that all is but opinion and conceit, for those things are plain and apparent, which were spoken unto Monimus the Cynic; and as plain and apparent is the use that may be made of those things, if that which is true and serious in them, be received as well as that which is sweet and pleasing.

XIV. A man's soul doth wrong and disrespect itself first and especially, when as much as in itself lies it becomes an aposteme, and as it were an excrescency of the world, for to be grieved and displeased with anything that happens in the world, is direct apostacy from the nature of the universe; part of which, all particular natures of the world, are. Secondly, when she either is averse from any man, or led by contrary desires or affections, tending to his hurt and prejudice; such as are the souls of them that are angry. Thirdly, when she is overcome by any pleasure or pain. Fourthly, when she doth dissemble, and covertly and falsely either doth or saith anything. Fifthly, when she doth either affect or endeavour anything to no certain end, but rashly and without due ratiocination and consideration, how consequent or inconsequent it is to the common end. For even the least things ought not to be done, without relation unto the end; and the end of the reasonable creatures is, to follow and obey him, who is the reason as it were, and the law of this great city, and ancient commonwealth.

XV. The time of a man's life is as a point; the substance of it ever flowing, the sense obscure; and the whole composition of the body tending to corruption. His soul is restless, fortune uncertain, and fame doubtful; to be brief, as a stream so are all things belonging to the body; as a dream, or as a smoke, so are all that belong unto the soul. Our life is a warfare, and a mere pilgrimage. Fame after life is no better than oblivion. What is it then that will adhere and follow? Only one thing, philosophy. And philosophy doth consist in this, for a man to preserve that spirit which is within him, from all manner of contumelies and injuries, and above all pains or pleasures; never to do anything either rashly, or feignedly, or hypocritically: wholly to depend from himself and his own proper actions: all things that happen unto him to embrace contentedly, as coming from Him from whom he himself also came; and above all things, with all meekness and a calm cheerfulness, to expect death, as being nothing else but the resolution of those elements, of which every creature is composed. And if the elements themselves suffer nothing by this their perpetual conversion of one into another, that dissolution, and alteration, which is so common unto all, why should it be feared by any? Is not this according to nature? But nothing that is according to nature can be evil, whilst I was at Carnuntzim.

The Third Book

I. A man must not only consider how daily his life wasteth and decreaseth, but this also, that if he live long, he cannot be certain, whether his understanding shall continue so able and sufficient, for either discreet consideration, in matter of businesses; or for contemplation: it being the thing, whereon true knowledge of things both divine and human, doth depend. For if once he shall begin to dote, his respiration, nutrition, his imaginative, and appetitive, and other natural faculties, may still continue the same: he shall find no want of them. But how to make that right use of himself that he should, how to observe exactly in all things that which is right and just, how to redress and rectify all wrong, or sudden apprehensions and imaginations, and even of this particular, whether he should live any longer or no, to consider duly; for all such things, wherein the best strength and vigour of the mind is most requisite; his power and ability will be past and gone. Thou must hasten therefore; not only because thou art every day nearer unto death than other, but also because that intellective faculty in thee, whereby thou art enabled to know the true nature of things, and to order all thy actions by that knowledge, doth daily waste and decay: or, may fail thee before thou die.

II. This also thou must observe, that whatsoever it is that naturally doth happen to things natural, hath somewhat in itself that is pleasing and delightful: as a great loaf when it is baked, some parts of it cleave as it were, and part asunder, and make the crust of it rugged and unequal, and yet those parts of it, though in some sort it be against the art and intention of baking itself, that they are thus cleft and parted, which should have been and were first made all even and uniform, they become it well nevertheless, and have a certain peculiar property, to stir the appetite. So figs are accounted fairest and ripest then, when they begin to shrink, and wither as it were. So ripe olives, when they are next to putrefaction, then are they in their proper beauty. The hanging down of grapes—the brow of a lion, the froth of a foaming wild boar, and many other like things, though by themselves considered, they are far from any beauty, yet because they happen naturally, they both are comely, and delightful; so that if a man shall with a profound mind and apprehension, consider all things in the world, even among all those things which are but mere accessories and natural appendices as it were, there will scarce appear anything unto him, wherein he will not find matter of pleasure and delight. So will he behold with as much pleasure the true rictus of wild beasts, as those which by skilful painters and other artificers are imitated. So will he be able to perceive the proper ripeness and beauty of old age, whether in man or woman: and whatsoever else it is that is beautiful and alluring in whatsoever is, with chaste and continent eyes he will soon find out and discern. Those and many other things will he discern, not credible unto every one, but unto them only who are truly and familiarly acquainted, both with nature itself, and all natural things.

III. Hippocrates having cured many sicknesses, fell sick himself and died. The Chaldeans and Astrologians having foretold the deaths of divers, were afterwards themselves surprised by the fates. Alexander and Pompeius, and Caius Caesar, having destroyed so many towns, and cut off in the field so many thousands both of horse and foot, yet they themselves at last were fain to part with their own lives. Heraclitus having written so many natural tracts concerning the last and general conflagration of the world, died afterwards all filled with water within, and all bedaubed with dirt and dung without. Lice killed Democritus; and Socrates, another sort of vermin, wicked ungodly men. How then stands the case? Thou hast taken ship, thou hast sailed, thou art come to land, go out, if to another life, there also shalt thou find gods, who are everywhere. If all life and sense shall cease, then shalt thou cease also to be subject to either pains or pleasures; and to serve and tend this vile cottage; so much the viler, by how much that which ministers unto it doth excel; the one being a rational substance, and a spirit, the other nothing but earth and blood.

IV. Spend not the remnant of thy days in thoughts and fancies concerning other men, when it is not in relation to some common good, when by it thou art hindered from some other better work. That is, spend not thy time in thinking, what such a man doth, and to what end: what he saith, and what he thinks, and what he is about, and such other things or curiosities, which make a man to rove and wander from the care and observation of that part of himself, which is rational, and overruling. See therefore in the whole series and connection of thy thoughts, that thou be careful to prevent whatsoever is idle and impertinent: but especially, whatsoever is curious and malicious: and thou must use thyself to think only of such things, of which if a man upon a sudden should ask thee, what it is that thou art now thinking, thou mayest answer This, and That, freely and boldly, that so by thy thoughts it may presently appear that in all thee is sincere, and peaceable; as becometh one that is made for society, and regards not pleasures, nor gives way to any voluptuous imaginations at all: free from all contentiousness, envy, and suspicion, and from whatsoever else thou wouldest blush to confess thy thoughts were set upon. He that is such, is he surely that doth not put off to lay hold on that which is best indeed, a very priest and minister of the gods, well acquainted and in good correspondence with him especially that is seated and placed within himself, as in a temple and sacrary: to whom also he keeps and preserves himself unspotted by pleasure, undaunted by pain; free from any manner of wrong, or contumely, by himself offered unto himself: not capable of any evil from others: a wrestler of the best sort, and for the highest prize, that he may not be cast down by any passion or affection of his own; deeply dyed and drenched in righteousness, embracing and accepting with his whole heart whatsoever either happeneth or is allotted unto him. One who not often, nor without some great necessity tending to some public good, mindeth what any other, either speaks, or doth, or purposeth: for those things only that are in his own power, or that are truly his own, are the objects of his employments, and his thoughts are ever taken up with those things, which of the whole universe are by the fates or Providence destinated and appropriated unto himself. Those things that are his own, and in his own power, he himself takes order, for that they be good: and as for those that happen unto him, he believes them to be so. For that lot and portion which is assigned to every one, as it is unavoidable and necessary, so is it always profitable. He remembers besides that whatsoever partakes of reason, is akin unto him, and that to care for all men generally, is agreeing to the nature of a man: but as for honour and praise, that they ought not generally to be admitted and accepted of from all, but from such only, who live according to nature. As for them that do not, what manner of men they be at home, or abroad; day or night, how conditioned themselves with what manner of conditions, or with men of what conditions they moil and pass away the time together, he knoweth, and remembers right well, he therefore regards not such praise and approbation, as proceeding from them, who cannot like and approve themselves.

V. Do nothing against thy will, nor contrary to the community, nor without due examination, nor with reluctancy. Affect not to set out thy thoughts with curious neat language. Be neither a great talker, nor a great undertaker. Moreover, let thy God that is in thee to rule over thee, find by thee, that he hath to do with a man; an aged man; a sociable man; a Roman; a prince; one that hath ordered his life, as one that expecteth, as it were, nothing but the sound of the trumpet, sounding a retreat to depart out of this life with all expedition. One who for his word or actions neither needs an oath, nor any man to be a witness.

VI. To be cheerful, and to stand in no need, either of other men's help or attendance, or of that rest and tranquillity, which thou must be beholding to others for. Rather like one that is straight of himself, or hath ever been straight, than one that hath been rectified.

VII. If thou shalt find anything in this mortal life better than righteous- ness, than truth, temperance, fortitude, and in general better than a mind contented both with those things which according to right and reason she doth, and in those, which without her will and knowledge happen unto thee by the providence; if I say, thou canst find out anything better than this, apply thyself unto it with thy whole heart, and that which is best wheresoever thou dost find it, enjoy freely. But if nothing thou shalt find worthy to be preferred to that spirit which is within thee; if nothing better than to subject unto thee thine own lusts and desires, and not to give way to any fancies or imaginations before thou hast duly considered of them, nothing better than to withdraw thyself (to use Socrates his words) from all sensuality, and submit thyself unto the gods, and to have care of all men in general: if thou shalt find that all other things in comparison of this, are but vile, and of little moment; then give not way to any other thing, which being once though but affected and inclined unto, it will no more be in thy power without all distraction as thou oughtest to prefer and to pursue after that good, which is thine own and thy proper good. For it is not lawful, that anything that is of another and inferior kind and nature, be it what it will, as either popular applause, or honour, or riches, or pleasures; should be suffered to confront and contest as it were, with that which is rational, and operatively good. For all these things, if once though but for a while, they begin to please, they presently prevail, and pervert a man's mind, or turn a man from the right way. Do thou therefore I say absolutely and freely make choice of that which is best, and stick unto it. Now, that they say is best, which is most profitable. If they mean profitable to man as he is a rational man, stand thou to it, and maintain it; but if they mean profitable, as he is a creature, only reject it; and from this thy tenet and conclusion keep off carefully all plausible shows and colours of external appearance, that thou mayest be able to discern things rightly.

VIII. Never esteem of anything as profitable, which shall ever constrain thee either to break thy faith, or to lose thy modesty; to hate any man, to suspect, to curse, to dissemble, to lust after anything, that requireth the secret of walls or veils. But he that preferreth before all things his rational part and spirit, and the sacred mysteries of virtue which issueth from it, he shall never lament and exclaim, never sigh; he shall never want either solitude or company: and which is chiefest of all, he shall live without either desire or fear. And as for life, whether for a long or short time he shall enjoy his soul thus compassed about with a body, he is altogether indifferent. For if even now he were to depart, he is as ready for it, as for any other action, which may be performed with modesty and decency. For all his life long, this is his only care, that his mind may always be occupied in such intentions and objects, as are proper to a rational sociable creature.

IX. In the mind that is once truly disciplined and purged, thou canst not find anything, either foul or impure, or as it were festered: nothing that is either servile, or affected: no partial tie; no malicious averseness; nothing obnoxious; nothing concealed. The life of such an one, death can never surprise as imperfect; as of an actor, that should die before he had ended, or the play itself were at an end, a man might speak.

X. Use thine opinative faculty with all honour and respect, for in her indeed is all: that thy opinion do not beget in thy understanding anything contrary to either nature, or the proper constitution of a rational creature. The end and object of a rational constitution is, to do nothing rashly, to be kindly affected towards men, and in all things willingly to submit unto the gods. Casting therefore all other things aside, keep thyself to these few, and remember withal that no man properly can be said to live more than that which is now present, which is but a moment of time. Whatsoever is besides either is already past, or uncertain. The time therefore that any man doth live, is but a little, and the place where he liveth, is but a very little corner of the earth, and the greatest fame that can remain of a man after his death, even that is but little, and that too, such as it is whilst it is, is by the succession of silly mortal men preserved, who likewise shall shortly die, and even whiles they live know not what in very deed they themselves are: and much less can know one, who long before is dead and gone.

XI. To these ever-present helps and mementoes, let one more be added, ever to make a particular description and delineation as it were of every object that presents itself to thy mind, that thou mayest wholly and throughly contemplate it, in its own proper nature, bare and naked; wholly, and severally; divided into its several parts and quarters: and then by thyself in thy mind, to call both it, and those things of which it doth consist, and in which it shall be resolved, by their own proper true names, and appellations. For there is nothing so effectual to beget true magnanimity, as to be able truly and methodically to examine and consider all things that happen in this life, and so to penetrate into their natures, that at the same time, this also may concur in our apprehensions: what is the true use of it? and what is the true nature of this universe, to which it is useful? how much in regard of the universe may it be esteemed? how much in regard of man, a citizen of the supreme city, of which all other cities in the world are as it were but houses and families?

XII. What is this, that now my fancy is set upon? of what things doth it consist? how long can it last? which of all the virtues is the proper virtue for this present use? as whether meekness, fortitude, truth, faith, sincerity, contentation, or any of the rest? Of everything therefore thou must use thyself to say, This immediately comes from God, this by that fatal connection, and concatenation of things, or (which almost comes to one) by some coincidental casualty. And as for this, it proceeds from my neighbour, my kinsman, my fellow: through his ignorance indeed, because he knows not what is truly natural unto him: but I know it, and therefore carry myself towards him according to the natural law of fellowship; that is kindly, and justly. As for those things that of themselves are altogether indifferent, as in my best judgment I conceive everything to deserve more or less, so I carry myself towards it.

XIII. If thou shalt intend that which is present, following the rule of right and reason carefully, solidly, meekly, and shalt not intermix any other businesses, but shall study this only to preserve thy spirit unpolluted, and pure, and shall cleave unto him without either hope or fear of anything, in all things that thou shalt either do or speak, contenting thyself with heroical truth, thou shalt live happily; and from this, there is no man that can hinder thee.

XIV. As physicians and chirurgeons have always their instruments ready at hand for all sudden cures; so have thou always thy dogmata in a readiness for the knowledge of things, both divine and human: and whatsoever thou dost, even in the smallest things that thou dost, thou must ever remember that mutual relation, and connection that is between these two things divine, and things human. For without relation unto God, thou shalt never speed in any worldly actions; nor on the other side in any divine, without some respect had to things human.

XV. **Be not deceived; for thou shalt never live to read thy moral** commentaries, nor the acts of the famous Romans and Grecians; nor those excerpta from several books; all which thou hadst provided and laid up for thyself against thine old age. Hasten therefore to an end, and giving over all vain hopes, help thyself in time if thou carest for thyself, as thou oughtest to do.

XVI. **To steal, to sow, to buy, to be at rest, to see what is to be done** (which is not seen by the eyes, but by another kind of sight:) what these words mean, and how many ways to be understood, they do not understand. The body, the soul, the understanding. As the senses naturally belong to the body, and the desires and affections to the soul, so do the dogmata to the understanding.

XVII. **To be capable of fancies and imaginations, is common to man** and beast. To be violently drawn and moved by the lusts and desires of the soul, is proper to wild beasts and monsters, such as Phalaris and Nero were. To follow reason for ordinary duties and actions is common to them also, who believe not that there be any gods, and for their advantage would make no conscience to betray their own country; and who when once the doors be shut upon them, dare do anything. If therefore all things else be common to these likewise, it follows, that for a man to like and embrace all things that happen and are destinated unto him, and not to trouble and molest that spirit which is seated in the temple of his own breast, with a multitude of vain fancies and imaginations, but to keep him propitious and to obey him as a god, never either speaking anything contrary to truth, or doing anything contrary to justice, is the only true property of a good man. And such a one, though no man should believe that he liveth as he doth, either sincerely and conscionably, or cheerful and contentedly; yet is he neither with any man at all angry for it, nor diverted by it from the way that leadeth to the end of his life, through which a man must pass pure, ever ready to depart, and willing of himself without any compulsion to fit and accommodate himself to his proper lot and portion.

The Fourth Book

I. That inward mistress part of man if it be in its own true natural temper, is towards all worldly chances and events ever so disposed and affected, that it will easily turn and apply itself to that which may be, and is within its own power to compass, when that cannot be which at first it intended. For it never doth absolutely addict and apply itself to any one object, but whatsoever it is that it doth now intend and prosecute, it doth prosecute it with exception and reservation; so that whatsoever it is that falls out contrary to its first intentions, even that afterwards it makes its proper object. Even as the fire when it prevails upon those things that are in his way; by which things indeed a little fire would have been quenched, but a great fire doth soon turn to its own nature, and so consume whatsoever comes in his way: yea by those very things it is made greater and greater.

II. Let nothing be done rashly, and at random, but all things according to the most exact and perfect rules of art.

III. They seek for themselves private retiring places, as country villages, the sea-shore, mountains; yea thou thyself art wont to long much after such places. But all this thou must know proceeds from simplicity in the highest degree. At what time soever thou wilt, it is in thy power to retire into thyself, and to be at rest, and free from all businesses. A man cannot any whither retire better than to his own soul; he especially who is beforehand provided of such things within, which whensoever he doth withdraw himself to look in, may presently afford unto him perfect ease and tranquillity. By tranquillity I understand a decent orderly disposition and carriage, free from all confusion and tumultuousness. Afford then thyself this retiring continually, and thereby refresh and renew thyself. Let these precepts be brief and fundamental, which as soon as thou dost call them to mind, may suffice thee to purge thy soul throughly, and to send thee away well pleased with those things whatsoever they be, which now again after this short withdrawing of thy soul into herself thou dost return unto. For what is it that thou art offended at? Can it be at the wickedness of men, when thou dost call to mind this conclusion, that all reasonable creatures are made one for another? and that it is part of justice to bear with them? and that it is against their wills that they offend? and how many already, who once likewise prosecuted their enmities, suspected, hated, and fiercely contended, are now long ago stretched out, and reduced unto ashes? It is time for thee to make an end. As for those things which among the common chances of the world happen unto thee as thy particular lot and portion, canst thou be displeased with any of them, when thou dost call that our ordinary dilemma to mind, either a providence, or Democritus his atoms; and with it, whatsoever we brought to prove that the whole world is as it were one city? And as for thy body, what canst thou fear, if thou dost consider that thy mind and understanding, when once it hath recollected itself, and knows its own power, hath in this life and breath (whether it run smoothly and gently, or whether harshly and rudely), no interest at all, but is altogether indifferent: and whatsoever else thou hast heard and assented unto concerning either pain or pleasure? But the care of thine honour and reputation will perchance distract thee? How can that be, if thou dost look back, and consider both how quickly all things that are, are forgotten, and what an immense chaos of eternity was before, and will follow after all things: and the vanity of praise, and the inconstancy and variableness of human judgments and opinions, and the narrowness of the place, wherein it is limited and circumscribed? For the whole earth is but as one point; and of it, this inhabited part of it, is but a very little part; and of this part, how many in number, and what manner of men are they, that will commend thee? What remains then, but that thou often put in practice this kind of retiring of thyself, to this little part of thyself; and above all things, keep thyself from distraction, and intend not anything vehemently, but be free and consider all things, as a man whose proper object is Virtue, as a man whose true nature is to be kind and sociable, as a citizen, as a mortal creature. Among other things, which to consider, and look into thou must use to withdraw thyself, let those two be among the most obvious and at hand. One, that the things or objects themselves reach not unto the soul, but stand without still and quiet, and that it is from the opinion only which is within, that all the tumult and all the trouble doth proceed. The next, that all these things, which now thou seest, shall within a very little while be changed, and be no more: and ever call to mind, how many changes and alterations in the world thou thyself hast already been an eyewitness of in thy time. This world is mere change, and this life, opinion.

IV. If to understand and to be reasonable be common unto all men, then is that reason, for which we are termed reasonable, common unto all. If reason is general, then is that reason also, which prescribeth what is to be done and what not, common unto all. If that, then law. If law, then are we fellow-citizens. If so, then are we partners in some one commonweal. If so, then the world is as it were a city. For which other commonweal is it, that all men can be said to be members of? From this common city it is, that understanding, reason, and law is derived unto us, for from whence else? For as that which in me is earthly I have from some common earth; and that which is moist from some other element is imparted; as my breath and life hath its proper fountain; and that likewise which is dry and fiery in me: (for there is nothing which doth not proceed from something; as also there is nothing that can be reduced unto mere nothing:) so also is there some common beginning from whence my understanding hath proceeded.

V. As generation is, so also death, a secret of nature's wisdom: a mixture of elements, resolved into the same elements again, a thing surely which no man ought to be ashamed of: in a series of other fatal events and consequences, which a rational creature is subject unto, not improper or incongruous, nor contrary to the natural and proper constitution of man himself.

VI. Such and such things, from such and such causes, must of necessity proceed. He that would not have such things to happen, is as he that would have the fig-tree grow without any sap or moisture. In sum, remember this, that within a very little while, both thou and he shall both be dead, and after a little while more, not so much as your names and memories shall be remaining.

VII. Let opinion be taken away, and no man will think himself wronged. If no man shall think himself wronged, then is there no more any such thing as wrong. That which makes not man himself the worse, cannot make his life the worse, neither can it hurt him either inwardly or outwardly. It was expedient in nature that it should be so, and therefore necessary.

VIII. Whatsoever doth happen in the world, doth happen justly, and so if thou dost well take heed, thou shalt find it. I say not only in right order by a series of inevitable consequences, but according to justice and as it were by way of equal distribution, according to the true worth of everything. Continue then to take notice of it, as thou hast begun, and whatsoever thou dost, do it not without this proviso, that it be a thing of that nature that a good man (as the word good is properly taken) may do it. This observe carefully in every action.

IX. Conceit no such things, as he that wrongeth thee conceiveth, or would have thee to conceive, but look into the matter itself, and see what it is in very truth.

X. These two rules, thou must have always in a readiness. First, do nothing at all, but what reason proceeding from that regal and supreme part, shall for the good and benefit of men, suggest unto thee. And secondly, if any man that is present shall be able to rectify thee or to turn thee from some erroneous persuasion, that thou be always ready to change thy mind, and this change to proceed, not from any respect of any pleasure or credit thereon depending, but always from some probable apparent ground of justice, or of some public good thereby to be furthered; or from some other such inducement.

XI. Hast thou reason? I have. Why then makest thou not use of it? For if thy reason do her part, what more canst thou require?

XII. As a part hitherto thou hast had a particular subsistence: and now shalt thou vanish away into the common substance of Him, who first begot thee, or rather thou shalt be resumed again into that original rational substance, out of which all others have issued, and are propagated. Many small pieces of frankincense are set upon the same altar, one drops first and is consumed, another after; and it comes all to one.

XIII. **Within ten days, if so happen, thou shalt be esteemed a god of** them, who now if thou shalt return to the dogmata and to the honouring of reason, will esteem of thee no better than of a mere brute, and of an ape.

XIV. Not as though thou hadst thousands of years to live. Death hangs over thee: whilst yet thou livest, whilst thou mayest, be good.

XV. Now much time and leisure doth he gain, who is not curious to know what his neighbour hath said, or hath done, or hath attempted, but only what he doth himself, that it may be just and holy? or to express it in Agathos' words, Not to look about upon the evil conditions of others, but to run on straight in the line, without any loose and extravagant agitation.

XVI. He who is greedy of credit and reputation after his death, doth not consider, that they themselves by whom he is remembered, shall soon after every one of them be dead; and they likewise that succeed those; until at last all memory, which hitherto by the succession of men admiring and soon after dying hath had its course, be quite extinct. But suppose that both they that shall remember thee, and thy memory with them should be immortal, what is that to thee? I will not say to thee after thou art dead; but even to thee living, what is thy praise? But only for a secret and politic consideration, which we call oikonomian or dispensation. For as for that, that it is the gift of nature, whatsoever is commended in thee, what might be objected from thence, let that now that we are upon another consideration be omitted as unseasonable. That which is fair and goodly, whatsoever it be, and in what respect soever it be, that it is fair and goodly, it is so of itself, and terminates in itself, not admitting praise as a part or member: that therefore which is praised, is not thereby made either better or worse. This I understand even of those things, that are commonly called fair and good, as those which are commended either for the matter itself, or for curious workmanship. As for that which is truly good, what can it stand in need of more than either justice or truth; or more than either kindness and modesty? Which of all those, either becomes good or fair, because commended; or dispraised suffers any damage? Doth the emerald become worse in itself, or more vile if it be not commended? Doth gold, or ivory, or purple? Is there anything that doth though never so common, as a knife, a flower, or a tree?

XVII. If so be that the souls remain after death (say they that will not believe it); how is the air from all eternity able to contain them? How is the earth (say I) ever from that time able to Contain the bodies of them that are buried? For as here the change and resolution of dead bodies into another kind of subsistence (whatsoever it be;) makes place for other dead bodies: so the souls after death transferred into the air, after they have conversed there a while, are either by way of transmutation, or transfusion, or conflagration, received again into that original rational substance, from which all others do proceed: and so give way to those souls, who before coupled and associated unto bodies, now begin to subsist single. This, upon a supposition that the souls after death do for a while subsist single, may be answered. And here, (besides the number of bodies, so buried and contained by the earth), we may further consider the number of several beasts, eaten by us men, and by other creatures. For notwithstanding that such a multitude of them is daily consumed, and as it were buried in the bodies of the eaters, yet is the same place and body able to contain them, by reason of their conversion, partly into blood, partly into air and fire. What in these things is the speculation of truth? to divide things into that which is passive and material; and that which is active and formal.

XVIII. Not to wander out of the way, but upon every motion and desire, to perform that which is just: and ever to be careful to attain to the true natural apprehension of every fancy, that presents itself.

XIX. Whatsoever is expedient unto thee, O World, is expedient unto me; nothing can either be 'unseasonable unto me, or out of date, which unto thee is seasonable. Whatsoever thy seasons bear, shall ever by me be esteemed as happy fruit, and increase. O Nature! from thee are all things, in thee all things subsist, and to thee all tend. Could he say of Athens, Thou lovely city of Cecrops; and shalt not thou say of the world, Thou lovely city of God?

XX. They will say commonly, Meddle not with many things, if thou wilt live cheerfully. Certainly there is nothing better, than for a man to confine himself to necessary actions; to such and so many only, as reason in a creature that knows itself born for society, will command and enjoin. This will not only procure that cheerfulness, which from the goodness, but that also, which from the paucity of actions doth usually proceed. For since it is so, that most of those things, which we either speak or do, are unnecessary; if a man shall cut them off, it must needs follow that he shall thereby gain much leisure, and save much trouble, and therefore at every action a man must privately by way of admonition suggest unto himself, What? may not this that now I go about, be of the number of unnecessary actions? Neither must he use himself to cut off actions only, but thoughts and imaginations also, that are unnecessary for so will unnecessary consequent actions the better be prevented and cut off.

XXI. Try also how a good man's life; (of one, who is well pleased with those things whatsoever, which among the common changes and chances of this world fall to his own lot and share; and can live well contented and fully satisfied in the justice of his own proper present action, and in the goodness of his disposition for the future:) will agree with thee. Thou hast had experience of that other kind of life: make now trial of this also. Trouble not thyself any more henceforth, reduce thyself unto perfect simplicity. Doth any man offend? It is against himself that he doth offend: why should it trouble thee? Hath anything happened unto thee? It is well, whatsoever it be, it is that which of all the common chances of the world from the very beginning in the series of all other things that have, or shall happen, was destinated and appointed unto thee. To comprehend all in a few words, our life is short; we must endeavour to gain the present time with best discretion and justice. Use recreation with sobriety.

XXII. Either this world is a kosmoz or comely piece, because all disposed and governed by certain order: or if it be a mixture, though confused, yet still it is a comely piece. For is it possible that in thee there should be any beauty at all, and that in the whole world there should be nothing but disorder and confusion? and all things in it too, by natural different properties one from another differenced and distinguished; and yet all through diffused, and by natural sympathy, one to another united, as they are?

XXIII. A black or malign disposition, an effeminate disposition; an hard inexorable disposition, a wild inhuman disposition, a sheepish disposition, a childish disposition; a blockish, a false, a scurril, a fraudulent, a tyrannical: what then? If he be a stranger in the world, that knows not the things that are in it; why not be a stranger as well, that wonders at the things that are done in it?

XXIV. He is a true fugitive, that flies from reason, by which men are sociable. He blind, who cannot see with the eyes of his understanding. He poor, that stands in need of another, and hath not in himself all things needful for this life. He an aposteme of the world, who by being discontented with those things that happen unto him in the world, doth as it were apostatise, and separate himself from common nature's rational administration. For the same nature it is that brings this unto thee, whatsoever it be, that first brought thee into the world. He raises sedition in the city, who by irrational actions withdraws his own soul from that one and common soul of all rational creatures.

XXV. There is, who without so much as a coat; and there is, who without so much as a book, doth put philosophy in practice. I am half naked, neither have I bread to eat, and yet I depart not from reason, saith one. But I say; I want the food of good teaching, and instructions, and yet I depart not from reason.

XXVI. What art and profession soever thou hast learned, endeavour to affect it, and comfort thyself in it; and pass the remainder of thy life as one who from his whole heart commits himself and whatsoever belongs unto him, unto the gods: and as for men, carry not thyself either tyrannically or servilely towards any.

XXVII. Consider in my mind, for example's sake, the times of Vespasian: thou shalt see but the same things: some marrying, some bringing up children, some sick, some dying, some fighting, some feasting, some merchandising, some tilling, some flattering, some boasting, some suspecting, some undermining, some wishing to die, some fretting and murmuring at their present estate, some wooing, some hoarding, some seeking after magistracies, and some after kingdoms. And is not that their age quite over, and ended? Again, consider now the times of Trajan. There likewise thou seest the very self-same things, and that age also is now over and ended. In the like manner consider other periods, both of times and of whole nations, and see how many men, after they had with all their might and main intended and prosecuted some one worldly thing or other did soon after drop away, and were resolved into the elements. But especially thou must call to mind them, whom thou thyself in thy lifetime hast known much distracted about vain things, and in the meantime neglecting to do that, and closely and unseparably (as fully satisfied with it) to adhere unto it, which their own proper constitution did require. And here thou must remember, that thy carriage in every business must be according to the worth and due proportion of it, for so shalt thou not easily be tired out and vexed, if thou shalt not dwell upon small matters longer than is fitting.

XXVIII. Those words which once were common and ordinary, are now become obscure and obsolete; and so the names of men once commonly known and famous, are now become in a manner obscure and obsolete names. Camillus, Cieso, Volesius, Leonnatus; not long after, Scipio, Cato, then Augustus, then Adrianus, then Antoninus Pius: all these in a short time will be out of date, and, as things of another world as it were, become fabulous. And this I say of them, who once shined as the wonders of their ages, for as for the rest, no sooner are they expired, than with them all their fame and memory. And what is it then that shall always be remembered? all is vanity. What is it that we must bestow our care and diligence upon? even upon this only: that our minds and wills be just; that our actions be charitable; that our speech be never deceitful, or that our understanding be not subject to error; that our inclination be always set to embrace whatsoever shall happen unto us, as necessary, as usual, as ordinary, as flowing from such a beginning, and such a fountain, from which both thou thyself and all things are. Willingly therefore, and wholly surrender up thyself unto that fatal concatenation, yielding up thyself unto the fates, to be disposed of at their pleasure.

XXIX. Whatsoever is now present, and from day to day hath its existence; all objects of memories, and the minds and memories themselves, incessantly consider, all things that are, have their being by change and alteration. Use thyself therefore often to meditate upon this, that the nature of the universe delights in nothing more, than in altering those things that are, and in making others like unto them. So that we may say, that whatsoever is, is but as it were the seed of that which shall be. For if thou think that that only is seed, which either the earth or the womb receiveth, thou art very simple.

XXX. Thou art now ready to die, and yet hast thou not attained to that perfect simplicity: thou art yet subject to many troubles and perturbations; not yet free from all fear and suspicion of external accidents; nor yet either so meekly disposed towards all men, as thou shouldest; or so affected as one, whose only study and only wisdom is, to be just in all his actions.

XXXI. Behold and observe, what is the state of their rational part; and those that the world doth account wise, see what things they fly and are afraid of; and what things they hunt after.

XXXII. In another man's mind and understanding thy evil Cannot subsist, nor in any proper temper or distemper of the natural constitution of thy body, which is but as it were the coat or cottage of thy soul. Wherein then, but in that part of thee, wherein the conceit, and apprehension of any misery can subsist? Let not that part therefore admit any such conceit, and then all is well. Though thy body which is so near it should either be cut or burnt, or suffer any corruption or putrefaction, yet let that part to which it belongs to judge of these, be still at rest; that is, let her judge this, that whatsoever it is, that equally may happen to a wicked man, and to a good man, is neither good nor evil. For that which happens equally to him that lives according to nature, and to him that doth not, is neither according to nature, nor against it; and by consequent, neither good nor bad.

XXXIII. Ever consider and think upon the world as being but one living substance, and having but one soul, and how all things in the world, are terminated into one sensitive power; and are done by one general motion as it were, and deliberation of that one soul; and how all things that are, concur in the cause of one another's being, and by what manner of connection and concatenation all things happen.

XXXIV. What art thou, that better and divine part excepted, but as Epictetus said well, a wretched soul, appointed to carry a carcass up and down?

XXXV. To suffer change can be no hurt; as no benefit it is, by change to attain to being. The age and time of the world is as it were a flood and swift current, consisting of the things that are brought to pass in the world. For as soon as anything hath appeared, and is passed away, another succeeds, and that also will presently out of sight.

XXXVI. Whatsoever doth happen in the world, is, in the course of nature, as usual and ordinary as a rose in the spring, and fruit in summer. Of the same nature is sickness and death; slander, and lying in wait, and whatsoever else ordinarily doth unto fools use to be occasion either of joy or sorrow. That, what-soever it is, that comes after, doth always very naturally, and as it were familiarly, follow upon that which was before. For thou must consider the things of the world, not as a loose independent number, consisting merely of necessary events; but as a discreet connection of things orderly and harmoniously dis-posed. There is then to be seen in the things of the world, not a bare succession, but an admirable correspondence and affinity.

XXXVII. Let that of Heraclitus never be out of thy mind, that the death of earth, is water, and the death of water, is air; and the death of air, is fire; and so on the contrary. Remember him also who was ignorant whither the way did lead, and how that reason being the thing by which all things in the world are administered, and which men are continually and most inwardly conversant with: yet is the thing, which ordinarily they are most in opposition with, and how those things which daily happen among them, cease not daily to be strange unto them, and that we should not either speak, or do anything as men in their sleep, by opinion and bare imagination: for then we think we speak and do, and that we must not be as children, who follow their father's example; for best reason alleg-ing their bare successive tradition from our forefathers we have received it.

XXXVIII. Even as if any of the gods should tell thee, Thou shalt certainly die to-morrow, or next day, thou wouldst not, except thou wert ex-tremely base and pusillanimous, take it for a great benefit, rather to die the next day after, than to-morrow; (for alas, what is the difference!) so, for the same reason, think it no great matter to die rather many years after, than the very next day.

XXXIX. Let it be thy perpetual meditation, how many physicians who once looked so grim, and so theatrically shrunk their brows upon their patients, are dead and gone themselves. How many astrologers, after that in great osten-tation they had foretold the death of some others, how many philosophers after so many elaborate tracts and volumes concerning either mortality or immortality; how many brave captains and commanders, after the death and slaughter of so many; how many kings and tyrants, after they had with such horror and insolency abused their power upon men's lives, as though themselves had been immortal; how many, that I may so speak, whole cities both men and towns: Helice, Pom-peii, Herculaneum, and others innumerable are dead and gone. Run them over also, whom thou thyself, one after another, hast known in thy time to drop away. Such and such a one took care of such and such a one's burial, and soon after was buried himself. So one, so another: and all things in a short time. For herein lieth all indeed, ever to look upon all worldly things, as things for their continu-ance, that are but for a day: and for their worth, most vile, and contemptible, as for example, What is man? That which but the other day when he was conceived was vile snivel; and within few days shall be either an embalmed carcass, or mere ashes. Thus must thou according to truth and nature, throughly consider how man's life is but for a very moment of time, and so depart meek and contented: even as if a ripe olive falling should praise the ground that bare her, and give thanks to the tree that begat her.

XL. Thou must be like a promontory of the sea, against which though the waves beat continually, yet it both itself stands, and about it are those swelling waves stilled and quieted.

XLI. Oh, wretched I, to whom this mischance is happened! nay, happy I, to whom this thing being happened, I can continue without grief; neither wounded by that which is present, nor in fear of that which is to come. For as for this, it might have happened unto any man, but any man having such a thing befallen him, could not have continued without grief. Why then should that rather be an unhappiness, than this a happiness? But however, canst thou, O man! term that unhappiness, which is no mischance to the nature of man I Canst thou think that a mischance to the nature of man, which is not contrary to the end and will of his nature? What then hast thou learned is the will of man's nature? Doth that then which hath happened unto thee, hinder thee from being just? or magnanimous? or temperate? or wise? or circumspect? or true? or modest? or free? or from anything else of all those things in the present enjoying and possession whereof the nature of man, (as then enjoying all that is proper unto her,) is fully satisfied? Now to conclude; upon all occasion of sorrow remember henceforth to make use of this dogma, that whatsoever it is that hath happened unto thee, is in very deed no such thing of itself, as a misfortune; but that to bear it generously, is certainly great happiness.

XLII. It is but an ordinary coarse one, yet it is a good effectual remedy against the fear of death, for a man to consider in his mind the examples of such, who greedily and covetously (as it were) did for a long time enjoy their lives. What have they got more, than they whose deaths have been untimely? Are not they themselves dead at the last? as Cadiciant's, Fabius, Julianus Lepidus, or any other who in their lifetime having buried many, were at the last buried themselves. The whole space of any man's life, is but little; and as little as it is, with what troubles, with what manner of dispositions, and in the society of how wretched a body must it be passed! Let it be therefore unto thee altogether as a matter of indifferency. For if thou shalt look backward; behold, what an infinite chaos of time doth present itself unto thee; and as infinite a chaos, if thou shalt look forward. In that which is so infinite, what difference can there be between that which liveth but three days, and that which liveth three ages?

XLIII. Let thy course ever be the most compendious way. The most compendious, is that which is according to nature: that is, in all both words and deeds, ever to follow that which is most sound and perfect. For such a resolution will free a man from all trouble, strife, dissembling, and ostentation.

The Fifth Book

I. In the morning when thou findest thyself unwilling to rise, consider with thyself presently, it is to go about a man's work that I am stirred up. Am I then yet unwilling to go about that, for which I myself was born and brought forth into this world? Or was I made for this, to lay me down, and make much of myself in a warm bed? 'O but this is pleasing.' And was it then for this that thou wert born, that thou mightest enjoy pleasure? Was it not in very truth for this, that thou mightest always be busy and in action? Seest thou not how all things in the world besides, how every tree md plant, how sparrows and ants, spiders and bees: how all in their kind are intent as it were orderly to perform whatsoever (towards the preservation of this orderly universe) naturally doth become and belong unto thin? And wilt not thou do that, which belongs unto a man to do? Wilt not thou run to do that, which thy nature doth require? 'But thou must have some rest.' Yes, thou must. Nature hath of that also, as well as of eating and drinking, allowed thee a certain stint. But thou guest beyond thy stint, and beyond that which would suffice, and in matter of action, there thou comest short of that which thou mayest. It must needs be therefore, that thou dost not love thyself, for if thou didst, thou wouldst also love thy nature, and that which thy nature doth propose unto herself as her end. Others, as many as take pleasure in their trade and profession, can even pine themselves at their works, and neglect their bodies and their food for it; and doest thou less honour thy nature, than an ordinary mechanic his trade; or a good dancer his art? than a covetous man his silver, and vainglorious man applause? These to whatsoever they take an affection, can be content to want their meat and sleep, to further that every one which he affects: and shall actions tending to the common good of human society, seem more vile unto thee, or worthy of less respect and intention?

II. How easy a thing is it for a man to put off from him all turbulent adventitious imaginations, and presently to be in perfect rest and tranquillity!

III. Think thyself fit and worthy to speak, or to do anything that is according to nature, and let not the reproach, or report of some that may ensue upon it, ever deter thee. If it be right and honest to be spoken or done, undervalue not thyself so much, as to be discouraged from it. As for them, they have their own rational over-ruling part, and their own proper inclination: which thou must not stand and look about to take notice of, but go on straight, whither both thine own particular, and the common nature do lead thee; and the way of both these, is but one.

IV. I continue my course by actions according to nature, until I fall and cease, breathing out my last breath into that air, by which continually breathed in I did live; and falling upon that earth, out of whose gifts and fruits my father gathered his seed, my mother her blood, and my nurse her milk, out of which for so many years I have been provided, both of meat and drink. And lastly, which beareth me that tread upon it, and beareth with me that so many ways do abuse it, or so freely make use of it, so many ways to so many ends.

V. No man can admire thee for thy sharp acute language, such is thy natural disability that way. Be it so: yet there be many other good things, for the want of which thou canst not plead the want or natural ability. Let them be seen in thee, which depend wholly from thee; sincerity, gravity, laboriousness, contempt of pleasures; be not querulous, be Content with little, be kind, be free; avoid all superfluity, all vain prattling; be magnanimous. Doest not thou perceive, how many things there be, which notwithstanding any pretence of natural indisposition and unfitness, thou mightest have performed and exhibited, and yet still thou doest voluntarily continue drooping downwards? Or wilt thou say that it is through defect of thy natural constitution, that thou art constrained to murmur, to be base and wretched to flatter; now to accuse, and now to please, and pacify thy body: to be vainglorious, to be so giddy-headed., and unsettled in thy thoughts? nay (witnesses be the Gods) of all these thou mightest have been rid long ago: only, this thou must have been contented with, to have borne the blame of one that is somewhat slow and dull, wherein thou must so exercise thyself, as one who neither doth much take to heart this his natural defect, nor yet pleaseth himself in it.

VI. Such there be, who when they have done a good turn to any, are ready to set them on the score for it, and to require retaliation. Others there be, who though they stand not upon retaliation, to require any, yet they think with themselves nevertheless, that such a one is their debtor, and they know as their word is what they have done. Others again there be, who when they have done any such thing, do not so much as know what they have done; but are like unto the vine, which beareth her grapes, and when once she hath borne her own proper fruit, is contented and seeks for no further recompense. As a horse after a race, and a hunting dog when he hath hunted, and a bee when she hath made her honey, look not for applause and commendation; so neither doth that man that rightly doth understand his own nature when he hath done a good turn: but from one doth proceed to do another, even as the vine after she hath once borne fruit in her own proper season, is ready for another time. Thou therefore must be one of them, who what they do, barely do it without any further thought, and are in a manner insensible of what they do. 'Nay but,' will some reply perchance, 'this very thing a rational man is bound unto, to understand what it is, that he doeth.' For it is the property, say they, of one that is naturally sociable, to be sensible, that he doth operate sociably: nay, and to desire, that the party him self that is sociably dealt with, should be sensible of it too. I answer, That which thou sayest is true indeed, but the true meaning of that which is said, thou dost not understand. And therefore art thou one of those first, whom I mentioned. For they also are led by a probable appearance of reason. But if thou dost desire to understand truly what it is that is said, fear not that thou shalt therefore give over any sociable action.

VII. The form of the Athenians' prayer did run thus: 'O rain, rain, good Jupiter, upon all the grounds and fields that belong to the Athenians.' Either we should not pray at all, or thus absolutely and freely; and not every one for himself in particular alone.

VIII. As we say commonly, The physician hath prescribed unto this man, riding; unto another, cold baths; unto a third, to go barefoot: so it is alike to say, The nature of the universe hath prescribed unto this man sickness, or blindness, or some loss, or damage or some such thing. For as there, when we say of a physician, that he hath prescribed anything, our meaning is, that he hath appointed this for that, as subordinate and conducing to health: so here, whatsoever doth happen unto any, is ordained unto him as a thing subordinate unto the fates, and therefore do we say of such things, that they do happen, or fall together; as of square stones, when either in walls, or pyramids in a certain position they fit one another, and agree as it were in an harmony, the masons say, that they do (sumbainein) as if thou shouldest say, fall together: so that in the general, though the things be divers that make it, yet the consent or harmony itself is but one. And as the whole world is made up of all the particular bodies of the world, one perfect and complete body, of the same nature that particular bodies; so is the destiny of particular causes and events one general one, of the same nature that particular causes are. What I now say, even they that are mere idiots are not ignorant of: for they say commonly (touto eferen autw) that is, This his destiny hath brought upon him. This therefore is by the fates properly and particularly brought upon this, as that unto this in particular is by the physician prescribed. These therefore let us accept of in like manner, as we do those that are prescribed unto us our physicians. For them also in themselves shall We find to contain many harsh things, but we nevertheless, in hope of health, and recovery, accept of them. Let the fulfilling and accomplishment of those things which the common nature hath determined, be unto thee as thy health. Accept then, and be pleased with whatsoever doth happen, though otherwise harsh and un-pleasing, as tending to that end, to the health and welfare of the universe, and to Jove's happiness and prosperity. For this whatsoever it be, should not have been produced, had it not conduced to the good of the universe. For neither doth any ordinary particular nature bring anything to pass, that is not to whatsoever is within the sphere of its own proper administration and government agreeable and subordinate. For these two considerations then thou must be well pleased with anything that doth happen unto thee. First, because that for thee properly it was brought to pass, and unto thee it was prescribed; and that from the very beginning by the series and connection of the first causes, it hath ever had a reference unto thee. And secondly, because the good success and perfect welfare, and indeed the very continuance of Him, that is the Administrator of the whole, doth in a manner depend on it. For the whole (because whole, therefore entire and perfect) is maimed, and mutilated, if thou shalt cut off anything at all, whereby the coherence, and contiguity as of parts, so of causes, is maintained and preserved. Of which certain it is, that thou doest (as much as lieth in thee) cut off, and in some sort violently take somewhat away, as often as thou art displeased with anything that happeneth.

IX. Be not discontented, be not disheartened, be not out of hope, if often it succeed not so well with thee punctually and precisely to do all things according to the right dogmata, but being once cast off, return unto them again: and as for those many and more frequent occurrences, either of worldly distractions, or human infirmities, which as a man thou canst not but in some measure be subject unto, be not thou discontented with them; but however, love and affect that only which thou dust return unto: a philosopher's life, and proper occupation after the most exact manner. And when thou dust return to thy philosophy, return not unto it as the manner of some is, after play and liberty as it were, to their schoolmasters and pedagogues; but as they that have sore eyes to their sponge and egg: or as another to his cataplasm; or as others to their fomentations: so shalt not thou make it a matter of ostentation at all to obey reason but of ease and comfort. And remember that philosophy requireth nothing of thee, but what thy nature requireth, and wouldest thou thyself desire anything that is not according to nature? for which of these sayest thou; that which is according to nature or against it, is of itself more kind and pleasing? Is it not for that respect especially, that pleasure itself is to so many men's hurt and overthrow, most prevalent, because esteemed commonly most kind, and natural? But consider well whether magnanimity rather, and true liberty, and true simplicity, and equanimity, and holiness; whether these be not most kind and natural? And prudency itself, what more kind and amiable than it, when thou shalt truly consider with thyself, what it is through all the proper objects of thy rational intellectual faculty currently to go on without any fall or stumble? As for the things of the world, their true nature is in a manner so involved with obscurity, that unto many philosophers, and those no mean ones, they seemed altogether incomprehensible, and the Stoics themselves, though they judge them not altogether incomprehensible, yet scarce and not without much difficulty, comprehensible, so that all assent of ours is fallible, for who is he that is infallible in his conclusions? From the nature of things, pass now unto their subjects and matter: how temporary, how vile are they I such as may be in the power and possession of some abominable loose liver, of some common strumpet, of some notorious oppressor and extortioner. Pass from thence to the dispositions of them that thou doest ordinarily converse with, how hardly do we bear, even with the most loving and amiable! that I may not say, how hard it is for us to bear even with our own selves, in such obscurity, and impurity of things: in such and so continual a flux both of the substances and time; both of the motions themselves, and things moved; what it is that we can fasten upon; either to honour, and respect especially; or seriously, and studiously to seek after; I cannot so much as conceive, for indeed they are things contrary.

X. Thou must comfort thyself in the expectation of thy natural dissolution, and in the meantime not grieve at the delay; but rest contented in those two things. First, that nothing shall happen unto thee, which is not according to the nature of the universe. Secondly, that it is in thy power, to do nothing against thine own proper God, and inward spirit. For it is not in any man's power to constrain thee to transgress against him.

XI. What is the use that now at this present I make of my soul? Thus from time to time and upon all occasions thou must put this question to thyself; what is now that part of mine which they call the rational mistress part, employed about? Whose soul do I now properly possess? a child's? or a youth's? a woman's? or a tyrant's? some brute, or some wild beast's soul?

XII. What those things are in themselves, which by the greatest part are esteemed good, thou mayest gather even from this. For if a man shall hear things mentioned as good, which are really good indeed, such as are prudence, temperance, justice, fortitude, after so much heard and conceived, he cannot endure to hear of any more, for the word good is properly spoken of them. But as for those which by the vulgar are esteemed good, if he shall hear them mentioned as good, he doth hearken for more. He is well contented to hear, that what is spoken by the comedian, is but familiarly and popularly spoken, so that even the vulgar apprehend the difference. For why is it else, that this offends not and needs not to be excused, when virtues are styled good: but that which is spoken in commendation of wealth, pleasure, or honour, we entertain it only as merrily and pleasantly spoken? Proceed therefore, and inquire further, whether it may not be that those things also which being mentioned upon the stage were merrily, and with great applause of the multitude, scoffed at with this jest, that they that possessed them had not in all the world of their own, (such was their affluence and plenty) so much as a place where to avoid their excrements. Whether, I say, those ought not also in very deed to be much respected, and esteemed of, as the only things that are truly good.

XIII. All that I consist of, is either form or matter. No corruption can reduce either of these unto nothing: for neither did I of nothing become a subsistent creature. Every part of mine then will by mutation be disposed into a certain part of the whole world, and that in time into another part; and so in infinitum; by which kind of mutation, I also became what I am, and so did they that begot me, and they before them, and so upwards in infinitum. For so we may be allowed to speak, though the age and government of the world, be to some certain periods of time limited, and confined.

XIV. Reason, and rational power, are faculties which content themselves with themselves, and their own proper operations. And as for their first inclination and motion, that they take from themselves. But their progress is right to the end and object, which is in their way, as it were, and lieth just before them: that is, which is feasible and possible, whether it be that which at the first they proposed to themselves, or no. For which reason also such actions are termed katorqwseiz to intimate the directness of the way, by which they are achieved. Nothing must be thought to belong to a man, which doth not belong unto him as he is a man. These, the event of purposes, are not things required in a man. The nature of man doth not profess any such things. The final ends and consummations of actions are nothing at all to a man's nature. The end therefore of a man, or the summum bonum whereby that end is fulfilled, cannot consist in the consummation of actions purposed and intended. Again, concerning these outward worldly things, were it so that any of them did properly belong unto man, then would it not belong unto man, to condemn them and to stand in opposition with them. Neither would he be praiseworthy that can live without them; or he good, (if these were good indeed) who of his own accord doth deprive himself of any of them. But we see contrariwise, that the more a man doth withdraw himself from these wherein external pomp and greatness doth consist, or any other like these; or the better he doth bear with the loss of these, the better he is accounted.

XV. Such as thy thoughts and ordinary cogitations are, such will thy mind be in time. For the soul doth as it were receive its tincture from the fancies, and imaginations. Dye it therefore and thoroughly soak it with the assiduity of these cogitations. As for example. Wheresoever thou mayest live, there it is in thy power to live well and happy. But thou mayest live at the Court, there then also mayest thou live well and happy. Again, that which everything is made for, he is also made unto that, and cannot but naturally incline unto it. That which anything doth naturally incline unto, therein is his end. Wherein the end of everything doth consist, therein also doth his good and benefit consist. Society therefore is the proper good of a rational creature. For that we are made for society, it hath long since been demonstrated. Or can any man make any question of this, that whatsoever is naturally worse and inferior, is ordinarily subordinated to that which is better? and that those things that are best, are made one for another? And those things that have souls, are better than those that have none? and of those that have, those best that have rational souls?

XVI. To desire things impossible is the part of a mad man. But it is a thing impossible, that wicked man should not commit some such things. Neither doth anything happen to any man, which in the ordinary course of nature as natural unto him doth not happen. Again, the same things happen unto others also. And truly, if either he that is ignorant that such a thing hath happened unto him, or he that is ambitious to be commended for his magnanimity, can be patient, and is not grieved: is it not a grievous thing, that either ignorance, or a vain desire to please and to be commended, should be more powerful and effectual than true prudence? As for the things themselves, they touch not the soul, neither can they have any access unto it: neither can they of themselves any ways either affect it, or move it. For she herself alone can affect and move herself, and according as the dogmata and opinions are, which she doth vouchsafe herself; so are those things which, as accessories, have any co-existence with her.

XVII. After one consideration, man is nearest unto us; as we are bound to do them good, and to bear with them. But as he may oppose any of our true proper actions, so man is unto me but as a thing indifferent: even as the sun, or the wind, or some wild beast. By some of these it may be, that some operation or other of mine, may be hindered; however, of my mind and resolution itself, there can be no let or impediment, by reason of that ordinary constant both exception (or reservation wherewith it inclineth) and ready conversion of objects; from that which may not be, to that which may be, which in the prosecution of its inclinations, as occasion serves, it doth observe. For by these the mind doth turn and convert any impediment whatsoever, to be her aim and purpose. So that what before was the impediment, is now the principal object of her working; and that which before was in her way, is now her readiest way.

XVIII. Honour that which is chiefest and most powerful in the world, and that is it, which makes use of all things, and governs all things. So also in thyself; honour that which is chiefest, and most powerful; and is of one kind and nature with that which we now spake of. For it is the very same, which being in thee, turneth all other things to its own use, and by whom also thy life is governed.

XIX. That which doth not hurt the city itself; cannot hurt any citizen. This rule thou must remember to apply and make use of upon every conceit and apprehension of wrong. If the whole city be not hurt by this, neither am I certainly. And if the whole be not, why should I make it my private grievance? consider rather what it is wherein he is overseen that is thought to have done the wrong. Again, often meditate how swiftly all things that subsist, and all things that are done in the world, are carried away, and as it were conveyed out of sight: for both the substance themselves, we see as a flood, are in a continual flux; and all actions in a perpetual change; and the causes themselves, subject to a thousand alterations, neither is there anything almost, that may ever be said to be now settled and constant. Next unto this, and which follows upon it, consider both the infiniteness of the time already past, and the immense vastness of that which is to come, wherein all things are to be resolved and annihilated. Art not thou then a very fool, who for these things, art either puffed up with pride, or distracted with cares, or canst find in thy heart to make such moans as for a thing that would trouble thee for a very long time? Consider the whole universe whereof thou art but a very little part, and the whole age of the world together, whereof but a short and very momentary portion is allotted unto thee, and all the fates and destinies together, of which how much is it that comes to thy part and share! Again: another doth trespass against me. Let him look to that. He is master of his own disposition, and of his own operation. I for my part am in the meantime in possession of as much, as the common nature would have me to possess: and that which mine own nature would have me do, I do.

XX. Let not that chief commanding part of thy soul be ever subject to any variation through any corporal either pain or pleasure, neither suffer it to be mixed with these, but let it both circumscribe itself, and confine those affections to their own proper parts and members. But if at any time they do reflect and rebound upon the mind and understanding (as in an united and compacted body it must needs;) then must thou not go about to resist sense and feeling, it being natural. However let not thy understanding to this natural sense and feeling, which whether unto our flesh pleasant or painful, is unto us nothing properly, add an opinion of either good or bad and all is well.

XXI. To live with the Gods. He liveth with the Gods, who at all times affords unto them the spectacle of a soul, both contented and well pleased with whatsoever is afforded, or allotted unto her; and performing whatsoever is pleasing to that Spirit, whom (being part of himself) Jove hath appointed to every man as his overseer and governor.

XXII. Be not angry neither with him whose breath, neither with him whose arm holes, are offensive. What can he do? such is his breath naturally, and such are his arm holes; and from such, such an effect, and such a smell must of necessity proceed. 'O, but the man (sayest thou) hath understanding in him, and might of himself know, that he by standing near, cannot choose but offend.' And thou also (God bless thee!) hast understanding. Let thy reasonable faculty, work upon his reasonable faculty; show him his fault, admonish him. If he hearken unto thee, thou hast cured him, and there will be no more occasion of anger.

XXIII. 'Where there shall neither roarer be, nor harlot.' Why so? As thou dost purpose to live, when thou hast retired thyself to some such place, where neither roarer nor harlot is: so mayest thou here. And if they will not suffer thee, then mayest thou leave thy life rather than thy calling, but so as one that doth not think himself anyways wronged. Only as one would say, Here is a smoke; I will out of it. And what a great matter is this! Now till some such thing force me out, I will continue free; neither shall any man hinder me to do what I will, and my will shall ever be by the proper nature of a reasonable and sociable creature, regulated and directed.

XXIV. That rational essence by which the universe is governed, is for community and society; and therefore hath it both made the things that are worse, for the best, and hath allied and knit together those which are best, as it were in an harmony. Seest thou not how it hath sub-ordinated, and co-ordinated? and how it hath distributed unto everything according to its worth? and those which have the pre-eminency and superiority above all, hath it united together, into a mutual consent and agreement.

XXV. How hast thou carried thyself hitherto towards the Gods? towards thy parents? towards thy brethren? towards thy wife? towards thy children? towards thy masters? thy foster-fathers? thy friends? thy domestics? thy servants? Is it so with thee, that hitherto thou hast neither by word or deed wronged any of them? Remember withal through how many things thou hast already passed, and how many thou hast been able to endure; so that now the legend of thy life is full, and thy charge is accomplished. Again, how many truly good things have certainly by thee been discerned? how many pleasures, how many pains hast thou passed over with contempt? how many things eternally glorious hast thou despised? towards how many perverse unreasonable men hast thou carried thyself kindly, and discreetly?

XXVI. Why should imprudent unlearned souls trouble that which is both learned, and prudent? And which is that that is so? she that understandeth the beginning and the end, and hath the true knowledge of that rational essence, that passeth through all things subsisting, and through all ages being ever the same, disposing and dispensing as it were this universe by certain periods of time.

XXVII. Within a very little while, thou wilt be either ashes, or a sceletum; and a name perchance; and perchance, not so much as a name. And what is that but an empty sound, and a rebounding echo? Those things which in this life are dearest unto us, and of most account, they are in themselves but vain, putrid, contemptible. The most weighty and serious, if rightly esteemed, but as puppies, biting one another: or untoward children, now laughing and then crying. As for faith, and modesty, and justice, and truth, they long since, as one of the poets hath it, have abandoned this spacious earth, and retired themselves unto heaven. What is it then that doth keep thee here, if things sensible be so mutable and unsettled? and the senses so obscure, and so fallible? and our souls nothing but an exhalation of blood? and to be in credit among such, be but vanity? What is it that thou dost stay for? an extinction, or a translation; either of them with a propitious and contented mind. But still that time come, what will content thee? what else, but to worship and praise the Gods; and to do good unto men. To bear with them, and to forbear to do them any wrong. And for all external things belonging either to this thy wretched body, or life, to remember that they are neither thine, nor in thy power.

XXVIII. Thou mayest always speed, if thou wilt but make choice of the right way; if in the course both of thine opinions and actions, thou wilt observe a true method. These two things be common to the souls, as of God, so of men, and of every reasonable creature, first that in their own proper work they cannot be hindered by anything: and secondly, that their happiness doth consist in a disposition to, and in the practice of righteousness; and that in these their desire is terminated.

XXIX. If this neither be my wicked act, nor an act anyways depending from any wickedness of mine, and that by it the public is not hurt; what doth it concern me? And wherein can the public be hurt? For thou must not altogether be carried by conceit and common opinion: as for help thou must afford that unto them after thy best ability, and as occasion shall require, though they sustain damage, but in these middle or worldly things; but however do not thou conceive that they are truly hurt thereby: for that is not right. But as that old foster-father in the comedy, being now to take his leave doth with a great deal of ceremony, require his foster-child's rhombus, or rattle-top, remembering nevertheless that it is but a rhombus; so here also do thou likewise. For indeed what is all this pleading and public bawling for at the courts? O man, hast thou forgotten what those things are! yea but they are things that others much care for, and highly esteem of. Wilt thou therefore be a fool too? Once I was; let that suffice.

XXX. Let death surprise rue when it will, and where it will, I may be a happy man, nevertheless. For he is a happy man, who in his lifetime dealeth unto himself a happy lot and portion. A happy lot and portion is, good inclinations of the soul, good desires, good actions.

The Sixth Book

I. The matter itself, of which the universe doth consist, is of itself very tractable and pliable. That rational essence that doth govern it, hath in itself no cause to do evil. It hath no evil in itself; neither can it do anything that is evil: neither can anything be hurt by it. And all things are done and determined according to its will and prescript.

II. Be it all one unto thee, whether half frozen or well warm; whether only slumbering, or after a full sleep; whether discommended or commended thou do thy duty: or whether dying or doing somewhat else; for that also 'to die,' must among the rest be reckoned as one of the duties and actions of our lives.

III. Look in, let not either the proper quality, or the true worth of anything pass thee, before thou hast fully apprehended it.

IV. All substances come soon to their change, and either they shall be resolved by way of exhalation (if so be that all things shall be reunited into one substance), or as others maintain, they shall be scattered and dispersed. As for that Rational Essence by which all things are governed, as it best understandeth itself, both its own disposition, and what it doth, and what matter it hath to do with and accordingly doth all things; so we that do not, no wonder, if we wonder at many things, the reasons whereof we cannot comprehend.

V. The best kind of revenge is, not to become like unto them.

VI. Let this be thy only joy, and thy only comfort, from one sociable kind action without intermission to pass unto another, God being ever in thy mind.

VII. The rational commanding part, as it alone can stir up and turn itself; so it maketh both itself to be, and everything that happeneth, to appear unto itself, as it will itself.

VIII. According to the nature of the universe all things particular are determined, not according to any other nature, either about compassing and containing; or within, dispersed and contained; or without, depending. Either this universe is a mere confused mass, and an intricate context of things, which shall in time be scattered and dispersed again: or it is an union consisting of order, and administered by Providence. If the first, why should I desire to continue any longer in this fortuit confusion and commixtion? or why should I take care for anything else, but that as soon as may be I may be earth again? And why should I trouble myself any more whilst I seek to please the Gods? Whatsoever I do, dispersion is my end, and will come upon me whether I will or no. But if the latter be, then am not I religious in vain; then will I be quiet and patient, and put my trust in Him, who is the Governor of all.

IX. Whensoever by some present hard occurrences thou art constrained to be in some sort troubled and vexed, return unto thyself as soon as may be, and be not out of tune longer than thou must needs. For so shalt thou be the better able to keep thy part another time, and to maintain the harmony, if thou dost use thyself to this continually; once out, presently to have recourse unto it, and to begin again.

X. If it were that thou hadst at one time both a stepmother, and a natural mother living, thou wouldst honour and respect her also; nevertheless to thine own natural mother would thy refuge, and recourse be continually. So let the court and thy philosophy be unto thee. Have recourse unto it often, and comfort thyself in her, by whom it is that those other things are made tolerable unto thee, and thou also in those things not intolerable unto others.

XI. How marvellous useful it is for a man to represent unto himself meats, and all such things that are for the mouth, under a right apprehension and imagination! as for example: This is the carcass of a fish; this of a bird; and this of a hog. And again more generally; This phalernum, this excellent highly commended wine, is but the bare juice of an ordinary grape. This purple robe, but sheep's hairs, dyed with the blood of a shellfish. So for coitus, it is but the attrition of an ordinary base entrail, and the excretion of a little vile snivel, with a certain kind of convulsion: according to Hippocrates his opinion. How excellent useful are these lively fancies and representations of things, thus penetrating and passing through the objects, to make their true nature known and apparent! This must thou use all thy life long, and upon all occasions: and then especially, when matters are apprehended as of great worth and respect, thy art and care must be to uncover them, and to behold their vileness, and to take away from them all those serious circumstances and expressions, under which they made so grave a show. For outward pomp and appearance is a great juggler; and then especially art thou most in danger to be beguiled by it, when (to a man's thinking) thou most seemest to be employed about matters of moment.

XII. See what Crates pronounceth concerning Xenocrates himself.

XIII. Those things which the common sort of people do admire, are most of them such things as are very general, and may be comprehended under things merely natural, or naturally affected and qualified: as stones, wood, figs, vines, olives. Those that be admired by them that are more moderate and restrained, are comprehended under things animated: as flocks and herds. Those that are yet more gentle and curious, their admiration is commonly confined to reasonable creatures only; not in general as they are reasonable, but as they are capable of art, or of some craft and subtile invention: or perchance barely to reasonable creatures; as they that delight in the possession of many slaves. But he that honours a reasonable soul in general, as it is reasonable and naturally sociable, doth little regard anything else: and above all things is careful to preserve his own, in the continual habit and exercise both of reason and sociableness: and thereby doth co-operate with him, of whose nature he doth also participate; God.

XIV. Some things hasten to be, and others to be no more. And even whatsoever now is, some part thereof hath already perished. Perpetual fluxes and alterations renew the world, as the perpetual course of time doth make the age of the world (of itself infinite) to appear always fresh and new. In such a flux and course of all things, what of these things that hasten so fast away should any man regard, since among all there is not any that a man may fasten and fix upon? as if a man would settle his affection upon some ordinary sparrow living by him, who is no sooner seen, than out of sight. For we must not think otherwise of our lives, than as a mere exhalation of blood, or of an ordinary respiration of air. For what in our common apprehension is, to breathe in the air and to breathe it out again, which we do daily: so much is it and no more, at once to breathe out all thy respirative faculty into that common air from whence but lately (as being but from yesterday, and to-day), thou didst first breathe it in, and with it, life.

XV. Not vegetative spiration, it is not surely (which plants have) that in this life should be so dear unto us; nor sensitive respiration, the proper life of beasts, both tame and wild; nor this our imaginative faculty; nor that we are subject to be led and carried up and down by the strength of our sensual appetites; or that we can gather, and live together; or that we can feed: for that in effect is no better, than that we can void the excrements of our food. What is it then that should be dear unto us? to hear a clattering noise? if not that, then neither to be applauded by the tongues of men. For the praises of many tongues, is in effect no better than the clattering of so many tongues. If then neither applause, what is there remaining that should be dear unto thee? This I think: that in all thy motions and actions thou be moved, and restrained according to thine own true natural constitution and Construction only. And to this even ordinary arts and professions do lead us. For it is that which every art doth aim at, that whatsoever it is, that is by art effected and prepared, may be fit for that work that it is prepared for. This is the end that he that dresseth the vine, and he that takes upon him either to tame colts, or to train up dogs, doth aim at. What else doth the education of children, and all learned professions tend unto? Certainly then it is that, which should be dear unto us also. If in this particular it go well with thee, care not for the obtaining of other things. But is it so, that thou canst not but respect other things also? Then canst not thou truly be free? then canst thou not have self-content: then wilt thou ever be subject to passions. For it is not possible, but that thou must be envious, and jealous, and suspicious of them whom thou knowest can bereave thee of such things; and again, a secret under-miner of them, whom thou seest in present possession of that which is dear unto thee. To be short, he must of necessity be full of confusion within himself, and often accuse the Gods, whosoever stands in need of these things. But if thou shalt honour and respect thy mind only, that will make thee acceptable towards thyself, towards thy friends very tractable; and conformable and concordant with the Gods; that is, accepting with praises whatsoever they shall think good to appoint and allot unto thee.

XVI. Under, above, and about, are the motions of the elements; but the motion of virtue, is none of those motions, but is somewhat more excellent and divine. Whose way (to speed and prosper in it) must be through a way, that is not easily comprehended.

XVII. Who can choose but wonder at them? They will not speak well of them that are at the same time with them, and live with them; yet they them-selves are very ambitious, that they that shall follow, whom they have never seen, nor shall ever see, should speak well of them. As if a man should grieve that he hath not been commended by them, that lived before him.

XVIII. Do not ever conceive anything impossible to man, which by thee cannot, or not without much difficulty be effected; but whatsoever in gen-eral thou canst Conceive possible and proper unto any man, think that very possible unto thee also.

XIX. Suppose that at the palestra somebody hath all to-torn thee with his nails, and hath broken thy head. Well, thou art wounded. Yet thou dost not exclaim; thou art not offended with him. Thou dost not suspect him for it after-wards, as one that watcheth to do thee a mischief. Yea even then, though thou dost thy best to save thyself from him, yet not from him as an enemy. It is not by way of any suspicious indignation, but by way of gentle and friendly declina-tion. Keep the same mind and disposition in other parts of thy life also. For many things there be, which we must conceit and apprehend, as though we had had to do with an antagonist at the palestra. For as I said, it is very possible for us to avoid and decline, though we neither suspect, nor hate.

XX. If anybody shall reprove me, and shall make it apparent unto me, that in any either opinion or action of mine I do err, I will most gladly retract. For it is the truth that I seek after, by which I am sure that never any man was hurt; and as sure, that he is hurt that continueth in any error, or ignorance what-soever.

XXI. I for my part will do what belongs unto me; as for other things, whether things unsensible or things irrational; or if rational, yet deceived and ignorant of the true way, they shall not trouble or distract me. For as for those creatures which are not endued with reason and all other things and-matters of the world whatsoever I freely, and generously, as one endued with reason, of things that have none, make use of them. And as for men, towards them as naturally partakers of the same reason, my care is to carry myself sociably. But whatsoever it is that thou art about, remember to call upon the Gods. And as for the time how long thou shalt live to do these things, let it be altogether in-different unto thee, for even three such hours are sufficient.

XXII. Alexander of Macedon, and he that dressed his mules, when once dead both came to one. For either they were both resumed into those original rational essences from whence all things in the world are propagated; or both after one fashion were scattered into atoms.

XXIII Consider how many different things, whether they concern our bodies, or our souls, in a moment of time come to pass in every one of us, and so thou wilt not wonder if many more things or rather all things that are done, can at one time subsist, and coexist in that both one and general, which we call the world.

XXIV. If any should put this question unto thee, how this word Antoninus is written, wouldst thou not presently fix thine intention upon it, and utter out in order every letter of it? And if any shall begin to gainsay thee, and quarrel with thee about it; wilt thou quarrel with him again, or rather go on meekly as thou hast begun, until thou hast numbered out every letter? Here then likewise remember, that every duty that belongs unto a man doth consist of some certain letters or numbers as it were, to which without any noise or tumult keep-ing thyself thou must orderly proceed to thy proposed end, forbearing to quarrel with him that would quarrel and fall out with thee.

XXV. Is it not a cruel thing to forbid men to affect those things, which they conceive to agree best with their own natures, and to tend most to their own proper good and behoof? But thou after a sort deniest them this liberty, as often as thou art angry with them for their sins. For surely they are led unto those sins whatsoever they be, as to their proper good and commodity. But it is not so (thou wilt object perchance). Thou therefore teach them better, and make it appear unto them: but be not thou angry with them.

XXVI. Death is a cessation from the impression of the senses, the tyranny of the passions, the errors of the mind, and the servitude of the body.

XXVII. If in this kind of life thy body be able to hold out, it is a shame that thy soul should faint first, and give over, take heed, lest of a philosopher thou become a mere Caesar in time, and receive a new tincture from the court. For it may happen if thou dost not take heed. Keep thyself therefore, truly simple, good, sincere, grave, free from all ostentation, a lover of that which is just, religious, kind, tender-hearted, strong and vigorous to undergo anything that becomes thee. Endeavour to continue such, as philosophy (hadst thou wholly and constantly applied thyself unto it) would have made, and secured thee. Worship the Gods, procure the welfare of men, this life is short. Charitable actions, and a holy disposition, is the only fruit of this earthly life.

XXVIII. Do all things as becometh the disciple of Antoninus Pius. Remember his resolute constancy in things that were done by him according to reason, his equability in all things, his sanctity; the cheerfulness of his countenance, his sweetness, and how free he was from all vainglory; how careful to come to the true and exact knowledge of matters in hand, and how he would by no means give over till he did fully, and plainly understand the whole state of the business; and how patiently, and without any contestation he would bear with them, that did unjustly condemn him: how he would never be over-hasty in anything, nor give ear to slanders and false accusations, but examine and observe with best diligence the several actions and dispositions of men. Again, how he was no backbiter, nor easily frightened, nor suspicious, and in his language free from all affectation and curiosity: and how easily he would content himself with few things, as lodging, bedding, clothing, and ordinary nourishment, and attendance. How able to endure labour, how patient; able through his spare diet to continue from morning to evening without any necessity of withdrawing before his accustomed hours to the necessities of nature: his uniformity and constancy in matter of friendship. How he would bear with them that with all boldness and liberty opposed his opinions; and even rejoice if any man could better advise him: and lastly, how religious he was without superstition. All these things of him remember, that whensoever thy last hour shall come upon thee, it may find thee, as it did him, ready for it in the possession of a good conscience.

XXIX. Stir up thy mind, and recall thy wits again from thy natural dreams, and visions, and when thou art perfectly awoken, and canst perceive that they were but dreams that troubled thee, as one newly awakened out of another kind of sleep look upon these worldly things with the same mind as thou didst upon those, that thou sawest in thy sleep.

XXX. I consist of body and soul. Unto my body all things are indifferent, for of itself it cannot affect one thing more than another with apprehension of any difference; as for my mind, all things which are not within the verge of her own operation, are indifferent unto her, and for her own operations, those altogether depend of her; neither does she busy herself about any, but those that are present; for as for future and past operations, those also are now at this present indifferent unto her.

XXXI. As long as the foot doth that which belongeth unto it to do, and the hand that which belongs unto it, their labour, whatsoever it be, is not unnatural. So a man as long as he doth that which is proper unto a man, his labour cannot be against nature; and if it be not against nature, then neither is it hurtful unto him. But if it were so that happiness did consist in pleasure: how came notorious robbers, impure abominable livers, parricides, and tyrants, in so large a measure to have their part of pleasures?

XXXII. Dost thou not see, how even those that profess mechanic arts, though in some respect they be no better than mere idiots, yet they stick close to the course of their trade, neither can they find in their heart to decline from it: and is it not a grievous thing that an architect, or a physician shall respect the course and mysteries of their profession, more than a man the proper course and condition of his own nature, reason, which is common to him and to the Gods?

XXXIII. Asia, Europe; what are they, but as corners of the whole world; of which the whole sea, is but as one drop; and the great Mount Athos, but as a clod, as all present time is but as one point of eternity. All, petty things; all things that are soon altered, soon perished. And all things come from one beginning; either all severally and particularly deliberated and resolved upon, by the general ruler and governor of all; or all by necessary consequence. So that the dreadful hiatus of a gaping lion, and all poison, and all hurtful things, are but (as the thorn and the mire) the necessary consequences of goodly fair things. Think not of these therefore, as things contrary to those which thou dost much honour, and respect; but consider in thy mind the true fountain of all.

XXXIV He that seeth the things that are now, hath Seen all that either was ever, or ever shall be, for all things are of one kind; and all like one unto another. Meditate often upon the connection of all things in the world; and upon the mutual relation that they have one unto another. For all things are after a sort folded and involved one within another, and by these means all agree well together. For one thing is consequent unto another, by local motion, by natural conspiration and agreement, and by substantial union, or, reduction of all substances into one.

XXXV. Fit and accommodate thyself to that estate and to those occurrences, which by the destinies have been annexed unto thee; and love those men whom thy fate it is to live with; but love them truly. An instrument, a tool, an utensil, whatsoever it be, if it be fit for the purpose it was made for, it is as it should be though he perchance that made and fitted it, be out of sight and gone. But in things natural, that power which hath framed and fitted them, is and abideth within them still: for which reason she ought also the more to be respected, and we are the more obliged (if we may live and pass our time according to her purpose and intention) to think that all is well with us, and according to our own minds. After this manner also, and in this respect it is, that he that is all in all doth enjoy his happiness.

XXXVI. What things soever are not within the proper power and jurisdiction of thine own will either to compass or avoid, if thou shalt propose unto thyself any of those things as either good, or evil; it must needs be that according as thou shalt either fall into that which thou dost think evil, or miss of that which thou dost think good, so wilt thou be ready both to complain of the Gods, and to hate those men, who either shall be so indeed, or shall by thee be suspected as the cause either of thy missing of the one, or falling into the other. And indeed we must needs commit many evils, if we incline to any of these things, more or less, with an opinion of any difference. But if we mind and fancy those things only, as good and bad, which wholly depend of our own wills, there is no more occasion why we should either murmur against the Gods, or be at enmity with any man.

XXXVII. We all work to one effect, some willingly, and with a rational apprehension of what we do: others without any such knowledge. As I think Heraclitus in a place speaketh of them that sleep, that even they do work in their kind, and do confer to the general operations of the world. One man therefore doth co-operate after one sort, and another after another sort; but even he that doth murmur, and to his power doth resist and hinder; even he as much as any doth co-operate. For of such also did the world stand in need. Now do thou consider among which of these thou wilt rank thyself. For as for him who is the Administrator of all, he will make good use of thee whether thou wilt or no, and make thee (as a part and member of the whole) so to co-operate with him, that whatsoever thou doest, shall turn to the furtherance of his own counsels, and resolutions. But be not thou for shame such a part of the whole, as that vile and ridiculous verse (which Chrysippus in a place doth mention) is a part of the comedy.

XXXVIII. Doth either the sun take upon him to do that which belongs to the rain? or his son Aesculapius that, which unto the earth doth properly belong? How is it with every one of the stars in particular? Though they all differ one from another, and have their several charges and functions by themselves, do they not all nevertheless concur and co- operate to one end?

XXXIX. If so be that the Gods have deliberated in particular of those things that should happen unto me, I must stand to their deliberation, as discrete and wise. For that a God should be an imprudent God, is a thing hard even to conceive: and why should they resolve to do me hurt? for what profit either unto them or the universe (which they specially take care for) could arise from it? But if so be that they have not deliberated of me in particular, certainly they have of the whole in general, and those things which in consequence and coherence of this general deliberation happen unto me in particular, I am bound to embrace and accept of. But if so be that they have not deliberated at all (which indeed is very irreligious for any man to believe: for then let us neither sacrifice, nor pray, nor respect our oaths, neither let us any more use any of those things, which we persuaded of the presence and secret conversation of the Gods among us, daily use and practise:) but, I say, if so be that they have not indeed either in general, or particular deliberated of any of those things, that happen unto us in this world; yet God be thanked, that of those things that concern myself, it is lawful for me to deliberate myself, and all my deliberation is but concerning that which may be to me most profitable. Now that unto every one is most profitable, which is according to his own constitution and nature. And my nature is, to be rational in all my actions and as a good, and natural member of a city and commonwealth, towards my fellow members ever to be sociably and kindly disposed and affected. My city and country as I am Antoninus, is Rome; as a man, the whole world. Those things therefore that are expedient and profitable to those cities, are the only things that are good and expedient for me.

XL. Whatsoever in any kind doth happen to any one, is expedient to the whole. And thus much to content us might suffice, that it is expedient for the whole in general. But yet this also shalt thou generally perceive, if thou dost diligently take heed, that whatsoever doth happen to any one man or men.... And now I am content that the word expedient, should more generally be understood of those things which we otherwise call middle things, or things indifferent; as health, wealth, and the like.

XLI. As the ordinary shows of the theatre and of other such places, when thou art presented with them, affect thee; as the same things still seen, and in the same fashion, make the sight ingrateful and tedious; so must all the things that we see all our life long affect us. For all things, above and below, are still the same, and from the same causes. When then will there be an end?

XLII. Let the several deaths of men of all sorts, and of all sorts of professions, and of all sort of nations, be a perpetual object of thy thoughts,... so that thou mayst even come down to Philistio, Phoebus, and Origanion. Pass now to other generations. Thither shall we after many changes, where so many brave orators are; where so many grave philosophers; Heraclitus, Pythagoras, Socrates. Where so many heroes of the old times; and then so many brave captains of the latter times; and so many kings. After all these, where Eudoxus, Hipparchus, Archimedes; where so many other sharp, generous, industrious, subtile, peremptory dispositions; and among others, even they, that have been the greatest scoffers and deriders of the frailty and brevity of this our human life; as Menippus, and others, as many as there have been such as he. Of all these consider, that they long since are all dead, and gone. And what do they suffer by it! Nay they that have not so much as a name remaining, what are they the worse for it? One thing there is, and that only, which is worth our while in this world, and ought by us much to be esteemed; and that is, according to truth and right-eousness, meekly and lovingly to converse with false, and unrighteous men.

XLIII. When thou wilt comfort and cheer thyself, call to mind the several gifts and virtues of them, whom thou dost daily converse with; as for example, the industry of the one; the modesty of another; the liberality of a third; of another some other thing. For nothing can so much rejoice thee, as the re-semblances and parallels of several virtues, visible and eminent in the dispositions of those who live with thee; especially when, all at once, as near as may be, they represent themselves unto thee. And therefore thou must have them always in a readiness.

XLIV. Dost thou grieve that thou dost weigh but so many pounds, and not three hundred rather? Just as much reason hast thou to grieve that thou must live but so many years, and not longer. For as for bulk and substance thou dost content thyself with that proportion of it that is allotted unto thee, so shouldst thou for time.

XLV. Let us do our best endeavours to persuade them; but however, if reason and justice lead thee to it, do it, though they be never so much against it. But if any shall by force withstand thee, and hinder thee in it, convert thy virtu-ous inclination from one object unto another, from justice to contented equanimity, and cheerful patience: so that what in the one is thy hindrance, thou mayst make use of it for the exercise of another virtue: and remember that it was with due exception, and reservation, that thou didst at first incline and desire. For thou didst not set thy mind upon things impossible. Upon what then? that all thy desires might ever be moderated with this due kind of reservation. And this thou hast, and mayst always obtain, whether the thing desired be in thy power or no. And what do I care for more, if that for which I was born and brought forth into the world (to rule all my desires with reason and discretion) may be?

XLVI. The ambitious supposeth another man's act, praise and applause, to be his own happiness; the voluptuous his own sense and feeling; but he that is wise, his own action.

XLVII. It is in thy power absolutely to exclude all manner of conceit and opinion, as concerning this matter; and by the same means, to exclude all grief and sorrow from thy soul. For as for the things and objects themselves, they of themselves have no such power, whereby to beget and force upon us any opinion at all.

XLVIII. Use thyself when any man speaks unto thee, so to hearken **unto** him, as that in the interim thou give not way to any other thoughts; that so thou mayst (as far as is possible) seem fixed and fastened to his very soul, whosoever he be that speaks unto thee.

XLIX. That which is not good for the bee-hive, cannot be good for the bee.

L. Will either passengers, or patients, find fault and complain, either the one if they be well carried, or the others if well cured? Do they take care for any more than this; the one, that their shipmaster may bring them safe to land, and the other, that their physician may effect their recovery?

LI. How many of them who came into the world at the same time when I did, are already gone out of it?

LII. To them that are sick of the jaundice, honey seems bitter; and to them that are bitten by a mad dog, the water terrible; and to children, a little ball seems a fine thing. And why then should I be angry? or do I think that error and false opinion is less powerful to make men transgress, than either choler, being immoderate and excessive, to cause the jaundice; or poison, to cause rage?

LIII. No man can hinder thee to live as thy nature doth require. Nothing can happen unto thee, but what the common good of nature doth require.

LIV. What manner of men they be whom they seek to please, and what to get, and by what actions: how soon time will cover and bury all things, and how many it hath already buried!

The Seventh Book

I. What is wickedness? It is that which many time and often thou hast already seen and known in the world. And so oft as anything doth happen that might otherwise trouble thee, let this memento presently come to thy mind, that it is that which thou hast already often Seen and known. Generally, above and below, thou shalt find but the same things. The very same things whereof ancient stories, middle age stories, and fresh stories are full whereof towns are full, and houses full. There is nothing that is new. All things that are, are both usual and of little continuance.

II. What fear is there that thy dogmata, or philosophical resolutions and conclusions, should become dead in thee, and lose their proper power and efficacy to make thee live happy, as long as those proper and correlative fancies, and representations of things on which they mutually depend (which continually to stir up and revive is in thy power,) are still kept fresh and alive? It is in my power concerning this thing that is happened, what soever it be, to conceit that which is right and true. If it be, why then am I troubled? Those things that are without my understanding, are nothing to it at all: and that is it only, which doth properly concern me. Be always in this mind, and thou wilt be right.

III. That which most men would think themselves most happy for, and would prefer before all things, if the Gods would grant it unto them after their deaths, thou mayst whilst thou livest grant unto thyself; to live again. See the things of the world again, as thou hast already seen them. For what is it else to live again? Public shows and solemnities with much pomp and vanity, stage plays, flocks and herds; conflicts and contentions: a bone thrown to a company of hungry curs; a bait for greedy fishes; the painfulness, and continual burden-bearing of wretched ants, the running to and fro of terrified mice: little puppets drawn up and down with wires and nerves: these be the objects of the world among all these thou must stand steadfast, meekly affected, and free from all manner of indignation; with this right ratiocination and apprehension; that as the worth is of those things which a man doth affect, so is in very deed every man's worth more or less.

IV. Word after word, every one by itself, must the things that are spoken be conceived and understood; and so the things that are done, purpose after purpose, every one by itself likewise. And as in matter of purposes and actions, we must presently see what is the proper use and relation of every one; so of words must we be as ready, to consider of every one what is the true meaning, and signification of it according to truth and nature, however it be taken in common use.

V. Is my reason, and understanding sufficient for this, or no? If it be sufficient, without any private applause, or public ostentation as of an instrument, which by nature I am provided of, I will make use of it for the work in hand, as of an instrument, which by nature I am provided of. if it be not, and that otherwise it belong not unto me particularly as a private duty, I will either give it over, and leave it to some other that can better effect it: or I will endeavour it; but with the help of some other, who with the joint help of my reason, is able to bring somewhat to pass, that will now be seasonable and useful for the common good. For whatsoever I do either by myself, or with some other, the only thing that I must intend, is, that it be good and expedient for the public. For as for praise, consider how many who once were much commended, are now already quite forgotten, yea they that commended them, how even they themselves are long since dead and gone. Be not therefore ashamed, whensoever thou must use the help of others. For whatsoever it be that lieth upon thee to effect, thou must propose it unto thyself, as the scaling of walls is unto a soldier. And what if thou through either lameness or some other impediment art not able to reach unto the top of the battlements alone, which with the help of another thou mayst; wilt thou therefore give it over, or go about it with less courage and alacrity, because thou canst not effect it all alone?

VI. Let not things future trouble thee. For if necessity so require that they come to pass, thou shalt (whensoever that is) be provided for them with the same reason, by which whatsoever is now present, is made both tolerable and acceptable unto thee. All things are linked and knitted together, and the knot is sacred, neither is there anything in the world, that is not kind and natural in regard of any other thing, or, that hath not some kind of reference and natural correspondence with whatsoever is in the world besides. For all things are ranked together, and by that decency of its due place and order that each particular doth observe, they all concur together to the making of one and the same ["Kosmos" ed] or world: as if you said, a comely piece, or an orderly composition. For all things throughout, there is but one and the same order; and through all things, one and the same God, the same substance and the same law. There is one common reason, and one common truth, that belongs unto all reasonable creatures, for neither is there save one perfection of all creatures that are of the same kind, and partakers of the same reason.

VII. Whatsoever is material, doth soon vanish away into the common substance of the whole; and whatsoever is formal, or, whatsoever doth animate that which is material, is soon resumed into the common reason of the whole; and the fame and memory of anything, is soon swallowed up by the general age and duration of the whole.

VIII. To a reasonable creature, the same action is both according to nature, and according to reason.

IX. Straight of itself, not made straight.

X. As several members in one body united, so are reasonable creatures in a body divided and dispersed, all made and prepared for one common operation. And this thou shalt apprehend the better, if thou shalt use thyself often to say to thyself, I am meloz, or a member of the mass and body of reasonable substances. But if thou shalt say I am meroz, or a part, thou dost not yet love men from thy heart. The joy that thou takest in the exercise of bounty, is not yet grounded upon a due ratiocination and right apprehension of the nature of things. Thou dost exercise it as yet upon this ground barely, as a thing convenient and fitting; not, as doing good to thyself, when thou dost good unto others.

XI. Of things that are external, happen what will to that which can suffer by external accidents. Those things that suffer let them complain themselves, if they will; as for me, as long as I conceive no such thing, that that which is happened is evil, I have no hurt; and it is in my power not to conceive any such thing.

XII. Whatsoever any man either doth or saith, thou must be good; not for any man's sake, but for thine own nature's sake; as if either gold, or the emerald, or purple, should ever be saying to themselves, Whatsoever any man either doth or saith, I must still be an emerald, and I must keep my colour.

XIII. This may ever be my comfort and security: my understanding, that ruleth over all, will not of itself bring trouble and vexation upon itself. This I say; it will not put itself in any fear, it will not lead itself into any concupiscence. If it be in the power of any other to compel it to fear, or to grieve, it is free for him to use his power. But sure if itself do not of itself, through some false opinion or supposition incline itself to any such disposition; there is no fear. For as for the body, why should I make the grief of my body, to be the grief of my mind? If that itself can either fear or complain, let it. But as for the soul, which indeed, can only be truly sensible of either fear or grief; to which only it belongs according to its different imaginations and opinions, to admit of either of these, or of their contraries; thou mayst look to that thyself, that it suffer nothing. Induce her not to any such opinion or persuasion. The understanding is of itself sufficient unto itself, and needs not (if itself doth not bring itself to need) any other thing besides itself, and by consequent as it needs nothing, so neither can it be troubled or hindered by anything, if itself doth not trouble and hinder itself.

XIV. What is rv&nfLovia, or happiness: but a7~o~ &d~wv, or, a good da~rnon, or spirit? What then dost thou do here, O opinion? By the Gods I adjure thee, that thou get thee gone, as thou earnest: for I need thee not. Thou earnest indeed unto me according to thy ancient wonted manner. It is that, that all men have ever been subject unto. That thou camest therefore I am not angry with thee, only begone, now that I have found thee what thou art.

XV. Is any man so foolish as to fear change, to which all things that once were not owe their being? And what is it, that is more pleasing and more familiar to the nature of the universe? How couldst thou thyself use thy ordinary hot baths, should not the wood that heateth them first be changed? How couldst thou receive any nourishment from those things that thou hast eaten, if they should not be changed? Can anything else almost (that is useful and profitable) be brought to pass without change? How then dost not thou perceive, that for thee also, by death, to come to change, is a thing of the very same nature, and as necessary for the nature of the universe?

XVI. Through the substance of the universe, as through a torrent pass all particular bodies, being all of the same nature, and all joint workers with the universe itself as in one of our bodies so many members among themselves. How many such as Chrysippus, how many such as Socrates, how many such as Epictetus, hath the age of the world long since swallowed up and devoured? Let this, be it either men or businesses, that thou hast occasion to think of, to the end that thy thoughts be not distracted and thy mind too earnestly set upon anything, upon every such occasion presently come to thy mind. Of all my thoughts and cares, one only thing shall be the object, that I myself do nothing which to the proper constitution of man, (either in regard of the thing itself, or in regard of the manner, or of the time of doing,) is contrary. The time when thou shalt have forgotten all things, is at hand. And that time also is at hand, when thou thyself shalt be forgotten by all. Whilst thou art, apply thyself to that especially which unto man as he is a mart, is most proper and agreeable, and that is, for a man even to love them that transgress against him. This shall be, if at the same time that any such thing doth happen, thou call to mind, that they are thy kinsmen; that it is through ignorance and against their wills that they sin; and that within a very short while after, both thou and he shall be no more. But above all things, that he hath not done thee any hurt; for that by him thy mind and understanding is not made worse or more vile than it was before.

XVII. The nature of the universe, of the common substance of all things as it were of so much wax hath now perchance formed a horse; and then, destroying that figure, hath new tempered and fashioned the matter of it into the form and substance of a tree: then that again into the form and substance of a man: and then that again into some other. Now every one of these doth subsist but for a very little while. As for dissolution, if it be no grievous thing to the chest or trunk, to be joined together; why should it be more grievous to be put asunder?

XVIII. An angry countenance is much against nature, and it is oftentimes the proper countenance of them that are at the point of death. But were it so, that all anger and passion were so thoroughly quenched in thee, that it were altogether impossible to kindle it any more, yet herein must not thou rest satisfied, but further endeavour by good consequence of true ratiocination, perfectly to conceive and understand, that all anger and passion is against reason. For if thou shalt not be sensible of thine innocence; if that also shall be gone from thee, the comfort of a good conscience, that thou doest all things according to reason: what shouldest thou live any longer for? All things that now thou seest, are but for a moment. That nature, by which all things in the world are administered, will soon bring change and alteration upon them, and then of their substances make other things like unto them: and then soon after others again of the matter and substance of these: that so by these means, the world may still appear fresh and new.

XIX. Whensoever any man doth trespass against other, presently consider with thyself what it was that he did suppose to be good, what to be evil, when he did trespass. For this when thou knowest, thou wilt pity him thou wilt have no occasion either to wonder, or to be angry. For either thou thyself dust yet live in that error and ignorance, as that thou dust suppose either that very thing that he doth, or some other like worldly thing, to be good; and so thou art bound to pardon him if he have done that which thou in the like case wouldst have done thyself. Or if so be that thou dost not any more suppose the same things to be good or evil, that he doth; how canst thou but be gentle unto him that is in an error?

XX. Fancy not to thyself things future, as though they were present but of those that are present, take some aside, that thou takest most benefit of, and consider of them particularly, how wonderfully thou wouldst want them, if they were not present. But take heed withal, lest that whilst thou dust settle thy contentment in things present, thou grow in time so to overprize them, as that the want of them (whensoever it shall so fall out) should be a trouble and a vexation unto thee. Wind up thyself into thyself. Such is the nature of thy reasonable commanding part, as that if it exercise justice, and have by that means tranquillity within itself, it doth rest fully satisfied with itself without any other thing.

XXI. Wipe off all opinion stay the force and violence of unreasonable lusts and affections: circumscribe the present time examine whatsoever it be that is happened, either to thyself or to another: divide all present objects, either in that which is formal or material think of the last hour. That which thy neighbour hath committed, where the guilt of it lieth, there let it rest. Examine in order whatsoever is spoken. Let thy mind penetrate both into the effects, and into the causes. Rejoice thyself with true simplicity, and modesty; and that all middle things between virtue and vice are indifferent unto thee. Finally, love mankind; obey God.

XXII. All things (saith he) are by certain order and appointment. And what if the elements only. It will suffice to remember, that all things in general are by certain order and appointment: or if it be but few. And as concerning death, that either dispersion, or the atoms, or annihilation, or extinction, or translation will ensue. And as concerning pain, that that which is intolerable is soon ended by death; and that which holds long must needs be tolerable; and that the mind in the meantime (which is all in all) may by way of interclusion, or interception, by stopping all manner of commerce and sympathy with the body, still retain its own tranquillity. Thy understanding is not made worse by it. As for those parts that suffer, let them, if they can, declare their grief themselves. As for praise and commendation, view their mind and understanding, what estate they are in; what kind of things they fly, and what things they seek after: and that as in the seaside, whatsoever was before to be seen, is by the continual succession of new heaps of sand cast up one upon another, soon hid and covered; so in this life, all former things by those which immediately succeed.

XXIII. Out of Plato. 'He then whose mind is endowed with true magnanimity, who hath accustomed himself to the contemplation both of all times, and of all things in general; can this mortal life (thinkest thou) seem any great matter unto him? It is not possible, answered he. Then neither will such a one account death a grievous thing? By no means.'

XXIV. Out of Antisthenes. 'It is a princely thing to do well, and to be ill-spoken of. It is a shameful thing that the face should be subject unto the mind, to be put into what shape it will, and to be dressed by it as it will; and that the mind should not bestow so much care upon herself, as to fashion herself, and to dress herself as best becometh her.'

XXV. Out of several poets and comics. 'It will but little avail thee, to turn thine anger and indignation upon the things themselves that have fallen across unto thee. For as for them, they are not sensible of it, &c. Thou shalt but make thyself a laughing-stock; both unto the Gods and men, &c. Our life is reaped like a ripe ear of corn; one is yet standing and another is down, &c. But if so be that I and my children be neglected by the gods, there is some reason even for that, &c. As long as right and equity is of my side, &c. Not to lament with them, not to tremble, &c.'

XXVI. Out of Plato. 'My answer, full of justice and equity, should be this: Thy speech is not right, O man! if thou supposest that he that is of any worth at all, should apprehend either life or death, as a matter of great hazard and danger; and should not make this rather his only care, to examine his own actions, whether just or unjust: whether actions of a good, or of a wicked man, &c. For thus in very truth stands the case, O ye men of Athens. What place or station soever a man either hath chosen to himself, judging it best for himself; or is by lawful authority put and settled in, therein do I think (all appearance of danger notwithstanding) that he should continue, as one who feareth neither death, nor anything else, so much as he feareth to commit anything that is vicious and shameful, &c. But, O noble sir, consider I pray, whether true generosity and true happiness, do not consist in somewhat else rather, than in the preservation either of our, or other men's lives. For it is not the part of a man that is a man indeed, to desire to live long or to make much of his life whilst he liveth: but rather (he that is such) will in these things wholly refer himself unto the Gods, and believing that which every woman can tell him, that no man can escape death; the only thing that he takes thought and care for is this, that what time he liveth, he may live as well and as virtuously as he can possibly, &c. To look about, and with the eyes to follow the course of the stars and planets as though thou wouldst run with them; and to mind perpetually the several changes of the elements one into another. For such fancies and imaginations, help much to purge away the dross and filth of this our earthly life,' &c. That also is a fine passage of Plato's, where he speaketh of worldly things in these words: 'Thou must also as from some higher place look down, as it were, upon the things of this world, as flocks, armies, husbandmen's labours, marriages, divorces, generations, deaths: the tumults of courts and places of judicatures; desert places; the several nations of barbarians, public festivals, mournings, fairs, markets.' How all things upon earth are pell-mell; and how miraculously things contrary one to another, concur to the beauty and perfection of this universe.

XXVII. To look back upon things of former ages, as upon the manifold changes and conversions of several monarchies and commonwealths. We may also foresee things future, for they shall all be of the same kind; neither is it possible that they should leave the tune, or break the concert that is now begun, as it were, by these things that are now done and brought to pass in the world. It comes all to one therefore, whether a man be a spectator of the things of this life but forty years, or whether he see them ten thousand years together: for what shall he see more? 'And as for those parts that came from the earth, they shall return unto the earth again; and those that came from heaven, they also shall return unto those heavenly places.' Whether it be a mere dissolution and unbinding of the manifold intricacies and entanglements of the confused atoms; or some such dispersion of the simple and incorruptible elements... 'With meats and drinks and divers charms, they seek to divert the channel, that they might not die. Yet must we needs endure that blast of wind that cometh from above, though we toil and labour never so much.'

XXVIII. He hath a stronger body, and is a better wrestler than I. What then? Is he more bountiful? is he more modest? Doth he bear all adverse chances with more equanimity: or with his neighbour's offences with more meekness and gentleness than I?

XXIX. Where the matter may be effected agreeably to that reason, which both unto the Gods and men is common, there can be no just cause of grief or sorrow. For where the fruit and benefit of an action well begun and prosecuted according to the proper constitution of man may be reaped and obtained, or is sure and certain, it is against reason that any damage should there be suspected. In all places, and at all times, it is in thy power religiously to embrace whatsoever by God's appointment is happened unto thee, and justly to converse with those men, whom thou hast to do with, and accurately to examine every fancy that presents itself, that nothing may slip and steal in, before thou hast rightly apprehended the true nature of it.

XXX. Look not about upon other men's minds and understandings; but look right on forwards whither nature, both that of the universe, in those things that happen unto thee; and thine in particular, in those things that are done by thee: doth lead, and direct thee. Now every one is bound to do that, which is consequent and agreeable to that end which by his true natural constitution he was ordained unto. As for all other things, they are ordained for the use of reasonable creatures: as in all things we see that that which is worse and inferior, is made for that which is better. Reasonable creatures, they are ordained one for another. That therefore which is chief in every man's constitution, is, that he intend the common good. The second is, that he yield not to any lusts and motions of the flesh. For it is the part and privilege of the reasonable and intellective faculty, that she can so bound herself, as that neither the sensitive, nor the appetitive faculties, may not anyways prevail upon her. For both these are brutish. And therefore over both she challengeth mastery, and cannot anyways endure, if in her right temper, to be subject unto either. And this indeed most justly. For by nature she was ordained to command all in the body. The third thing proper to man by his constitution, is, to avoid all rashness and precipitancy; and not to be subject to error. To these things then, let the mind apply herself and go straight on, without any distraction about other things, and she hath her end, and by consequent her happiness.

XXXI. As one who had lived, and were now to die by right, whatsoever is yet remaining, bestow that wholly as a gracious overplus upon a virtuous life. Love and affect that only, whatsoever it be that happeneth, and is by the fates appointed unto thee. For what can be more reasonable? And as anything doth happen unto thee by way of cross, or calamity, call to mind presently and set before thine eyes, the examples of some other men, to whom the self-same thing did once happen likewise. Well, what did they? They grieved; they wondered; they complained. And where are they now? All dead and gone. Wilt thou also be like one of them? Or rather leaving to men of the world (whose life both in regard of themselves, and them that they converse with, is nothing but mere mutability; or men of as fickle minds, as fickle bodies; ever changing and soon changed themselves) let it be thine only care and study, how to make a right use of all such accidents. For there is good use to be made of them, and they will prove fit matter for thee to work upon, if it shall be both thy care and thy desire, that whatsoever thou doest, thou thyself mayst like and approve thyself for it.

And both these, see, that thou remember well, according as the diversity of the matter of the action that thou art about shall require. Look within; within is the fountain of all good. Such a fountain, where springing waters can never fail, so thou dig still deeper and deeper.

XXXII. Thou must use thyself also to keep thy body fixed and steady; free from all loose fluctuant either motion, or posture. And as upon thy face and looks, thy mind hath easily power over them to keep them to that which is grave and decent; so let it challenge the same power over the whole body also. But so observe all things in this kind, as that it be without any manner of affectation.

XXXIII. The art of true living in this world is more like a wrestler's, than a dancer's practice. For in this they both agree, to teach a man whatsoever falls upon him, that he may be ready for it, and that nothing may cast him down.

XXXIV. Thou must continually ponder and consider with thyself, what manner of men they be, and for their minds and understandings what is their present estate, whose good word and testimony thou dost desire. For then neither wilt thou see cause to complain of them that offend against their wills; or find any want of their applause, if once thou dost but penetrate into the true force and ground both of their opinions, and of their desires. 'No soul (saith he) is willingly bereft of the truth,' and by consequent, neither of justice, or temperance, or kindness, and mildness; nor of anything that is of the same kind. It is most needful that thou shouldst always remember this. For so shalt thou be far more gentle and moderate towards all men.

XXXV. What pain soever thou art in, let this presently come to thy mind, that it is not a thing whereof thou needest to be ashamed, neither is it a thing whereby thy understanding, that hath the government of all, can be made worse. For neither in regard of the substance of it, nor in regard of the end of it (which is, to intend the common good) can it alter and corrupt it. This also of Epicurus mayst thou in most pains find some help of, that it is 'neither intolerable, nor eternal;' so thou keep thyself to the true bounds and limits of reason and give not way to opinion. This also thou must consider, that many things there be, which oftentimes unsensibly trouble and vex thee, as not armed against them with patience, because they go not ordinarily under the name of pains, which in very deed are of the same nature as pain; as to slumber unquietly, to suffer heat, to want appetite: when therefore any of these things make thee discontented, check thyself with these words: Now hath pain given thee the foil; thy courage hath failed thee.

XXXVI. Take heed lest at any time thou stand so affected, though towards unnatural evil men, as ordinary men are commonly one towards another.

XXXVII. How know we whether Socrates were so eminent indeed, and of so extraordinary a disposition? For that he died more gloriously, that he disputed with the Sophists more subtilty; that he watched in the frost more assiduously; that being commanded to fetch innocent Salaminius, he refused to do it more generously; all this will not serve. Nor that he walked in the streets, with much gravity and majesty, as was objected unto him by his adversaries: which nevertheless a man may well doubt of, whether it were so or no, or, which above all the rest, if so be that it were true, a man would well consider of, whether commendable, or dis-commendable. The thing therefore that we must inquire into, is this; what manner of soul Socrates had: whether his disposition was such; as that all that he stood upon, and sought after in this world, was barely this, that he might ever carry himself justly towards men, and holily towards the Gods. Neither vexing himself to no purpose at the wickedness of others, nor yet ever condescending to any man's evil fact, or evil intentions, through either fear, or engagement of friendship. Whether of those things that happened unto him by God's appointment, he neither did wonder at any when it did happen, or thought it intolerable in the trial of it. And lastly, whether he never did suffer his mind to sympathise with the senses, and affections of the body. For we must not think that Nature hath so mixed and tempered it with the body, as that she hath not power to circumscribe herself, and by herself to intend her own ends and occasions.

XXXVIII. For it is a thing very possible, that a man should be a very divine man, and yet be altogether unknown. This thou must ever be mindful of, as of this also, that a man's true happiness doth consist in very few things. And that although thou dost despair, that thou shalt ever be a good either logician, or naturalist, yet thou art never the further off by it from being either liberal, or modest, or charitable, or obedient unto God.

XXXIX. Free from all compulsion in all cheerfulness and alacrity thou mayst run out thy time, though men should exclaim against thee never so much, and the wild beasts should pull in sunder the poor members of thy pampered mass of flesh. For what in either of these or the like cases should hinder the mind to retain her own rest and tranquillity, consisting both in the right judgment of those things that happen unto her, and in the ready use of all present matters and occasions? So that her judgment may say, to that which is befallen her by way of cross: this thou art in very deed, and according to thy true nature: notwithstanding that in the judgment of opinion thou dust appear otherwise: and her discretion to the present object; thou art that, which I sought for. For whatsoever it be, that is now present, shall ever be embraced by me as a fit and seasonable object, both for my reasonable faculty, and for my sociable, or charitable inclination to work upon. And that which is principal in this matter, is that it may be referred either unto the praise of God, or to the good of men. For either unto God or man, whatsoever it is that doth happen in the world hath in the ordinary course of nature its proper reference; neither is there anything, that in regard of nature is either new, or reluctant and intractable, but all things both usual and easy.

XL. Then hath a man attained to the estate of perfection in his life and conversation, when he so spends every day, as if it were his last day: never hot and vehement in his affections, nor yet so cold and stupid as one that had no sense; and free from all manner of dissimulation.

XLI. Can the Gods, who are immortal, for the continuance of so many ages bear without indignation with such and so many sinners, as have ever been, yea not only so, but also take such care for them, that they want nothing; and dust thou so grievously take on, as one that could bear with them no longer; thou that art but for a moment of time? yea thou that art one of those sinners thyself? A very ridiculous thing it is, that any man should dispense with vice and wickedness in himself, which is in his power to restrain; and should go about to suppress it in others, which is altogether impossible.

XLII. What object soever, our reasonable and sociable faculty doth meet with, that affords nothing either for the satisfaction of reason, or for the practice of charity, she worthily doth think unworthy of herself.

XLIII. When thou hast done well, and another is benefited by thy action, must thou like a very fool look for a third thing besides, as that it may appear unto others also that thou hast done well, or that thou mayest in time, receive one good turn for another? No man useth to be weary of that which is beneficial unto him. But every action according to nature, is beneficial. Be not weary then of doing that which is beneficial unto thee, whilst it is so unto others.

XLIV. The nature of the universe did once certainly before it was created, whatsoever it hath done since, deliberate and so resolve upon the creation of the world. Now since that time, whatsoever it is, that is and happens in the world, is either but a consequent of that one and first deliberation: or if so be that this ruling rational part of the world, takes any thought and care of things particular, they are surely his reasonable and principal creatures, that are the proper object of his particular care and providence. This often thought upon, will much conduce to thy tranquillity.

The Eighth Book

I. This also, among other things, may serve to keep thee from vainglory; if thou shalt consider, that thou art now altogether incapable of the commendation of one, who all his life long, or from his youth at least, hath lived a philosopher's life. For both unto others, and to thyself especially, it is well known, that thou hast done many things contrary to that perfection of life. Thou hast therefore been confounded in thy course, and henceforth it will be hard for thee to recover the title and credit of a philosopher. And to it also is thy calling and profession repugnant. If therefore thou dost truly understand, what it is that is of moment indeed; as for thy fame and credit, take no thought or care for that: let it suffice thee if all the rest of thy life, be it more or less, thou shalt live as thy nature requireth, or according to the true and natural end of thy making. Take pains therefore to know what it is that thy nature requireth, and let nothing else distract thee. Thou hast already had sufficient experience, that of those many things that hitherto thou hast erred and wandered about, thou couldst not find happiness in any of them. Not in syllogisms, and logical subtilties, not in wealth, not in honour and reputation, not in pleasure. In none of all these. Wherein then is it to be found? In the practice of those things, which the nature of man, as he is a man, doth require. How then shall he do those things? if his dogmata, or moral tenets and opinions (from which all motions and actions do proceed), be right and true. Which be those dogmata? Those that concern that which is good or evil, as that there is nothing truly good and beneficial unto man, but that which makes him just, temperate, courageous, liberal; and that there is nothing truly evil and hurtful unto man, but that which causeth the contrary effects.

II. Upon every action that thou art about, put this question to thyself; How will this when it is done agree with me? Shall I have no occasion to repent of it? Yet a very little while and I am dead and gone; and all things are at end. What then do I care for more than this, that my present action whatsoever it be, may be the proper action of one that is reasonable; whose end is, the common good; who in all things is ruled and governed by the same law of right and reason, by which God Himself is.

III. Alexander, Caius, Pompeius; what are these to Diogenes, Heraclitus, and Socrates? These penetrated into the true nature of things; into all causes, and all subjects: and upon these did they exercise their power and authority. But as for those, as the extent of their error was, so far did their slavery extend.

IV. What they have done, they will still do, although thou shouldst hang thyself. First; let it not trouble thee. For all things both good and evil: come to pass according to the nature and general condition of the universe, and within a very little while, all things will be at an end; no man will be remembered: as now of Africanus (for example) and Augustus it is already come to pass. Then secondly; fix thy mind upon the thing itself; look into it, and remembering thyself, that thou art bound nevertheless to be a good man, and what it is that thy nature requireth of thee as thou art a man, be not diverted from what thou art about, and speak that which seemeth unto thee most just: only speak it kindly, modestly, and without hypocrisy.

V. That which the nature of the universe doth busy herself about, is; that which is here, to transfer it thither, to change it, and thence again to take it away, and to carry it to another place. So that thou needest not fear any new thing. For all things are usual and ordinary; and all things are disposed by equality.

VI. Every particular nature hath content, when in its own proper course it speeds. A reasonable nature doth then speed, when first in matter of fancies and imaginations, it gives no consent to that which is either false uncertain. Secondly, when in all its motions and resolutions it takes its level at the common good only, and that it desireth nothing, and flieth from nothing, bet what is in its own power to compass or avoid. And lastly, when it willingly and gladly embraceth, whatsoever is dealt and appointed unto it by the common nature. For it is part of it; even as the nature of any one leaf, is part of the common nature of all plants and trees. But that the nature of a leaf, is part of a nature both unreasonable and unsensible, and which in its proper end may be hindered; or, which is servile and slavish: whereas the nature of man is part of a common nature which cannot be hindered, and which is both reasonable and just. From whence also it is, that accord ing to the worth of everything, she doth make such equal distribution of all things, as of duration, substance form, operation, and of events and accidents. But herein consider not whether thou shalt find this equality in everything absolutely and by itself; but whether in all the particulars of some one thing taken together, and compared with all the particulars of some other thing, and them together likewise.

VII. Thou hast no time nor opportunity to read. What then? Hast thou not time and opportunity to exercise thyself, not to wrong thyself; to strive against all carnal pleasures and pains, and to aet the upper hand of them; to contemn honour and vainglory; and not only, not to be angry with them, whom towards thee thou doest find unsensible and unthankful; but also to have a care of them still, and of their welfare?

VIII. Forbear henceforth to complain of the trouble of a courtly life, either in public before others, or in private by thyself.

IX. Repentance is an inward and self-reprehension for the neglect or omission of somewhat that was profitable. Now whatsoever is good, is also profitable, and it is the part of an honest virtuous man to set by it, and to make reckoning of it accordingly. But never did any honest virtuous man repent of the neglect or omission of any carnal pleasure: no carnal pleasure then is either good or profitable.

X. This, what is it in itself, and by itself, according to its proper constitution? What is the substance of it? What is the matter, or proper use? What is the form or efficient cause? What is it for in this world, and how long will it abide? Thus must thou examine all things, that present themselves unto thee.

XI. When thou art hard to be stirred up and awaked out of thy sleep, admonish thyself and call to mind, that, to perform actions tending to the common good is that which thine own proper constitution, and that which the nature of man do require. But to sleep, is common to unreasonable creatures also. And what more proper and natural, yea what more kind and pleasing, than that which is according to nature?

XII. As every fancy and imagination presents itself unto thee, consider (if it be possible) the true nature, and the proper qualities of it, and reason with thyself about it.

XIII. At thy first encounter with any one, say presently to thyself: This man, what are his opinions concerning that which is good or evil? as concerning pain, pleasure, and the causes of both; concerning honour, and dishonour, concerning life and death? thus and thus. Now if it be no wonder that a man should have such and such opinions, how can it be a wonder that he should do such and such things? I will remember then, that he cannot but do as he doth, holding those opinions that he doth. Remember, that as it is a shame for any man to wonder that a fig tree should bear figs, so also to wonder that the world should bear anything, whatsoever it is which in the ordinary course of nature it may bear. To a physician also and to a pilot it is a shame either for the one to wonder, that such and such a one should have an ague; or for the other, that the winds should prove Contrary.

XIV. Remember, that to change thy mind upon occasion, and to follow him that is able to rectify thee, is equally ingenuous, as to find out at the first, what is right and just, without help. For of thee nothing is required, ti, is beyond the extent of thine own deliberation and jun. merit, and of thine own understanding.

XV. If it were thine act and in thine own power, wouldest thou do it? If it were not, whom dost tin accuse? the atoms, or the Gods? For to do either, the part of a mad man. Thou must therefore blame nobody, but if it be in thy power, redress what is amiss; if it be not, to what end is it to complain? For nothing should be done but to some certain end.

XVI. Whatsoever dieth and falleth, however and wheresoever it die and fall, it cannot fall out of the world, here it have its abode and change, here also shall it have its dissolution into its proper elements. The same are the world's elements, and the elements of which thou dost consist. And they when they are changed, they murmur not; why shouldest thou?

XVII. Whatsoever is, was made for something: as a horse, a vine. Why wonderest thou? The sun itself will say of itself, I was made for something; and so hath every god its proper function. What then were then made for? to disport and delight thyself? See how even common sense and reason cannot brook it.

XVIII. Nature hath its end as well in the end and final consummation of anything that is, as in the begin-nine and continuation of it.

XIX. As one that tosseth up a ball. And what is a ball the better, if the motion of it be upwards; or the worse if it be downwards; or if it chance to fall upon the ground? So for the bubble; if it continue, what it the better? and if it dissolve, what is it the worse And so is it of a candle too. And so must thou reason with thyself, both in matter of fame, and in matter of death. For as for the body itself, (the subject of death) wouldest thou know the vileness of it? Turn it about that thou mayest behold it the worst sides upwards as well, as in its more ordinary pleasant shape; how doth it look, when it is old and withered? when sick and pained? when in the act of lust, and fornication? And as for fame. This life is short. Both he that praiseth, and he that is praised; he that remembers, and he that is remembered, will soon be dust and ashes. Besides, it is but in one corner of this part of the world that thou art praised; and yet in this corner, thou hast not the joint praises of all men; no nor scarce of any one constantly. And yet the whole earth itself, what is it but as one point, in regard of the whole world?

XX. That which must be the subject of thy consideration, is either the matter itself, or the dogma, or the operation, or the true sense and signification.

XXI. Most justly have these things happened unto thee: why dost not thou amend? O but thou hadst rather become good to-morrow, than to be so to-day.

XXII. Shall I do it? I will; so the end of my action be to do good unto men. Doth anything by way of cross or adversity happen unto me? I accept it, with reference unto the Gods, and their providence; the fountain of all things, from which whatsoever comes to pass, doth hang and depend.

XXIII. By one action judge of the rest: this bathing which usually takes up so much of our time, what is it? Oil, sweat, filth; or the sordes of the body: an excrementitious viscosity, the excrements of oil and other ointments used about the body, and mixed with the sordes of the body: all base and loathsome. And such almost is every part of our life; and every worldly object.

XXIV. Lucilla buried Verus; then was Lucilla herself buried by others. So Secunda Maximus, then Secunda herself. So Epitynchanus, Diotimus; then Epitynchanus himself. So Antoninus Pius, Faustina his wife; then Antoninus himself. This is the course of the world. First Celer, Adrianus; then Adrianus himself. And those austere ones; those that foretold other men's deaths; those that were so proud and stately, where are they now? Those austere ones I mean, such as were Charax, and Demetrius the Platonic, and Eudaemon, and others like unto those. They were all but for one day; all dead and gone long since. Some of them no sooner dead, than forgotten. Others soon turned into fables. Of others, even that which was fabulous, is now long since forgotten. This thereafter thou must remember, that whatsoever thou art compounded of, shall soon be dispersed, and that thy life and breath, or thy soul, shall either be no more or shall ranslated (sp.), and appointed to some certain place and station.

XXV. The true joy of a man, is to do that which properly belongs unto a man. That which is most proper unto a man, is, first, to be kindly affected towards them that are of the same kind and nature as he is himself to contemn all sensual motions and appetites, to discern rightly all plausible fancies and imaginations, to contemplate the nature of the universe; both it, and things that are done in it. In which kind of contemplation three several relations are to be observed The first, to the apparent secondary cause. The Second to the first original cause, God, from whom originally proceeds whatsoever doth happen in the world. The third and last, to them that we live and converse with: what use may be made of it, to their use and benefit.

XXVI. If pain be an evil, either it is in regard of the body; (and that cannot be, because the body of itself is altogether insensible:) or in regard of the soul But it is in the power of the soul, to preserve her own peace and tranquillity, and not to suppose that pain is evil. For all judgment and deliberation; all prosecution, or aversation is from within, whither the sense of evil (except it be let in by opinion) cannot penetrate.

XXVII. Wipe off all idle fancies, and say unto thyself incessantly; Now if I will, it is in my power to keep out of this my soul all wickedness, all lust, and concupiscences, all trouble and confusion. But on the contrary to behold and consider all things according to their true nature, and to carry myself towards everything according to its true worth. Remember then this thy power that nature hath given thee.

XXVIII. Whether thou speak in the Senate or whether thou speak to any particular, let thy speech In always grave and modest. But thou must not openly and vulgarly observe that sound and exact form of speaking, concerning that which is truly good and truly civil; the vanity of the world, and of worldly men: which otherwise truth and reason doth prescribe.

XXIX. Augustus his court; his wife, his daughter, his nephews, his sons-in-law his sister, Agrippa, his kinsmen, his domestics, his friends; Areus, Maecenas, his slayers of beasts for sacrifice and divination: there thou hast the death of a whole court together. Proceed now on to the rest that have been since that of Augustus. Hath death dwelt with them otherwise, though so many and so stately whilst they lived, than it doth use to deal with any one particular man? Consider now the death of a whole kindred and family, as of that of the Pompeys, as that also that useth to be written upon some monuments, HE WAS THE LAST OF HIS OWN KINDRED. O what care did his predecessors take, that they might leave a successor, yet behold at last one or other must of necessity be THE LAST. Here again therefore consider the death of a whole kindred.

XXX. Contract thy whole life to the measure and proportion of one single action. And if in every particular action thou dost perform what is fitting to the utmost of thy power, let it suffice thee. And who can hinder thee, but that thou mayest perform what is fitting? But there may be some outward let and impediment. Not any, that can hinder thee, but that whatsoever thou dost, thou may do it, justly, temperately, and with the praise of God. Yea, but there may be somewhat, whereby some operation or other of thine may be hindered. And then, with that very thing that doth hinder, thou mayest he well pleased, and so by this gentle and equanimious conversion of thy mind unto that which may be, instead of that which at first thou didst intend, in the room of that former action there succeedeth another, which agrees as well with this contraction of thy life, that we now speak of.

XXXI. Receive temporal blessings without ostentation, when they are sent and thou shalt be able to part with them with all readiness and facility when they are taken from thee again.

XXXII. If ever thou sawest either a hand, or a foot, or a head lying by itself, in some place or other, as cut off from the rest of the body, such must thou conceive him to make himself, as much as in him lieth, that either is offended with anything that is happened, (whatsoever it be) and as it were divides himself from it: or that commits anything against the natural law of mutual correspondence, and society among men: or, he that, commits any act of uncharitableness. Whosoever thou art, thou art such, thou art cast forth I know not whither out of the general unity, which is according to nature. Thou went born indeed a part, but now thou hast cut thyself off. However, herein is matter of joy and exultation, that thou mayst be united again. God hath not granted it unto any other part, that once separated and cut off, it might be reunited, and come together again. But, behold, that GOODNESS how great and immense it is! which hath so much esteemed MAN. As at first he was so made, that he needed not, except he would himself, have divided himself from the whole; so once divided and cut off, IT hath so provided and ordered it, that if he would himself, he might return, and grow together again, and be admitted into its former rank and place of a part, as he was before.

XXXIII. As almost all her other faculties and properties the nature of the universe hath imparted unto every reasonable creature, so this in particular we have received from her, that as whatsoever doth oppose itself unto her, and doth withstand her in her purposes and intentions, she doth, though against its will and intention, bring it about to herself, to serve herself of it in the execution of her own destinated ends; and so by this though not intended co-operation of it with herself makes it part of herself whether it will or no. So may every reasonable creature, what crosses and impediments soever it meets with in the course of this mortal life, it may use them as fit and proper objects, to the furtherance of whatsoever it intended and absolutely proposed unto itself as its natural end and happiness.

XXXIV. Let not the general representation unto thyself of the wretchedness of this our mortal life, trouble thee. Let not thy mind wander up and down, and heap together in her thoughts the many troubles and grievous calamities which thou art as subject unto as any other. But as everything in particular doth happen, put this question unto thyself, and say: What is it that in this present matter, seems unto thee so intolerable? For thou wilt be ashamed to confess it. Then upon this presently call to mind, that neither that which is future, nor that which is past can hurt thee; but that only which is present. (And that also is much lessened, if thou dost lightly circumscribe it:) and then check thy mind if for so little a while, (a mere instant), it cannot hold out with patience.

XXXV. What? are either Panthea or Pergamus abiding to this day by their masters' tombs? or either Chabrias or Diotimus by that of Adrianus? O foolery! For what if they did, would their masters be sensible of It? or if sensible, would they be glad of it? or if glad, were these immortal? Was not it appointed unto them also (both men and women,) to become old in time, and then to die? And these once dead, what would become of these former? And when all is done, what is all this for, but for a mere bag of blood and corruption?

XXXVI. If thou beest quick-sighted, be so in matter of judgment, and best discretion, saith he.

XXXVII. In the whole constitution of man, I see not any virtue contrary to justice, whereby it may be resisted and opposed. But one whereby pleasure and voluptuousness may be resisted and opposed, I see: continence.

XXXVIII. If thou canst but withdraw conceit and opinion concerning that which may seem hurtful and offensive, thou thyself art as safe, as safe may be. Thou thyself? and who is that? Thy reason. 'Yea, but I am not reason.' Well, be it so. However, let not thy reason or understanding admit of grief, and if there be anything in thee that is grieved, let that, (whatsoever it be,) conceive its own grief, if it can.

XXXIX. That which is a hindrance of the senses, is an evil to the sensitive nature. That which is a hindrance of the appetitive and prosecutive faculty, is an evil to the sensitive nature. As of the sensitive, so of the vegetative constitution, whatsoever is a hindrance unto it, is also in that respect an evil unto the same. And so likewise, whatsoever is a hindrance unto the mind and understanding, must needs be the proper evil of the reasonable nature. Now apply all those things unto thyself. Do either pain or pleasure seize on thee? Let the senses look to that. Hast thou met with Some obstacle or other in thy purpose and intention? If thou didst propose without due reservation and exception now hath thy reasonable part received a blow indeed But if in general thou didst propose unto thyself what soever might be, thou art not thereby either hurt, nor properly hindered. For in those things that properly belong unto the mind, she cannot be hindered by any man. It is not fire, nor iron; nor the power of a tyrant nor the power of a slandering tongue; nor anything else that can penetrate into her.

XL. If once round and solid, there is no fear that ever it will change.

XLI. Why should I grieve myself; who never did willingly grieve any other! One thing rejoices one and another thing another. As for me, this is my joy, if my understanding be right and sound, as neither averse from any man, nor refusing any of those things which as a man I am subject unto; if I can look upon all things in the world meekly and kindly; accept all things and carry myself towards everything according to to true worth of the thing itself.

XLII. This time that is now present, bestow thou upon thyself. They that rather hunt for fame after death, do not consider, that those men that shall be hereafter, will be even such, as these whom now they can so hardly bear with. And besides they also will be mortal men. But to consider the thing in itself, if so many with so many voices, shall make such and such a sound, or shall have such and such an opinion concerning thee, what is it to thee?

XLIII. Take me and throw me where thou wilt: I am indifferent. For there also I shall have that spirit which is within me propitious; that is well pleased and fully contented both in that constant disposition, and with those particular actions, which to its own proper constitution are suitable and agreeable.

XLIV. Is this then a thing of that worth, that for it my soul should suffer, and become worse than it was? as either basely dejected, or disordinately affected, or confounded within itself, or terrified? What can there be, that thou shouldest so much esteem?

XLV. Nothing can happen unto thee, which is not incidental unto thee, as thou art a man. As nothing can happen either to an ox, a vine, or to a stone, which is not incidental unto them; unto every one in his own kind. If therefore nothing can happen unto anything, which is not both usual and natural; why art thou displeased? Sure the common nature of all would not bring anything upon any, that were intolerable. If therefore it be a thing external that causes thy grief, know, that it is not that properly that doth cause it, but thine own conceit and opinion concerning the thing: which thou mayest rid thyself of, when thou wilt. But if it be somewhat that is amiss in thine own disposition, that doth grieve thee, mayest thou not rectify thy moral tenets and opinions. But if it grieve thee, that thou doest not perform that which seemeth unto thee right and just, why doest not thou choose rather to perform it than to grieve? But somewhat that is stronger than thyself doth hinder thee. Let it not grieve thee then, if it be not thy fault that the thing is not performed. 'Yea but it is a thing of that nature, as that thy life is not worth the while, except it may be performed.' If it be so, upon condition that thou be kindly and lovingly disposed towards all men, thou mayest be gone. For even then, as much as at any time, art thou in a very good estate of performance, when thou doest die in charity with those, that are an obstacle unto thy performance.

XLVI. Remember that thy mind is of that nature as that it becometh altogether unconquerable, when once recollected in herself, she seeks no other content than this, that she cannot be forced: yea though it so fall out, that it be even against reason itself, that it cloth bandy. How much less when by the help of reason she is able to judge of things with discretion? And therefore let thy chief fort and place of defence be, a mind free from passions. A stronger place, (whereunto to make his refuge, and so to become impregnable) and better fortified than this, hath no man. He that seeth not this is unlearned. He that seeth it, and betaketh not himself to this place of refuge, is unhappy.

XLVII. Keep thyself to the first bare and naked apprehensions of things, as they present themselves unto thee, and add not unto them. It is reported unto thee, that such a one speaketh ill of thee. Well; that he speaketh ill of thee, so much is reported. But that thou art hurt thereby, is not reported: that is the addition of opinion, which thou must exclude. I see that my child is sick. That he is sick, I see, but that he is in danger of his life also, I see it not. Thus thou must use to keep thyself to the first motions and apprehensions of things, as they present themselves outwardly; and add not unto them from within thyself through mere conceit and opinion. Or rather add unto them: hut as one that understandeth the true nature of all things that happen in the world.

XLVIII. Is the cucumber bitter? set it away. Brambles are in the way? avoid them. Let this suffice. Add not presently speaking unto thyself, What serve these things for in the world? For, this, one that is acquainted with the mysteries of nature, will laugh at thee for it; as a carpenter would or a shoemaker, if meeting in either of their shops with some shavings, or small remnants of their work, thou shouldest blame them for it. And yet those men, it is not for want of a place where to throw them that they keep them in their shops for a while: but the nature of the universe hath no such out-place; but herein doth consist the wonder of her art and skill, that she having once circumscribed herself within some certain bounds and limits, whatsoever is within her that seems either corrupted, or old, or unprofitable, she can change it into herself, and of these very things can make new things; so that she needeth not to seek elsewhere out of herself either for a new supply of matter and substance, or for a place where to throw out whatsoever is irrecoverably putrid and corrupt. Thus she, as for place, so for matter and art, is herself sufficient unto herself.

XLIX. Not to be slack and negligent; or loose, and wanton in thy actions; nor contentious, and troublesome in thy conversation; nor to rove and wander in thy fancies and imaginations. Not basely to contract thy soul; nor boisterously to sally out with it, or furiously to launch out as it were, nor ever to want employment.

L. 'They kill me, they cut my flesh; they persecute my person with curses.' What then? May not thy mind for all this continue pure, prudent, temperate, just? As a fountain of sweet and clear water, though she be cursed by some stander by, yet do her springs nevertheless still run as sweet and clear as before; yea though either dirt or dung be thrown in, yet is it no sooner thrown, than dispersed, and she cleared. She cannot be dyed or infected by it. What then must I do, that I may have within myself an overflowing fountain, and not a well? Beget thyself by continual pains and endeavours to true liberty with charity, and true simplicity and modesty.

LI. He that knoweth not what the world is, knoweth not where he himself is. And he that knoweth not what the world was made for, cannot possibly know either what are the qualities, or what is the nature of the world. Now he that in either of these is to seek, for what he himself was made is ignorant also. What then dost thou think of that man, who proposeth unto himself, as a matter of great moment, the noise and applause of men, who both where they are, and what they are themselves, are altogether ignorant? Dost thou desire to be commended of that man, who thrice in one hour perchance, doth himself curse himself? Dost thou desire to please him, who pleaseth not himself? or dost thou think that he pleaseth himself, who doth use to repent himself almost of everything that he doth?

LII. Not only now henceforth to have a common breath, or to hold correspondency of breath, with that air, that compasseth us about; but to have a common mind, or to hold correspondency of mind also with that rational substance, which compasseth all things. For, that also is of itself, and of its own nature (if a man can but draw it in as he should) everywhere diffused; and passeth through all things, no less than the air doth, if a man can but suck it in.

LIII. Wickedness in general doth not hurt the world. Particular wickedness doth not hurt any other: only unto him it is hurtful, whosoever he be that offends, unto whom in great favour and mercy it is granted, that whensoever he himself shall but first desire it, he may be presently delivered of it. Unto my free-will my neighbour's free-will, whoever he be, (as his life, or his bode), is altogether indifferent. For though we are all made one for another, yet have our minds and understandings each of them their own proper and limited jurisdiction. For else another man's wickedness might be my evil which God would not have, that it might not be in another man's power to make me unhappy: which nothing now can do but mine own wickedness.

LIV. The sun seemeth to be shed abroad. And indeed it is diffused but not effused. For that diffusion of it is a [-r~Jo-tc] or an extension. For therefore are the beams of it called [~i-~m'~] from the word [~KTEIVEO-Oa,,] to be stretched out and extended. Now what a sunbeam is, thou mayest know if thou observe the light of the sun, when through some narrow hole it pierceth into some room that is dark. For it is always in a direct line. And as by any solid body, that it meets with in the way that is not penetrable by air, it is divided and abrupted, and yet neither slides off, or falls down, but stayeth there nevertheless: such must the diffusion in the mind be; not an effusion, but an extension. What obstacles and impediments soever she meeteth within her way, she must not violently, and by way of an impetuous onset light upon them; neither must she fall down; but she must stand, and give light unto that which doth admit of it. For as for that which doth not, it is its own fault and loss, if it bereave itself of her light.

LV. He that feareth death, either feareth that he shall have no sense at all, or that his senses will not be the same. Whereas, he should rather comfort himself, that either no sense at all, and so no sense of evil; or if any sense, then another life, and so no death properly.

LVI. All men are made one for another: either then teach them better, or bear with them.

LVII. The motion of the mind is not as the motion of a dart. For the mind when it is wary and cautelous, and by way of diligent circumspection turneth herself many ways, may then as well be said to go straight on to the object, as when it useth no such circumspection.

LVIII. To pierce and penetrate into the estate of every one's understanding that thou hast to do with: as also to make the estate of thine own open, and penetrable to any other.

The Ninth Book

I. He that is unjust, is also impious. For the nature of the universe, having made all reasonable creatures one for another, to the end that they should do one another good; more or less according to the several persons and occasions but in nowise hurt one another: it is manifest that he that doth transgress against this her will, is guilty of impiety towards the most ancient and venerable of all the deities. For the nature of the universe, is the nature the common parent of all, and therefore piously to be observed of all things that are, and that which now is, to whatsoever first was, and gave it its being, hath relation of blood and kindred. She is also called truth and is the first cause of all truths. He therefore that willingly and wittingly doth lie, is impious in that he doth receive, and so commit injustice: but he that against his will, in that he disagreeth from the nature of the universe, and in that striving with the nature of the world he doth in his particular, violate the general order of the world. For he doth no better than strive and war against it, who contrary to his own nature applieth himself to that which is contrary to truth. For nature had before furnished him with instincts and opportunities sufficient for the attainment of it; which he having hitherto neglected, is not now able to discern that which is false from that which is true. He also that pursues after pleasures, as that which is truly good and flies from pains, as that which is truly evil: is impious. For such a one must of necessity oftentimes accuse that common nature, as distributing many things both unto the evil, and unto the good, not according to the deserts of either: as unto the bad oftentimes pleasures, and the causes of pleasures; so unto the good, pains, and the occasions of pains. Again, he that feareth pains and crosses in this world, feareth some of those things which some time or other must needs happen in the world. And that we have already showed to be impious. And he that pursueth after pleasures, will not spare, to compass his desires, to do that which is unjust, and that is manifestly impious. Now those things which unto nature are equally indifferent (for she had not created both, both pain and pleasure, if both had not been unto her equally indifferent): they that will live according to nature, must in those things (as being of the same mind and disposition that she is) be as equally indifferent. Whosoever therefore in either matter of pleasure and pain; death and life; honour and dishonour, (which things nature in the administration of the world, indifferently doth make use of), is not as indifferent, it is apparent that he is impious. When I say that common nature doth indifferently make use of them, my meaning is, that they happen indifferently in the ordinary course of things, which by a necessary consequence, whether as principal or accessory, come to pass in the world, according to that first and ancient deliberation of Providence, by which she from some certain beginning, did resolve upon the creation of such a world, conceiving then in her womb as it were some certain rational generative seeds and faculties of things future, whether subjects, changes, successions; both such and such, and just so many.

II. It were indeed more happy and comfortable, for a man to depart out of this world, having lived all his life long clear from all falsehood, dissimulation, voluptuousness, and pride. But if this cannot be, yet it is some comfort for a man joyfully to depart as weary, and out of love with those; rather than to desire to live, and to continue long in those wicked courses. Hath not yet experience taught thee to fly from the plague? For a far greater plague is the corruption of the mind, than any certain change and distemper of the common air can be. This is a plague of creatures, as they are living creatures; but that of men as they are men or reasonable.

III. Thou must not in matter of death carry thyself scornfully, but as one that is well pleased with it, as being one of those things that nature hath appointed. For what thou dost conceive of these, of a boy to become a young man, to wax old, to grow, to ripen, to get teeth, or a beard, or grey hairs to beget, to bear, or to be delivered; or what other action soever it be, that is natural unto man according to the several seasons of his life; such a thing is it also to be dissolved. It is therefore the part of a wise man, in matter of death, not in any wise to carry himself either violently, or proudly but patiently to wait for it, as one of nature's operations: that with the same mind as now thou dost expect when that which yet is but an embryo in thy wife's belly shall come forth, thou mayst expect also when thy soul shall fall off from that outward coat or skin: wherein as a child in the belly it lieth involved and shut up. But thou desirest a more popular, and though not so direct and philosophical, yet a very powerful and penetrative recipe against the fear of death, nothing can make they more willing to part with thy life, than if thou shalt consider, both what the subjects themselves are that thou shalt part with, and what manner of disposition thou shalt no more have to do with. True it is, that, offended with them thou must not be by no means, but take care of them, and meekly bear with them However, this thou mayst remember, that whensoever it happens that thou depart, it shall not be from men that held the same opinions that thou dost. For that indeed, (if it were so) is the only thing that might make thee averse from death, and willing to continue here, if it were thy hap to live with men that had obtained the same belief that thou hast. But now, what a toil it is for thee to live with men of different opinions, thou seest: so that thou hast rather occasion to say, Hasten, I thee pray, O Death; lest I also in time forget myself.

IV. He that sinneth, sinneth unto himself. He that is unjust, hurts himself, in that he makes himself worse than he was before. Not he only that committeth, but he also that omitteth something, is oftentimes unjust.

V. If my present apprehension of the object be right, and my present action charitable, and this, towards whatsoever doth proceed from God, be my present disposition, to be well pleased with it, it sufficeth.

VI. To wipe away fancy, to use deliberation, to quench concupiscence, to keep the mind free to herself.

VII. Of all unreasonable creatures, there is but one unreasonable soul; and of all that are reasonable, but one reasonable soul, divided betwixt them all. As of all earthly things there is but one earth, and but one light that we see by; and but one air that we breathe in, as many as either breathe or see. Now whatsoever partakes of some common thing, naturally affects and inclines unto that whereof it is part, being of one kind and nature with it. Whatsoever is earthly, presseth downwards to the common earth. Whatsoever is liquid, would flow together. And whatsoever is airy, would be together likewise. So that without some obstacle, and some kind of violence, they cannot well be kept asunder. Whatsoever is fiery, doth not only by reason of the elementary fire tend upwards; but here also is so ready to join, and to burn together, that whatsoever doth want sufficient moisture to make resistance, is easily set on fire. Whatsoever therefore is partaker of that reasonable common nature, naturally doth as much and more long after his own kind. For by how much in its own nature it excels all other things, by so much more is it desirous to be joined and united unto that, which is of its own nature. As for unreasonable creatures then, they had not long been, but presently begun among them swarms, and flocks, and broods of young ones, and a kind of mutual love and affection. For though but unreasonable, yet a kind of soul these had, and therefore was that natural desire of union more strong and intense in them, as in creatures of a more excellent nature, than either in plants, or stones, or trees. But among reasonable creatures, begun commonwealths, friendships, families, public meetings, and even in their wars, conventions, and truces. Now among them that were yet of a more excellent nature, as the stars and planets, though by their nature far distant one from another, yet even among them began some mutual correspondency and unity. So proper is it to excellency in a high degree to affect unity, as that even in things so far distant, it could operate unto a mutual sympathy. But now behold, what is now come to pass. Those creatures that are reasonable, are now the only creatures that have forgotten their natural affection and inclination of one towards another. Among them alone of all other things that are of one kind, there is not to be found a general disposition to flow together. But though they fly from nature, yet are they stopt in their course, and apprehended. Do they what they can, nature doth prevail. And so shalt thou confess, if thou dost observe it. For sooner mayst thou find a thing earthly, where no earthly thing is, than find a man that naturally can live by himself alone.

VIII. Man, God, the world, every one in their kind, bear some fruits. All things have their proper time to bear. Though by custom, the word itself is in a manner become proper unto the vine, and the like, yet is it so nevertheless, as we have said. As for reason, that beareth both common fruit for the use of others; and peculiar, which itself doth enjoy. Reason is of a diffusive nature, what itself is in itself, it begets in others, and so doth multiply.

IX. **Either teach them better if it be in thy power; or if it be not,** remember that for this use, to bear with them patiently, was mildness and goodness granted unto thee. The Gods themselves are good unto such; yea and in some things, (as in matter of health, of wealth, of honour,) are content often to further their endeavours: so good and gracious are they. And mightest thou not be so too? or, tell me, what doth hinder thee?

X. **Labour not as one to whom it is appointed to be wretched, nor as** one that either would be pitied, or admired; but let this be thine only care and desire; so always and in all things to prosecute or to forbear, as the law of charity, or mutual society doth require.

XI. **This day I did come out of all my trouble. Nay I have cast out all** my trouble; it should rather be for that which troubled thee, whatsoever it was, was not without anywhere that thou shouldest come out of it, but within in thine own opinions, from whence it must be cast out, before thou canst truly and constantly be at ease.

XII. **All those things, for matter of experience are usual and ordinary;** for their continuance but for a day; and for their matter, most base and filthy. As they were in the days of those whom we have buried, so are they now also, and no otherwise.

XIII. **The things themselves that affect us, they stand without doors,** neither knowing anything themselves nor able to utter anything unto others concerning themselves. What then is it, that passeth verdict on them? The understanding.

XIV. **As virtue and wickedness consist not in passion, but in action; so** neither doth the true good or evil of a reasonable charitable man consist in passion, but in operation and action.

XV. **To the stone that is cast up, when it comes down it is no hurt unto** it; as neither benefit, when it doth ascend.

XVI. **Sift their minds and understandings, and behold what men they** be, whom thou dost stand in fear of what they shall judge of thee, what they themselves judge of themselves.

XVII. All things that are in the world, are always in the estate of alteration. Thou also art in a perpetual change, yea and under corruption too, in some part: and so is the whole world.

XVIII. it is not thine, but another man's sin. Why should it trouble thee? Let him look to it, whose sin it is.

XIX. Of an operation and of a purpose there is an ending, or of an action and of a purpose we say commonly, that it is at an end: from opinion also there is an absolute cessation, which is as it were the death of it. In all this there is no hurt. Apply this now to a man's age, as first, a child; then a youth, then a young man, then an old man; every change from one age to another is a kind of death And all this while here no matter of grief yet. Pass now unto that life first, that which thou livedst under thy grandfather, then under thy mother, then under thy father. And thus when through the whole course of thy life hitherto thou hast found and observed many alterations, many changes, many kinds of endings and cessations, put this question to thyself What matter of grief or sorrow dost thou find in any of these? Or what doest thou suffer through any of these? If in none of these, then neither in the ending and consummation of thy whole life, which is also but a cessation and change.

XX. As occasion shall require, either to thine own understanding, or to that of the universe, or to his, whom thou hast now to do with, let thy refuge be with all speed. To thine own, that it resolve upon nothing against justice. To that of the universe, that thou mayest remember, part of whom thou art. Of his, that thou mayest consider whether in the estate of ignorance, or of knowledge. And then also must thou call to mind, that he is thy kinsman.

XXI. As thou thyself, whoever thou art, were made for the perfection and consummation, being a member of it, of a common society; so must every action of thine tend to the perfection and consummation of a life that is truly sociable. What action soever of thine therefore that either immediately or afar off, hath not reference to the common good, that is an exorbitant and disorderly action; yea it is seditious; as one among the people who from such and such a consent and unity, should factiously divide and separate himself.

XXII. Children's anger, mere babels; wretched souls bearing up dead bodies, that they may not have their fall so soon: even as it is in that common dirge song.

XXIII. Go to the quality of the cause from which the effect doth proceed. Behold it by itself bare and naked, separated from all that is material. Then consider the utmost bounds of time that that cause, thus and thus qualified, can subsist and abide.

XXIV. Infinite are the troubles and miseries, that thou hast already been put to, by reason of this only, because that for all happiness it did not suffice thee, or, that thou didst not account it sufficient happiness, that thy understanding did operate according to its natural constitution.

XXV. When any shall either impeach thee with false accusations, or hatefully reproach thee, or shall use any such carriage towards thee, get thee presently to their minds and understandings, and look in them, and behold what manner of men they be. Thou shalt see, that there is no such occasion why it should trouble thee, what such as they are think of thee. Yet must thou love them still, for by nature they are thy friends. And the Gods themselves, in those things that they seek from them as matters of great moment, are well content, all manner of ways, as by dreams and oracles, to help them as well as others.

XXVI. Up and down, from one age to another, go the ordinary things of the world; being still the same. And either of everything in particular before it come to pass, the mind of the universe doth consider with itself and deliberate: and if so, then submit for shame unto the determination of such an excellent understanding: or once for all it did resolve upon all things in general; and since that whatsoever happens, happens by a necessary consequence, and all things indivisibly in a manner and inseparably hold one of another. In sum, either there is a God, and then all is well; or if all things go by chance and fortune, yet mayest thou use thine own providence in those things that concern thee properly; and then art thou well.

XXVII. Within a while the earth shall cover us all, and then she herself shall have her change. And then the course will be, from one period of eternity unto another, and so a perpetual eternity. Now can any man that shall consider with himself in his mind the several rollings or successions of so many changes and alterations, and the swiftness of all these rulings; can he otherwise but contemn in his heart and despise all worldly things? The cause of the universe is as it were a strong torrent, it carrieth all away.

XXVIII. And these your professed politicians, the only true practical philosophers of the world, (as they think of themselves) so full of affected gravity, or such professed lovers of virtue and honesty, what wretches be they in very deed; how vile and contemptible in themselves? O man! what ado doest thou keep? Do what thy nature doth now require. Resolve upon it, if thou mayest: and take no thought, whether anybody shall know it or no. Yea, but sayest thou, I must not expect a Plato's commonwealth. If they profit though never so little, I must be content; and think much even of that little progress. Doth then any of them forsake their former false opinions that I should think they profit? For without a change of opinions, alas! what is all that ostentation, but mere wretchedness of slavish minds, that groan privately, and yet would make a show of obedience to reason, and truth? Go too now and tell me of Alexander and

Philippus, and Demetrius Phalereus. Whether they understood what the common nature requireth, and could rule themselves or no, they know best themselves. But if they kept a life, and swaggered; I (God be thanked) am not bound to imitate them. The effect of true philosophy is, unaffected simplicity and modesty. Persuade me not to ostentation and vainglory.

XXIX. From some high place as it were to look down, and to behold here flocks, and there sacrifices, without number; and all kind of navigation; some in a rough and stormy sea, and some in a calm: the general differences, or different estates of things, some, that are now first upon being; the several and mutual relations of those things that are together; and some other things that are at their last. Their lives also, who were long ago, and theirs who shall be hereafter, and the present estate and life of those many nations of barbarians that are now in the world, thou must likewise consider in thy mind. And how many there be, who never so much as heard of thy name, how many that will soon forget it; how many who but even now did commend thee, within a very little while perchance will speak ill of thee. So that neither fame, nor honour, nor anything else that this world doth afford, is worth the while. The sum then of all; whatsoever doth happen unto thee, whereof God is the cause, to accept it contentedly: whatsoever thou doest, whereof thou thyself art the cause, to do it justly: which will be, if both in thy resolution and in thy action thou have no further end, than to do good unto others, as being that, which by thy natural constitution, as a man, thou art bound unto.

XXX. Many of those things that trouble and straiten thee, it is in thy power to cut off, as wholly depending from mere conceit and opinion; and then thou shalt have room enough.

XXXI. To comprehend the whole world together in thy mind, and the whole course of this present age to represent it unto thyself, and to fix thy thoughts upon the sudden change of every particular object. How short the time is from the generation of anything, unto the dissolution of the same; but how immense and infinite both that which was before the generation, and that which after the generation of it shall be. All things that thou seest, will soon be perished, and they that see their corruptions, will soon vanish away themselves. He that dieth a hundred years old, and he that dieth young, shall come all to one.

XXXII. What are their minds and understandings; and what the things that they apply themselves unto: what do they love, and what do they hate for? Fancy to thyself the estate of their souls openly to be seen. When they think they hurt them shrewdly, whom they speak ill of; and when they think they do them a very good turn, whom they commend and extol: O how full are they then of conceit, and opinion!

XXXIII. Loss and corruption, is in very deed nothing else but change and alteration; and that is it, which the nature of the universe doth most delight in, by which, and according to which, whatsoever is done, is well done. For that was the estate of worldly things from the beginning, and so shall it ever be. Or wouldest thou rather say, that all things in the world have gone ill from the beginning for so many ages, and shall ever go ill? And then among so many deities, could no divine power be found all this while, that could rectify the things of the world? Or is the world, to incessant woes and miseries, for ever condemned?

XXXIV. How base and putrid, every common matter is! Water, dust, and from the mixture of these bones, and all that loathsome stuff that our bodies do consist of: so subject to be infected, and corrupted. And again those other things that are so much prized and admired, as marble stones, what are they, but as it were the kernels of the earth? gold and silver, what are they, but as the more gross faeces of the earth? Thy most royal apparel, for matter, it is but as it were the hair of a silly sheep, and for colour, the very blood of a shell-fish; of this nature are all other things. Thy life itself, is some such thing too; a mere exhalation of blood: and it also, apt to be changed into some other common thing.

XXXV. Will this querulousness, this murmuring, this complaining and dissembling never be at an end? What then is it, that troubleth thee? Doth any new thing happen unto thee? What doest thou so wonder at? At the cause, or the matter? Behold either by itself, is either of that weight and moment indeed? And besides these, there is not anything. But thy duty towards the Gods also, it is time thou shouldst acquit thyself of it with more goodness and simplicity.

XXXVI. It is all one to see these things for a hundred of years together or but for three years.

XXXVII. If he have sinned, his is the harm, not mine. But perchance he hath not.

XXXVIII. Either all things by the providence of reason happen unto every particular, as a part of one general body; and then it is against reason that a part should complain of anything that happens for the good of the whole; or if, according to Epicurus, atoms be the cause of all things and that life be nothing else but an accidentary confusion of things, and death nothing else, but a mere dispersion and so of all other things: what doest thou trouble thyself for?

XXXIX. Sayest thou unto that rational part, Thou art dead; corruption hath taken hold on thee? Doth it then also void excrements? Doth it like either oxen, or sheep, graze or feed; that it also should be mortal, as well as the body?

XL. Either the Gods can do nothing for us at all, or they can still and allay all the distractions and distempers of thy mind. If they can do nothing, why doest thou pray? If they can, why wouldst not thou rather pray, that they will grant unto thee, that thou mayst neither fear, nor lust after any of those worldly things which cause these distractions and distempers of it? Why not rather, that thou mayst not at either their absence or presence, be grieved and discontented: than either that thou mayst obtain them, or that thou mayst avoid them? For certainly it must needs be, that if the Gods can help us in anything, they may in this kind also. But thou wilt say perchance, 'In those things the Gods have given me my liberty: and it is in mine own power to do what I will.' But if thou mayst use this liberty, rather to set thy mind at true liberty, than wilfully with baseness and servility of mind to affect those things, which either to compass or to avoid is not in thy power, wert not thou better? And as for the Gods, who hath told thee, that they may not help us up even in those things that they have put in our own power? whether it be so or no, thou shalt soon perceive, if thou wilt but try thyself and pray. One prayeth that he may compass his desire, to lie with such or such a one, pray thou that thou mayst not lust to lie with her. Another how he may be rid of such a one; pray thou that thou mayst so patiently bear with him, as that thou have no such need to be rid of him. Another, that he may not lose his child. Pray thou that thou mayst not fear to lose him. To this end and purpose, let all thy prayer be, and see what will be the event.

XLI. 'In my sickness' (saith Epicurus of himself:) 'my discourses were not concerning the nature of my disease, neither was that, to them that came to visit me, the subject of my talk; but in the consideration and contemplation of that, which was of especial weight and moment, was all my time bestowed and spent, and among others in this very thing, how my mind, by a natural and una-voidable sympathy partaking in some sort with the present indisposition of my body, might nevertheless keep herself free from trouble, and in present posses-sion of her own proper happiness. Neither did I leave the ordering of my body to the physicians altogether to do with me what they would, as though I expected any great matter from them, or as though I thought it a matter of such great consequence, by their means to recover my health: for my present estate, me-thought, liked me very well, and gave me good content.' Whether therefore in sickness (if thou chance to sicken) or in what other kind of extremity soever, endeavour thou also to be in thy mind so affected, as he doth report of himself: not to depart from thy philosophy for anything that can befall thee, nor to give ear to the discourses of silly people, and mere naturalists.

XLII. It is common to all trades and professions to mind and intend that only, which now they are about, and the instrument whereby they work.

XLIII. When at any time thou art offended with any one's impudency, put presently this question to thyself: 'What? Is it then possible, that there should not be any impudent men in the world! Certainly it is not possible.' Desire not then that which is impossible. For this one, (thou must think) whosoever he be, is one of those impudent ones, that the world cannot be without. So of the subtile and crafty, so of the perfidious, so of every one that offendeth, must thou ever be ready to reason with thyself. For whilst in general thou dost thus reason with thyself, that the kind of them must needs be in the world, thou wilt be the better able to use meekness towards every particular. This also thou shalt find of very good use, upon every such occasion, presently to consider with thyself, what proper virtue nature hath furnished man with, against such a vice, or to encounter with a disposition vicious in this kind. As for example, against the unthankful, it hath given goodness and meekness, as an antidote, and so against another vicious in another kind some other peculiar faculty. And generally, is it not in thy power to instruct him better, that is in an error? For whosoever sinneth, doth in that decline from his purposed end, and is certainly deceived, And again, what art thou the worse for his sin? For thou shalt not find that any one of these, against whom thou art incensed, hath in very deed done anything whereby thy mind (the only true subject of thy hurt and evil) can be made worse than it was. And what a matter of either grief or wonder is this, if he that is unlearned, do the deeds of one that is unlearned? Should not thou rather blame thyself, who, when upon very good grounds of reason, thou mightst have thought it very probable, that such a thing would by such a one be committed, didst not only not foresee it, but moreover dost wonder at it, that such a thing should be. But then especially, when thou dost find fault with either an unthankful, or a false man, must thou reflect upon thyself. For without all question, thou thyself art much in fault, if either of one that were of such a disposition, thou didst expect that he should be true unto thee: or when unto any thou didst a good turn, thou didst not there bound thy thoughts, as one that had obtained his end; nor didst not think that from the action itself thou hadst received a full reward of the good that thou hadst done. For what wouldst thou have more? Unto him that is a man, thou hast done a good turn: doth not that suffice thee? What thy nature required, that hast thou done. Must thou be rewarded for it? As if either the eye for that it seeth, or the feet that they go, should require satisfaction. For as these being by nature appointed for such an use, can challenge no more, than that they may work according to their natural constitution: so man being born to do good unto others whensoever he doth a real good unto any by helping them out of error; or though but in middle things, as in matter of wealth, life, preferment, and the like, doth help to further their desires he doth that for which he was made, and therefore can require no more.

The Tenth Book

I. O my soul, the time I trust will be, when thou shalt be good, simple, single, more open and visible, than that body by which it is enclosed. Thou wilt one day be sensible of their happiness, whose end is love, and their affections dead to all worldly things. Thou shalt one day be full, and in want of no external thing: not seeking pleasure from anything, either living or insensible, that this world can afford; neither wanting time for the continuation of thy pleasure, nor place and opportunity, nor the favour either of the weather or of men. When thou shalt have content in thy present estate, and all things present shall add to thy content: when thou shalt persuade thyself, that thou hast all things; all for thy good, and all by the providence of the Gods: and of things future also shalt be as confident, that all will do well, as tending to the maintenance and preservation in some sort, of his perfect welfare and happiness, who is perfection of life, of goodness, and beauty; who begets all things, and containeth all things in himself, and in himself doth recollect all things from all places that are dissolved, that of them he may beget others again like unto them. Such one day shall be thy disposition, that thou shalt be able, both in regard of the Gods, and in regard of men, so to fit and order thy conversation, as neither to complain of them at any time, for anything that they do; nor to do anything thyself, for which thou mayest justly be condemned.

II. As one who is altogether governed by nature, let it be thy care to observe what it is that thy nature in general doth require. That done, if thou find not that thy nature, as thou art a living sensible creature, will be the worse for it, thou mayest proceed. Next then thou must examine, what thy nature as thou art a living sensible creature, doth require. And that, whatsoever it be, thou mayest admit of and do it, if thy nature as thou art a reasonable living creature, will not be the worse for it. Now whatsoever is reasonable, is also sociable, Keep thyself to these rules, and trouble not thyself about idle things.

III. Whatsoever doth happen unto thee, thou art naturally by thy natural constitution either able, or not able to bear. If thou beest able, be not offended, but bear it according to thy natural constitution, or as nature hath enabled thee. If thou beest not able, be not offended. For it will soon make an end of thee, and itself, (whatsoever it be) at the same time end with thee. But remember, that whatsoever by the strength of opinion, grounded upon a certain apprehension of both true profit and duty, thou canst conceive tolerable; that thou art able to bear that by thy natural constitution.

IV. Him that offends, to teach with love and meek ness, and to show him his error. But if thou canst not, then to blame thyself; or rather not thyself neither, if thy will and endeavours have not been wanting.

V. Whatsoever it be that happens unto thee, it is that which from all time was appointed unto thee. For by the same coherence of causes, by which thy substance from all eternity was appointed to be, was also whatsoever should happen unto it, destinated and appointed.

VI. Either with Epicurus, we must fondly imagine the atoms to be the cause of all things, or we must needs grant a nature. Let this then be thy first ground, that thou art part of that universe, which is governed by nature. Then secondly, that to those parts that are of the same kind and nature as thou art, thou hast relation of kindred. For of these, if I shall always be mindful, first as I am a part, I shall never be displeased with anything, that falls to my particular share of the common chances of the world. For nothing that is behoveful unto the whole, can be truly hurtful to that which is part of it. For this being the common privilege of all natures, that they contain nothing in themselves that is hurtful unto them; it cannot be that the nature of the universe (whose privilege beyond other particular natures, is, that she cannot against her will by any higher external cause be constrained,) should beget anything and cherish it in her bosom that should tend to her own hurt and prejudice. As then I bear in mind that I am a part of such an universe, I shall not be displeased with anything that happens. And as I have relation of kindred to those parts that are of the same kind and nature that I am, so I shall be careful to do nothing that is prejudicial to the community, but in all my deliberations shall they that are of my kind ever be; and the common good, that, which all my intentions and resolutions shall drive unto, as that which is contrary unto it, I shall by all means endeavour to prevent and avoid. These things once so fixed and concluded, as thou wouldst think him a happy citizen, whose constant study and practice were for the good and benefit of his fellow citizens, and the carriage of the city such towards him, that he were well pleased with it; so must it needs be with thee, that thou shalt live a happy life.

VII. All parts of the world, (all things I mean that are contained within the whole world), must of necessity at some time or other come to corruption. Alteration I should say, to speak truly and properly; but that I may be the better understood, I am content at this time to use that more common word. Now say I, if so be that this be both hurtful unto them, and yet unavoidable, would not, thinkest thou, the whole itself be in a sweet case, all the parts of it being subject to alteration, yea and by their making itself fitted for corruption, as consisting of things different and contrary? And did nature then either of herself thus project and purpose the affliction and misery of her parts, and therefore of purpose so made them, not only that haply they might, but of necessity that they should fall into evil; or did not she know what she did, when she made them? For either of these two to say, is equally absurd. But to let pass nature in general, and to reason of things particular according to their own particular natures; how absurd and ridiculous is it, first to say that all parts of the whole are, by their proper natural constitution, subject to alteration; and then when any such thing doth happen, as when one doth fall sick and dieth, to take on and wonder as though some strange thing had happened? Though this besides might move not so grievously to take on when any such thing doth happen, that whatsoever is dissolved, it is dissolved into those things, whereof it was compounded. For every dissolution is either a mere dispersion, of the elements into those elements again whereof everything did consist, or a change, of that which is more solid into earth; and of that which is pure and subtile or spiritual, into air. So that by this means nothing is lost, but all resumed again into those rational generative seeds of the universe; and this universe, either after a certain period of time to lie consumed by fire, or by continual changes to be renewed, and so for ever to endure. Now that solid and spiritual that we speak of, thou must not conceive it to be that very same, which at first was, when thou wert born. For alas! all this that now thou art in either kind, either for matter of substance, or of life, hath but two or three days ago partly from meats eaten, and partly from air breathed in, received all its influx, being the same then in no other respect, than a running river, maintained by the perpetual influx and new supply of waters, is the same. That therefore which thou hast since received, not that which came from thy mother, is that which comes to change and corruption. But suppose that that for the general substance, and more solid part of it, should still cleave unto thee never so close, yet what is that to the proper qualities and affections of it, by which persons are distinguished, which certainly are quite different?

VIII. Now that thou hast taken these names upon thee of good, modest, true; of emfrwn, sumfrwn, uperfrwn; take heed lest at any times by doing anything that is contrary, thou be but improperly so called, and lose thy right to these appellations. Or if thou do, return unto them again with all possible speed. And remember, that the word emfrwn notes unto thee an intent and intelligent consideration of every object that presents itself unto thee, without distraction. And the word emfrwn a ready and contented acceptation of whatsoever by the appointment of the common nature, happens unto thee. And the word sumfrwn, a super-extension, or a transcendent, and outreaching disposition of thy mind, whereby it passeth by all bodily pains and pleasures, honour and credit, death and whatsoever is of the same nature, as matters of absolute indifferency, and in no wise to be stood upon by a wise man. These then if inviolably thou shalt observe, and shalt not be ambitious to be so called by others, both thou thyself shalt become a new man, and thou shalt begin a new life. For to continue such as hitherto thou hast been, to undergo those distractions and distempers as thou must needs for such a life as hitherto thou hast lived, is the part of one that is very foolish, and is overfond of his life. Whom a man might compare to one of those half-eaten wretches, matched in the amphitheatre with wild beasts; who as full as they are all the body over with wounds and blood, desire for a great favour, that they may be reserved till the next day, then also, and in the same estate to be exposed to the same nails and teeth as before. Away therefore, ship thyself; and from the troubles and distractions of thy former life convey thyself as it were unto these few names; and if thou canst abide in them, or be constant in the practice and possession of them, continue there as glad and joyful as one that were translated unto some such place of bliss and happiness as that which by Hesiod and Plato is called the Islands of the Blessed, by others called the Elysian Fields. And whensoever thou findest thyself; that thou art in danger of a relapse, and that thou art not able to master and overcome those difficulties and temptations that present themselves in thy present station: get thee into any private corner, where thou mayst be better able. Or if that will not serve forsake even thy life rather. But so that it be not in passion but in a plain voluntary modest way: this being the only commendable action of thy whole life that thus thou art departed, or this having been the main work and business of thy whole life, that thou mightest thus depart. Now for the better remembrance of those names that we have spoken of, thou shalt find it a very good help, to remember the Gods as often as may be: and that, the thing which they require at our hands of as many of us, as are by nature reasonable creation is not that with fair words, and outward show of piety and devotion we should flatter them, but that we should become like unto them: and that as all other natural creatures, the fig tree for example; the dog the bee: both do, all of them, and apply themselves unto that which by their natural constitution, is proper unto them; so man likewise should do that, which by his nature, as he is a man, belongs unto him.

IX. Toys and fooleries at home, wars abroad: sometimes terror, sometimes torpor, or stupid sloth: this is thy daily slavery. By little and little, if thou doest not better look to it, those sacred dogmata will be blotted out of thy mind. How many things be there, which when as a mere naturalist, thou hast barely considered of according to their nature, thou doest let pass without any further use? Whereas thou shouldst in all things so join action and contemplation, that thou mightest both at the same time attend all present occasions, to perform everything duly and carefully and yet so intend the contemplative part too, that no part of that delight and pleasure, which the contemplative knowledge of everything according to its true nature doth of itself afford, might be lost. Or, that the true and contemnplative knowledge of everything according to its own nature, might of itself, (action being subject to many lets and impediments) afford unto thee sufficient pleasure and happiness. Not apparent indeed, but not concealed. And when shalt thou attain to the happiness of true simplicity, and unaffected gravity? When shalt thou rejoice in the certain knowledge of every particular object according to its true nature: as what the matter and substance of it is; what use it is for in the world: how long it can subsist: what things it doth consist of: who they be that are capable of it, and who they that can give it, and take it away?

X. As the spider, when it hath caught the fly that it hunted after, is not little proud, nor meanly conceited of herself: as he likewise that hath caught an hare, or hath taken a fish with his net: as another for the taking of a boar, and another of a bear: so may they be proud, and applaud themselves for their valiant acts against the Sarmatai, or northern nations lately defeated. For these also, these famous soldiers and warlike men, if thou dost look into their minds and opinions, what do they for the most part but hunt after prey?

XI. To find out, and set to thyself some certain way and method of contemplation, whereby thou mayest clearly discern and represent unto thyself, the mutual change of all things, the one into the other. Bear it in thy mind evermore, and see that thou be throughly well exercised in this particular. For there is not anything more effectual to beget true magnanimity.

XII. He hath got loose from the bonds of his body, and perceiving that within a very little while he must of necessity bid the world farewell, and leave all these things behind him, he wholly applied himself, as to righteousness in all his actions, so to the common nature in all things that should happen unto him. And contenting himself with these two things, to do all things justly, and whatsoever God doth send to like well of it: what others shall either say or think of him, or shall do against him, he doth not so much as trouble his thoughts with it. To go on straight, whither right and reason directed him, and by so doing to follow God, was the only thing that he did mind, that, his only business and occupation.

XIII. What use is there of suspicion at all? or, why should thoughts of mistrust, and suspicion concerning that which is future, trouble thy mind at all? What now is to be done, if thou mayest search and inquiry into that, what needs thou care for more? And if thou art well able to perceive it alone, let no man divert thee from it. But if alone thou doest not so well perceive it, suspend thine action, and take advice from the best. And if there be anything else that doth hinder thee, go on with prudence and discretion, according to the present occasion and opportunity, still proposing that unto thyself, which thou doest conceive most right and just. For to hit that aright, and to speed in the prosecution of it, must needs be happiness, since it is that only which we can truly and properly be said to miss of, or miscarry in.

XIV. What is that that is slow, and yet quick? merry, and yet grave? He that in all things doth follow reason for his guide.

XV. In the morning as soon as thou art awaked, when thy judgment, **before** either thy affections, or external objects have wrought upon it, is yet most free and impartial: put this question to thyself, whether if that which is right and just be done, the doing of it by thyself, or by others when thou art not able thyself; be a thing material or no. For sure it is not. And as for these that keep such a life, and stand so much upon the praises, or dispraises of other men, hast thou forgotten what manner of men they be? that such and such upon their beds, and such at their board: what their ordinary actions are: what they pursue after, and what they fly from: what thefts and rapines they commit, if not with their hands and feet, yet with that more precious part of theirs, their minds: which (would it but admit of them) might enjoy faith, modesty, truth, justice, a good spirit.

XVI. Give what thou wilt, and take away what thou wilt, saith he that is well taught and truly modest, to Him that gives, and takes away. And it is not out of a stout and peremptory resolution, that he saith it, but in mere love, and humble submission.

XVII. So live as indifferent to the world and all worldly objects, as one who liveth by himself alone upon some desert hill. For whether here, or there, if the whole world be but as one town, it matters not much for the place. Let them behold and see a man, that is a man indeed, living according to the true nature of man. If they cannot bear with me, let them kill me. For better were it to die, than so to live as they would have thee.

XVIII. Make it not any longer a matter of dispute or discourse, what are the signs and proprieties of a good man, but really and actually to be such.

XIX. Ever to represent unto thyself; and to set before thee, both the general age and time of the world, and the whole substance of it. And how all things particular in respect of these are for their substance, as one of the least seeds that is: and for their duration, as the turning of the pestle in the mortar once about. Then to fix thy mind upon every particular object of the world, and to conceive it, (as it is indeed,) as already being in the state of dissolution, and of change; tending to some kind of either putrefaction or dispersion; or whatsoever else it is, that is the death as it were of everything in his own kind.

XX. Consider them through all actions and occupations, of their lives: as when they eat, and when they sleep: when they are in the act of necessary exoneration, and when in the act of lust. Again, when they either are in their greatest exultation; and in the middle of all their pomp and glory; or being angry and displeased, in great state and majesty, as from an higher place, they chide and rebuke. How base and slavish, but a little while ago, they were fain to be, that they might come to this; and within a very little while what will be their estate, when death hath once seized upon them.

XXI. That is best for every one, that the common nature of all doth send unto every one, and then is it best, when she doth send it.

XXII. The earth, saith the poet, doth often long after the rain. So is the glorious sky often as desirous to fall upon the earth, which argues a mutual kind of love between them. And so (say I) doth the world bear a certain affection of love to whatsoever shall come to pass With thine affections shall mine concur, O world. The same (and no other) shall the object of my longing be which is of thine. Now that the world doth love it is true indeed so is it as commonly said, and acknowledged ledged, when, according to the Greek phrase, imitated by the Latins, of things that used to be, we say commonly, that they love to be.

XXIII. Either thou dost Continue in this kind of life and that is it, which so long thou hast been used unto and therefore tolerable: or thou doest retire, or leave the world, and that of thine own accord, and then thou hast thy mind: or thy life is cut off; and then mayst thou rejoice that thou hast ended thy charge. One of these must needs be. Be therefore of good comfort.

XXIV Let it always appear and be manifest unto thee that solitariness, and desert places, by many philosophers so much esteemed of and affected, are of themselves but thus and thus; and that all things are them to them that live in towns, and converse with others as they are the same nature everywhere to be seen and observed: to them that have retired themselves to the top of mountains, and to desert havens, or what other desert and inhabited places soever. For anywhere it thou wilt mayest thou quickly find and apply that to thyself; which Plato saith of his philosopher, in a place: as private and retired, saith he, as if he were shut up and enclosed about in some shepherd's lodge, on the top of a hill. There by thyself to put these questions to thyself or to enter in these considerations: What is my chief and principal part, which hath power over the rest? What is now the present estate of it, as I use it; and what is it, that I employ it about? Is it now void of reason ir no? Is it free, and separated; or so affixed, so congealed and grown together as it were with the flesh, that it is swayed by the motions and inclinations of it?

XXV. He that runs away from his master is a fugitive. But the law is every man's master. He therefore that forsakes the law, is a fugitive. So is he, whosoever he be, that is either sorry, angry, or afraid, or for anything that either hath been, is, or shall be by his appointment, who is the Lord and Governor of the universe. For he truly and properly is Nomoz, or the law, as the only nemwn (sp.), or distributor and dispenser of all things that happen unto any one in his lifetime—Whatsoever then is either sorry, angry, or afraid, is a fugitive.

XXVI. From man is the seed, that once cast into the womb man hath no more to do with it. Another cause succeedeth, and undertakes the work, and in time brings a child (that wonderful effect from such a beginning!) to perfection. Again, man lets food down through his throat; and that once down, he hath no more to do with it. Another cause succeedeth and distributeth this food into the senses, and the affections: into life, and into strength; and doth with it those other many and marvellous things, that belong unto man. These things therefore that are so secretly and invisibly wrought and brought to pass, thou must use to behold and contemplate; and not the things themselves only, but the power also by which they are effected; that thou mayst behold it, though not with the eyes of the body, yet as plainly and visibly as thou canst see and discern the outward efficient cause of the depression and elevation of anything.

XXVII. Ever to mind and consider with thyself; how all things that now are, have been heretofore much after the same sort, and after the same fashion that now they are: and so to think of those things which shall be hereafter also. Moreover, whole dramata, and uniform scenes, or scenes that comprehend the lives and actions of men of one calling and profession, as many as either in thine own experience thou hast known, or by reading of ancient histories; (as the whole court of Adrianus, the whole court of Antoninus Pius, the whole court of Philippus, that of Alexander, that of Croesus): to set them all before thine eyes. For thou shalt find that they are all but after one sort and fashion: only that the actors were others.

XXVIII. As a pig that cries and flings when his throat is cut, fancy to thyself every one to be, that grieves for any worldly thing and takes on. Such a one is he also, who upon his bed alone, doth bewail the miseries of this our mortal life. And remember this, that Unto reasonable creatures only it is granted that they may willingly and freely submit unto Providence: but absolutely to submit, is a necessity imposed upon all creatures equally.

XXIX. Whatsoever it is that thou goest about, consider of it by thyself, and ask thyself, What? because I shall do this no more when I am dead, should therefore death seem grievous unto me?

XXX. When thou art offended with any man's transgression, presently reflect upon thyself; and consider what thou thyself art guilty of in the same kind. As that thou also perchance dost think it a happiness either to be rich, or to live in pleasure, or to be praised and commended, and so of the rest in particular. For this if thou shalt call to mind, thou shalt soon forget thine anger; especially when at the same time this also shall concur in thy thoughts, that he was constrained by his error and ignorance so to do: for how can he choose as long as he is of that opinion? Do thou therefore if thou canst, take away that from him, that forceth him to do as he doth.

XXXI. When thou seest Satyro, think of Socraticus and Eutyches, or Hymen, and when Euphrates, think of Eutychio, and Sylvanus, when Alciphron, of Tropaeophorus, when Xenophon, of Crito, or Severus. And when thou doest look upon thyself, fancy unto thyself some one or other of the Caesars; and so for every one, some one or other that hath been for estate and profession answerable unto him. Then let this come to thy mind at the same time; and where now are they all? Nowhere or anywhere? For so shalt thou at all time be able to perceive how all worldly things are but as the smoke, that vanisheth away: or, indeed, mere nothing. Especially when thou shalt call to mind this also, that whatsoever is once changed, shall never be again as long as the world endureth. And thou then, how long shalt thou endure? And why doth it not suffice thee, if virtuously, and as becometh thee, thou mayest pass that portion of time, how little soever it be, that is allotted unto thee?

XXXII. What a subject, and what a course of life is it, that thou doest so much desire to be rid of. For all these things, what are they, but fit objects for an understanding, that beholdeth everything according to its true nature, to exercise itself upon? Be patient, therefore, until that (as a strong stomach that turns all things into his own nature; and as a great fire that turneth in flame and light, whatsoever thou doest cast into it) thou have made these things also familiar, and as it were natural unto thee.

XXXIII. Let it not be in any man's power, to say truly of thee, that thou art not truly simple, or sincere and open, or not good. Let him be deceived whosoever he be that shall have any such opinion of thee. For all this doth depend of thee. For who is it that should hinder thee from being either truly simple or good? Do thou only resolve rather not to live, than not to be such. For indeed neither doth it stand with reason that he should live that is not such. What then is it that may upon this present occasion according to best reason and discretion, either be said or done? For whatsoever it be, it is in thy power either to do it, or to say it, and therefore seek not any pretences, as though thou wert hindered. Thou wilt never cease groaning and complaining, until such time as that, what pleasure is unto the voluptuous, be unto thee, to do in everything that presents itself, whatsoever may be done conformably and agreeably to the proper constitution of man, or, to man as he is a man. For thou must account that pleasure, whatsoever it be, that thou mayest do according to thine own nature. And to do this, every place will fit thee. Unto the cylindrus, or roller, it is not granted to move everywhere according to its own proper motion, as neither unto the water, nor unto the fire, nor unto any other thing, that either is merely natural, or natural and sensitive; but not rational for many things there be that can hinder their operations. But of the mind and understanding this is the proper privilege, that according to its own nature, and as it will itself, it can pass through every obstacle that it finds, and keep straight on forwards. Setting therefore before thine eyes this happiness and felicity of thy mind, whereby it is able to pass through all things, and is capable of all motions, whether as the fire, upwards; or as the stone downwards, or as the cylindrus through that which is sloping: content thyself with it, and seek not after any other thing. For all other kind of hindrances that are not hindrances of thy mind either they are proper to the body, or merely proceed from the opinion, reason not making that resistance that it should, but basely, and cowardly suffering itself to be foiled; and of themselves can neither wound, nor do any hurt at all. Else must he of necessity, whosoever he be that meets with any of them, become worse than he was before. For so is it in all other subjects, that that is thought hurtful unto them, whereby they are made worse. But here contrariwise, man (if he make that good use of them that he should) is rather the better and the more praiseworthy for any of those kind of hindrances, than otherwise. But generally remember that nothing can hurt a natural citizen, that is not hurtful unto the city itself, nor anything hurt the city, that is not hurtful unto the law itself. But none of these casualties, or external hindrances, do hurt the law itself; or, are contrary to that course of justice and equity, by which public societies are maintained: neither therefore do they hurt either city or citizen.

XXXIV. As he that is bitten by a mad dog, is afraid of everything almost that he seeth: so unto him, whom the dogmata have once bitten, or in whom true knowledge hath made an impression, everything almost that he sees or reads be it never so short or ordinary, doth afford a good memento; to put him out of all grief and fear, as that of the poet, 'The winds blow upon the trees, and their leaves fall upon the ground. Then do the trees begin to bud again, and by the spring-time they put forth new branches. So is the generation of men; some come into the world, and others go out of it.' Of these leaves then thy children are. And they also that applaud thee so gravely, or, that applaud thy speeches, with that their usual acclamation, axiopistwz, O wisely spoken I and speak well of thee, as on the other side, they that stick not to curse thee, they that privately and secretly dispraise and deride thee, they also are but leaves. And they also that shall follow, in whose memories the names of men famous after death, is preserved, they are but leaves neither. For even so is it of all these worldly things. Their spring comes, and they are put forth. Then blows the wind, and they go down. And then in lieu of them grow others out of the wood or common matter of all things, like unto them. But, to endure but for a while, is common unto all. Why then shouldest thou so earnestly either seek after these things, or fly from them, as though they should endure for ever? Yet a little while, and thine eyes will be closed up, and for him that carries thee to thy grave shall another mourn within a while after.

XXXV. A good eye must be good to see whatsoever is to be seen, and not green things only. For that is proper to sore eyes. So must a good ear, and a good smell be ready for whatsoever is either to be heard, or smelt: and a good stomach as indifferent to all kinds of food, as a millstone is, to whatsoever she was made for to grind. As ready therefore must a sound understanding be for whatsoever shall happen. But he that saith, O that my children might live! and, O that all men might commend me for whatsoever I do! is an eye that seeks after green things; or as teeth, after that which is tender.

XXXVI. There is not any man that is so happy in his death, but that some of those that are by him when he dies, will be ready to rejoice at his supposed calamity. Is it one that was virtuous and wise indeed? will there not some one or other be found, who thus will say to himself; 'Well now at last shall I be at rest from this pedagogue. He did not indeed otherwise trouble us much: but I know well enough that in his heart, he did much condemn us.' Thus will they speak of the virtuous. But as for us, alas I how many things be there, for which there be many that glad would be to be rid of us. This therefore if thou shalt think of whensoever thou diest, thou shalt die the more willingly, when thou shalt think with thyself; I am now to depart from that world, wherein those that have been my nearest friends and acquaintances, they whom I have so much suffered for, so often prayed for, and for whom I have taken such care, even they would have me die, hoping that after my death they shall live happier, than they did before. What then should any man desire to continue here any longer? Nevertheless, whensoever thou diest, thou must not be less kind and loving unto them for it; but as before, see them, continue to be their friend, to wish them well, and meekly, and gently to carry thyself towards them, but yet so that on the other side, it make thee not the more unwilling to die. But as it fareth with them that die an easy quick death, whose soul is soon separated from their bodies, so must thy separation from them be. To these had nature joined and annexed me: now she parts us; I am ready to depart, as from friends and kinsmen, but yet without either reluctancy or compulsion. For this also is according to Nature.

XXXVII. Use thyself; as often, as thou seest any man do anything, presently (if it be possible) to say unto thyself, What is this man's end in this his action? But begin this course with thyself first of all, and diligently examine thyself concerning whatsoever thou doest.

XXXVIII. Remember, that that which sets a man at work, and hath power over the affections to draw them either one way, or the other way, is not any external thing properly, but that which is hidden within every man's dogmata, and opinions: That, that is rhetoric; that is life; that (to speak true) is man himself. As for thy body, which as a vessel, or a case, compasseth thee about, and the many and curious instruments that it hath annexed unto it, let them not trouble thy thoughts. For of themselves they are but as a carpenter's axe, but that they are born with us, and naturally sticking unto us. But otherwise, without the inward cause that hath power to move them, and to restrain them, those parts are of themselves of no more use unto us, than the shuttle is of itself to the weaver, or the pen to the writer, or the whip to the coachman.

The Eleventh Book

I. The natural properties, and privileges of a reasonable soul are: That she seeth herself; that she can order, and compose herself: that she makes herself as she will herself: that she reaps her own fruits whatsoever, whereas plants, trees, unreasonable creatures, what fruit soever (be it either fruit properly, or analogically only) they bear, they bear them unto others, and not to themselves. Again; whensoever, and wheresoever, sooner or later, her life doth end, she hath her own end nevertheless. For it is not with her, as with dancers and players, who if they be interrupted in any part of their action, the whole action must needs be imperfect: but she in what part of time or action soever she be surprised, can make that which she hath in her hand whatsoever it be, complete and full, so that she may depart with that comfort, 'I have lived; neither want I anything of that which properly did belong unto me.' Again, she compasseth the whole world, and penetrateth into the vanity, and mere outside (wanting substance and solidity) of it, and stretcheth herself unto the infiniteness of eternity; and the revolution or restoration of all things after a certain period of time, to the same state and place as before, she fetcheth about, and doth comprehend in herself; and considers withal, and sees clearly this, that neither they that shall follow us, shall see any new thing, that we have not seen, nor they that went before, anything more than we: but that he that is once come to forty (if he have any wit at all) can in a manner (for that they are all of one kind) see all things, both past and future. As proper is it, and natural to the soul of man to love her neighbour, to be true and modest; and to regard nothing so much as herself: which is also the property of the law: whereby by the way it appears, that sound reason and justice comes all to one, and therefore that justice is the chief thing, that reasonable creatures ought to propose unto themselves as their end.

II. A pleasant song or dance; the Pancratiast's exercise, sports that thou art wont to be much taken with, thou shalt easily contemn; if the harmonious voice thou shalt divide into so many particular sounds whereof it doth consist, and of every one in particular shall ask thyself; whether this or that sound is it, that doth so conquer thee. For thou wilt be ashamed of it. And so for shame, if accordingly thou shalt consider it, every particular motion and posture by itself: and so for the wrestler's exercise too. Generally then, whatsoever it be, besides virtue, and those things that proceed from virtue that thou art subject to be much affected with, remember presently thus to divide it, and by this kind of division, in each particular to attain unto the contempt of the whole. This thou must transfer and apply to thy whole life also.

III. That soul which is ever ready, even now presently (if need be) from the body, whether by way of extinction, or dispersion, or continuation in another place and estate to be separated, how blessed and happy is it! But this readiness of it, it must proceed, not from an obstinate and peremptory resolution of the mind, violently and passionately set upon Opposition, as Christians are wont; but from a peculiar judgment; with discretion and gravity, so that others may be persuaded also and drawn to the like example, but without any noise and passionate exclamations.

IV. Have I done anything charitably? then am I benefited by it. See that this upon all occasions may present itself unto thy mind, and never cease to think of it. What is thy profession? to be good. And how should this be well brought to pass, but by certain theorems and doctrines; some Concerning the nature of the universe, and some Concerning the proper and particular constitution of man?

V. Tragedies were at first brought in and instituted, to put men in mind of worldly chances and casualties: that these things in the ordinary course of nature did so happen: that men that were much pleased and delighted by such accidents upon this stage, would not by the same things in a greater stage be grieved and afflicted: for here you see what is the end of all such things; and that even they that cry out so mournfully to Cithaeron, must bear them for all their cries and exclamations, as well as others. And in very truth many good things are spoken by these poets; as that (for example) is an excellent passage: 'But if so be that I and my two children be neglected by the Gods, they have some reason even for that,' &c. And again, 'It will but little avail thee to storm and rage against the things themselves,' &c. Again, 'To reap one's life, as a ripe ear of corn;' and whatsoever else is to be found in them, that is of the same kind. After the tragedy, the ancient comedy was brought in, which had the liberty to inveigh against personal vices; being therefore through this her freedom and liberty of speech of very good use and effect, to restrain men from pride and arrogancy. To which end it was, that Diogenes took also the same liberty. After these, what were either the Middle, or New Comedy admitted for, but merely, (Or for the most part at least) for the delight and pleasure of curious and excellent imitation? 'It will steal away; look to it,' &c. Why, no man denies, but that these also have some good things whereof that may be one: but the whole drift and foundation of that kind of dramatical poetry, what is it else, but as we have said?

VI. How clearly doth it appear unto thee, that no other course of thy life could fit a true philosopher's practice better, than this very course, that thou art now already in?

VII. A branch cut off from the continuity of that which was next unto it, must needs be cut off from the whole tree: so a man that is divided from another man, is divided from the whole society. A branch is cut off by another, but he that hates and is averse, cuts himself off from his neighbour, and knows not that at the same time he divides himself from the whole body, or corporation. But herein is the gift and mercy of God, the Author of this society, in that, once cut off we may grow together and become part of the whole again. But if this happen often the misery is that the further a man is run in this division, the harder he is to be reunited and restored again: and however the branch which, once cut of afterwards was graffed in, gardeners can tell you is not like that which sprouted together at first, and still continued in the unity of the body.

VIII. To grow together like fellow branches in matter of good correspondence and affection; but not in matter of opinions. They that shall oppose thee in thy right courses, as it is not in their power to divert thee from thy good action, so neither let it be to divert thee from thy good affection towards them. But be it thy care to keep thyself constant in both; both in a right judgment and action, and in true meekness towards them, that either shall do their endeavour to hinder thee, or at least will be displeased with thee for what thou hast done. For to fail in either (either in the one to give over for fear, or in the other to forsake thy natural affection towards him, who by nature is both thy friend and thy kinsman) is equally base, and much savouring of the disposition of a cowardly fugitive soldier.

IX. It is not possible that any nature should be inferior unto art, since that all arts imitate nature. If this be so; that the most perfect and general nature of all natures should in her operation come short of the skill of arts, is most improbable. Now common is it to all arts, to make that which is worse for the better's sake. Much more then doth the common nature do the same. Hence is the first ground of justice. From justice all other virtues have their existence. For justice cannot be preserved, if either we settle our minds and affections upon worldly things; or be apt to be deceived, or rash, and inconstant.

X. The things themselves (which either to get or to avoid thou art put to so much trouble) come not unto thee themselves; but thou in a manner goest unto them. Let then thine own judgment and opinion concerning those things be at rest; and as for the things themselves, they stand still and quiet, without any noise or stir at all; and so shall all pursuing and flying cease.

XI. Then is the soul as Empedocles doth liken it, like unto a sphere or globe, when she is all of one form and figure: when she neither greedily stretcheth out herself unto anything, nor basely contracts herself, or lies flat and dejected; but shineth all with light, whereby she does see and behold the true nature, both that of the universe, and her own in particular.

XII. Will any contemn me? let him look to that, upon what grounds he does it: my care shall be that I may never be found either doing or speaking anything that doth truly deserve contempt. Will any hate me? let him look to that. I for my part will be kind and loving unto all, and even unto him that hates me, whom-soever he be, will I be ready to show his error, not by way of exprobation or ostentation of my patience, but ingenuously and meekly: such as was that famous Phocion, if so be that he did not dissemble. For it is inwardly that these things must be: that the Gods who look inwardly, and not upon the outward appearance, may behold a man truly free from all indignation and grief. For what hurt can it be unto thee whatsoever any man else doth, as long as thou mayest do that which is proper and suitable to thine own nature? Wilt not thou (a man wholly appointed to be both what, and as the common good shall require) accept of that which is now seasonable to the nature of the universe?

XIII. They contemn one another, and yet they seek to please one another: and whilest they seek to surpass one another in worldly pomp and greatness, they most debase and prostitute themselves in their better part one to another.

XIV. How rotten and insincere is he, that saith, I am resolved to carry myself hereafter towards you with all ingenuity and simplicity. O man, what doest thou mean! what needs this profession of thine? the thing itself will show it. It ought to be written upon thy forehead. No sooner thy voice is heard, than thy countenance must be able to show what is in thy mind: even as he that is loved knows presently by the looks of his sweetheart what is in her mind. Such must he be for all the world, that is truly simple and good, as he whose armholes are offensive, that whosoever stands by, as soon as ever he comes near him, may as it were smell him whether he will or no. But the affectation of simplicity is nowise laudable. There is nothing more shameful than perfidious friendship. Above all things, that must be avoided. However true goodness, simplicity, and kindness cannot so be hidden, but that as we have already said in the very eyes and countenance they will show themselves.

XV. To live happily is an inward power of the soul, when she is affected with indifferency, towards those things that are by their nature indifferent. To be thus affected she must consider all worldly objects both divided and whole: remembering withal that no object can of itself beget any opinion in us, neither can come to us, but stands without still and quiet; but that we ourselves beget, and as it were print in ourselves opinions concerning them. Now it is in our power, not to print them; and if they creep in and lurk in some corner, it is in our power to wipe them off. Remembering moreover, that this care and circumspection of thine, is to continue but for a while, and then thy life will be at an end. And what should hinder, but that thou mayest do well with all these things? For if they be according to nature, rejoice in them, and let them be pleasing and acceptable unto thee. But if they be against nature, seek thou that which is according to thine own nature, and whether it be for thy credit or no, use all possible speed for the attainment of it: for no man ought to be blamed, for seeking his own good and happiness.

XVI. Of everything thou must consider from whence it came, of what things it doth consist, and into what it will be changed: what will be the nature of it, or what it will be like unto when it is changed; and that it can suffer no hurt by this change. And as for other men's either foolishness or wickedness, that it may not trouble and grieve thee; first generally thus; What reference have I unto these? and that we are all born for one another's good: then more particularly after another consideration; as a ram is first in a flock of sheep, and a bull in a herd of cattle, so am I born to rule over them. Begin yet higher, even from this: if atoms be not the beginning of all things, than which to believe nothing can be more absurd, then must we needs grant that there is a nature, that doth govern the universe. If such a nature, then are all worse things made for the better's sake; and all better for one another's sake. Secondly, what manner of men they be, at board, and upon their beds, and so forth. But above all things, how they are forced by their opinions that they hold, to do what they do; and even those things that they do, with what pride and self-conceit they do them. Thirdly, that if they do these things rightly, thou hast no reason to be grieved. But if not rightly, it must needs be that they do them against their wills, and through mere ignorance. For as, according to Plato's opinion, no soul doth willingly err, so by consequent neither doth it anything otherwise than it ought, but against her will. Therefore are they grieved, whensoever they hear themselves charged, either of injustice, or unconscionableness, or covetousness, or in general, of any injurious kind of dealing towards their neighbours. Fourthly, that thou thyself doest transgress in many things, and art even such another as they are. And though perchance thou doest forbear the very act of some sins, yet hast thou in thyself an habitual disposition to them, but that either through fear, or vainglory, or some such other ambitious foolish respect, thou art restrained. Fifthly, that whether they have sinned or no, thou doest not understand perfectly. For many things are done by way of discreet policy; and generally a man must know many things first, before he be able truly and judiciously to judge of another man's action. Sixthly, that whensoever thou doest take on grievously, or makest great woe, little doest thou remember then that a man's life is but for a moment of time, and that within a while we shall all be in our graves. Seventhly, that it is not the sins and transgressions themselves that trouble us properly; for they have their existence in their minds and understandings only, that commit them; but our own opinions concerning those sins. Remove then, and be content to part with that conceit of thine, that it is a grievous thing, and thou hast removed thine anger. But how should I remove it? How? reasoning with thyself that it is not shameful. For if that which is shameful, be not the only true evil that is, thou also wilt be driven whilest thou doest follow the common instinct of nature, to avoid that which is evil, to commit many unjust things, and to become a thief, and anything, that will make to the attainment of thy intended worldly ends. Eighthly, how many things may and do oftentimes follow upon such fits of anger and grief; far more grievous in themselves, than those very things which we are so grieved or angry for. Ninthly, that meekness is a thing unconquerable, if it be true and natural, and not affected or hypocritical. For how shall even the most fierce and malicious that thou shalt conceive, be able to hold on against thee, if thou shalt still continue meek and loving unto him; and that even at that time, when he is about to do thee wrong, thou shalt be well disposed, and in good temper, with all meekness to teach him, and to instruct him better? As for example; My son, we were not born for this, to hurt and annoy one another; it will be thy hurt not mine, my son: and so to show him forcibly and fully, that it is so in very deed: and that neither bees do it one to another, nor any other creatures that are naturally sociable. But this thou must do, not scoffingly, not by way of exprobation, but tenderly without any harshness of words. Neither must thou do it by way of exercise, or ostentation, that they that are by and hear thee, may admire thee: but so always that nobody be privy to it, but himself alone: yea, though there be more present at the same time. These nine particular heads, as so many gifts from the Muses, see that thou remember well: and begin one day, whilest thou art yet alive, to be a man indeed. But on the other side thou must take heed, as much to flatter them, as to be angry with them: for both are equally uncharitable, and equally hurtful. And in thy passions, take it presently to thy consideration, that to be angry is not the part of a man, but that to be meek and gentle, as it savours of more humanity, so of more manhood. That in this, there is strength and nerves, or vigour and fortitude: whereof anger and indignation is altogether void. For the nearer everything is unto unpassionateness, the nearer it is unto power. And as grief doth proceed from weakness, so doth anger. For both, both he that is angry and that grieveth, have received a wound, and cowardly have as it were yielded themselves unto their affections. If thou wilt have a tenth also, receive this tenth gift from Hercules the guide and leader of the Muses: that is a mad man's part, to look that there should be no wicked men in the world, because it is impossible. Now for a man to brook well enough, that there should be wicked men in the world, but not to endure that any should transgress against himself, is against all equity, and indeed tyrannical.

XVII. Four several dispositions or inclinations there be of the mind and understanding, which to be aware of, thou must carefully observe: and whensoever thou doest discover them, thou must rectify them, saying to thyself concerning every one of them, This imagination is not necessary; this is uncharitable: this thou shalt speak as another man's slave, or instrument; than which nothing can be more senseless and absurd: for the fourth, thou shalt sharply check and upbraid thyself; for that thou doest suffer that more divine part in thee, to become subject and obnoxious to that more ignoble part of thy body, and the gross lusts and concupiscences thereof.

XVIII. What portion soever, either of air or fire there be in thee, although by nature it tend upwards, submitting nevertheless to the ordinance of the universe, it abides here below in this mixed body. So whatsoever is in thee, either earthy, or humid, although by nature it tend downwards, yet is it against its nature both raised upwards, and standing, or consistent. So obedient are even the elements themselves to the universe, abiding patiently wheresoever (though against their nature) they are placed, until the sound as it were of their retreat, and separation. Is it not a grievous thing then, that thy reasonable part only should be disobedient, and should not endure to keep its place: yea though it be nothing enjoined that is contrary unto it, but that only which is according to its nature? For we cannot say of it when it is disobedient, as we say of the fire, or air, that it tends upwards towards its proper element, for then goes it the quite contrary way. For the motion of the mind to any injustice, or incontinency, or to sorrow, or to fear, is nothing else but a separation from nature. Also when the mind is grieved for anything that is happened by the divine providence, then doth it likewise forsake its own place. For it was ordained unto holiness and godliness, which specially consist in an humble submission to God and His providence in all things; as well as unto justice: these also being part of those duties, which as naturally sociable, we are bound unto; and without which we cannot happily converse one with another: yea and the very ground and fountain indeed of all just actions.

XIX. He that hath not one and the self-same general end always as long as he liveth, cannot possibly be one and the self-same man always. But this will not suffice except thou add also what ought to be this general end. For as the general conceit and apprehension of all those things which upon no certain ground are by the greater part of men deemed good, cannot be uniform and agreeable, but that only which is limited and restrained by some certain proprieties and conditions, as of community: that nothing be conceived good, which is not commonly and publicly good: so must the end also that we propose unto ourselves, be common and sociable. For he that doth direct all his own private motions and purposes to that end, all his actions will be agreeable and uniform; and by that means will be still the same man.

XX. Remember the fable of the country mouse and the city mouse, and the great fright and terror that this was put into.

XXI. Socrates was wont to call the common conceits and opinions of men, the common bugbears of the world: the proper terror of silly children.

XXII. The Lacedaemonians at their public spectacles were wont to appoint seats and forms for their strangers in the shadow, they themselves were content to sit anywhere.

XXIII. What Socrates answered unto Perdiccas, why he did not come unto him, Lest of all deaths I should die the worst kind of death, said he: that is, not able to requite the good that hath been done unto me.

XXIV. In the ancient mystical letters of the Ephesians, there was an item, that a man should always have in his mind some one or other of the ancient worthies.

XXV. The Pythagoreans were wont betimes in the morning the first thing they did, to look up unto the heavens, to put themselves in mind of them who constantly and invariably did perform their task: as also to put themselves in mind of orderliness, or good order, and of purity, and of naked simplicity. For no star or planet hath any cover before it.

XXVI. How Socrates looked, when he was fain to gird himself with a skin, Xanthippe his wife having taken away his clothes, and carried them abroad with her, and what he said to his fellows and friends, who were ashamed; and out of respect to him, did retire themselves when they saw him thus decked.

XXVII. In matter of writing or reading thou must needs be taught before thou can do either: much more in matter of life. 'For thou art born a mere slave, to thy senses and brutish affections;' destitute without teaching of all true knowledge and sound reason.

XXVIII. 'My heart smiled within me.' 'They will accuse even virtue herself; with heinous and opprobrious words.'

XXIX. As they that long after figs in winter when they cannot be had; so are they that long after children, before they be granted them.

XXX. 'As often as a father kisseth his child, he should say secretly with himself' (said Epictetus,) 'tomorrow perchance shall he die.' But these words be ominous. No words ominous (said he) that signify anything that is natural: in very truth and deed not more ominous than this, 'to cut down grapes when they are ripe.' Green grapes, ripe grapes, dried grapes, or raisins: so many changes and mutations of one thing, not into that which was not absolutely, but rather so many several changes and mutations, not into that which hath no being at all, but into that which is not yet in being.

XXXI. 'Of the free will there is no thief or robber:' out of Epictetus; Whose is this also: that we should find a certain art and method of assenting; and that we should always observe with great care and heed the inclinations of our minds, that they may always be with their due restraint and reservation, always charitable, and according to the true worth of every present object. And as for earnest longing, that we should altogether avoid it: and to use averseness in those things only, that wholly depend of our own wills. It is not about ordinary petty matters, believe it, that all our strife and contention is, but whether, with the vulgar, we should be mad, or by the help of philosophy wise and sober, said he.

XXXII. Socrates said, 'What will you have? the souls of reasonable, or unreasonable creatures? Of reasonable. But what? Of those whose reason is sound and perfect? or of those whose reason is vitiated and corrupted? Of those whose reason is sound and perfect. Why then labour ye not for such? Because we have them already. What then do ye so strive and contend between you?'

The Twelfth Book

I. Whatsoever thou doest hereafter aspire unto, thou mayest even now enjoy and possess, if thou doest not envy thyself thine own happiness. And that will be, if thou shalt forget all that is past, and for the future, refer thyself wholly to the Divine Providence, and shalt bend and apply all thy present thoughts and intentions to holiness and righteousness. To holiness, in accepting willingly whatsoever is sent by the Divine Providence, as being that which the nature of the universe hath appointed unto thee, which also hath appointed thee for that, whatsoever it be. To righteousness, in speaking the truth freely, and without ambiguity; and in doing all things justly and discreetly. Now in this good course, let not other men's either wickedness, or opinion, or voice hinder thee: no, nor the sense of this thy pampered mass of flesh: for let that which suffers, look to itself. If therefore whensoever the time of thy departing shall come, thou shalt readily leave all things, and shalt respect thy mind only, and that divine part of thine, and this shall be thine only fear, not that some time or other thou shalt cease to live, but thou shalt never begin to live according to nature: then shalt thou be a man indeed, worthy of that world, from which thou hadst thy beginning; then shalt thou cease to be a stranger in thy country, and to wonder at those things that happen daily, as things strange and unexpected, and anxiously to depend of divers things that are not in thy power.

II. God beholds our minds and understandings, bare and naked from these material vessels, and outsides, and all earthly dross. For with His simple and pure understanding, He pierceth into our inmost and purest parts, which from His, as it were by a water pipe and channel, first flowed and issued. This if thou also shalt use to do, thou shalt rid thyself of that manifold luggage, wherewith thou art round about encumbered. For he that does regard neither his body, nor his clothing, nor his dwelling, nor any such external furniture, must needs gain unto himself great rest and ease. Three things there be in all, which thou doest consist of; thy body, thy life, and thy mind. Of these the two former, are so far forth thine, as that thou art bound to take care for them. But the third alone is that which is properly thine. If then thou shalt separate from thyself, that is from thy mind, whatsoever other men either do or say, or whatsoever thou thyself hast heretofore either done or said; and all troublesome thoughts concerning the future, and whatsoever, (as either belonging to thy body or life:) is without the jurisdiction of thine own will, and whatsoever in the ordinary course of human chances and accidents doth happen unto thee; so that thy mind (keeping herself loose and free from all outward coincidental entanglements; always in a readiness to depart:) shall live by herself, and to herself, doing that which is just, accepting whatsoever doth happen, and speaking the truth always; if, I say, thou shalt separate from thy mind, whatsoever by sympathy might adhere unto it, and all time both past and future, and shalt make thyself in all points and respects, like unto Empedocles his allegorical sphere, 'all round and circular,' &c., and shalt think of no longer life than that which is now present: then shalt thou be truly able to pass the remainder of thy days without troubles and distractions; nobly and generously disposed, and in good favour and correspondency, with that spirit which is within thee.

III. I have often wondered how it should come to pass, that every man loving himself best, should more regard other men's opinions concerning himself than his own. For if any God or grave master standing by, should command any of us to think nothing by himself but what he should presently speak out; no man were able to endure it, though but for one day. Thus do we fear more what our neighbours will think of us, than what we ourselves.

IV. how come it to pass that the Gods having ordered all other things so well and so lovingly, should be overseen in this one only thing, that whereas then hath been some very good men that have made many covenants as it were with God and by many holy actions and outward services contracted a kind of familiarity with Him; that these men when once they are dead, should never be restored to life, but be extinct for ever. But this thou mayest be sure of, that this (if it be so indeed) would never have been so ordered by the Gods, had it been fit otherwise. For certainly it was possible, had it been more just so and had it been according to nature, the nature of the universe would easily have borne it. But now because it is not so, (if so be that it be not so indeed) be therefore confident that it was not fit it should be so for thou seest thyself, that now seeking after this matter, how freely thou doest argue and contest with God. But were not the Gods both just and good in the highest degree, thou durst not thus reason with them. Now if just and good, it could not be that in the creation of the world, they should either unjustly or unreasonably oversee anything.

V. Use thyself even unto those things that thou doest at first despair of. For the left hand we see, which for the most part lieth idle because not used; yet doth it hold the bridle with more strength than the right, because it hath been used unto it.

VI. Let these be the objects of thy ordinary meditation: to consider, what manner of men both for soul and body we ought to be, whensoever death shall surprise us: the shortness of this our mortal life: the immense vastness of the time that hath been before, and will he after us: the frailty of every worldly material object: all these things to consider, and behold clearly in themselves, all disguisement of external outside being removed and taken away. Again, to consider the efficient causes of all things: the proper ends and references of all actions: what pain is in itself; what pleasure, what death: what fame or honour, how every man is the true and proper ground of his own rest and tranquillity, and that no man can truly be hindered by any other: that all is but conceit and opinion. As for the use of thy dogmata, thou must carry thyself in the practice of them, rather like unto a pancratiastes, or one that at the same time both fights and wrestles with hands and feet, than a gladiator. For this, if he lose his sword that he fights with, he is gone: whereas the other hath still his hand free, which he may easily turn and manage at his will.

VII. All worldly things thou must behold and consider, dividing them into matter, form, and reference, or their proper end.

VIII. How happy is man in this his power that hath been granted unto him: that he needs not do anything but what God shall approve, and that he may embrace contentedly, whatsoever God doth send unto him?

IX. Whatsoever doth happen in the ordinary course and consequence of natural events, neither the Gods, (for it is not possible, that they either wittingly or unwittingly should do anything amiss) nor men, (for it is through ignorance, and therefore against their wills that they do anything amiss) must be accused. None then must be accused.

X. How ridiculous and strange is he, that wonders at anything that happens in this life in the ordinary course of nature!

XI. Either fate, (and that either an absolute necessity, and unavoidable decree; or a placable and flexible Providence) or all is a mere casual confusion, void of all order and government. If an absolute and unavoidable necessity, why doest thou resist? If a placable and exorable Providence, make thyself worthy of the divine help and assistance. If all be a mere confusion without any moderator, or governor, then hast thou reason to congratulate thyself; that in such a general flood of confusion thou thyself hast obtained a reasonable faculty, whereby thou mayest govern thine own life and actions. But if thou beest carried away with the flood, it must be thy body perchance, or thy life, or some other thing that belongs unto them that is carried away: thy mind and understanding cannot. Or should it be so, that the light of a candle indeed is still bright and lightsome until it be put out: and should truth, and righteousness, and temperance cease to shine in thee whilst thou thyself hast any being?

XII. At the conceit and apprehension that such and such a one hath sinned, thus reason with thyself; What do I know whether this be a sin indeed, as it seems to be? But if it be, what do I know but that he himself hath already condemned himself for it? And that is all one as if a man should scratch and tear his own face, an object of compassion rather than of anger. Again, that he that would not have a vicious man to sin, is like unto him that would not have moisture in the fig, nor children to welp nor a horse to neigh, nor anything else that in the course of nature is necessary. For what shall he do that hath such an habit? If thou therefore beest powerful and eloquent, remedy it if thou canst.

XIII. If it be not fitting, do it not. If it be not true, speak it not. Ever maintain thine own purpose and resolution free from all compulsion and necessity.

XIV. Of everything that presents itself unto thee, to consider what the true nature of it is, and to unfold it, as it were, by dividing it into that which is formal: that which is material: the true use or end of it, and the just time that it is appointed to last.

XV. It is high time for thee, to understand that there is somewhat in thee, better and more divine than either thy passions, or thy sensual appetites and affections. What is now the object of my mind, is it fear, or suspicion, or lust, or any such thing? To do nothing rashly without some certain end; let that be thy first care. The next, to have no other end than the common good. For, alas! yet a little while, and thou art no more: no more will any, either of those things that now thou seest, or of those men that now are living, be any more. For all things are by nature appointed soon to be changed, turned, and corrupted, that other things might succeed in their room.

XVI. Remember that all is but opinion, and all opinion depends of the mind. Take thine opinion away, and then as a ship that hath stricken in within the arms and mouth of the harbour, a present calm; all things safe and steady: a bay, not capable of any storms and tempests: as the poet hath it.

XVII. No operation whatsoever it he, ceasing for a while, can be truly said to suffer any evil, because it is at an end. Neither can he that is the author of that operation; for this very respect, because his operation is at an end, be said to suffer any evil. Likewise then, neither can the whole body of all our actions (which is our life) if in time it cease, be said to suffer any evil for this very reason, because it is at an end; nor he truly be said to have been ill affected, that did put a period to this series of actions. Now this time or certain period, depends of the determination of nature: sometimes of particular nature, as when a man dieth old; but of nature in general, however; the parts whereof thus changing one after another, the whole world still continues fresh and new. Now that is ever best and most seasonable, which is for the good of the whole. Thus it appears that death of itself can neither be hurtful to any in particular, because it is not a shameful thing (for neither is it a thing that depends of our own will, nor of itself contrary to the common good) and generally, as it is both expedient and seasonable to the whole, that in that respect it must needs be good. It is that also, which is brought unto us by the order and appointment of the Divine Providence; so that he whose will and mind in these things runs along with the Divine ordinance, and by this concurrence of his will and mind with the Divine Providence, is led and driven along, as it were by God Himself; may truly be termed and esteemed the *OEo~p7poc*, or divinely led and inspired.

XVIII. These three things thou must have always in a readiness: first concerning thine own actions, whether thou doest nothing either idly, or otherwise, than justice and equity do require: and concerning those things that happen unto thee externally, that either they happen unto thee by chance, or by providence; of which two to accuse either, is equally against reason. Secondly, what like unto our bodies are whilest yet rude and imperfect, until they be animated: and from their animation, until their expiration: of what things they are compounded, and into what things they shall be dissolved. Thirdly, how vain all things will appear unto thee when, from on high as it were, looking down thou shalt contemplate all things upon earth, and the wonderful mutability, that they are subject unto: considering withal, the infinite both greatness and variety of things aerial and things celestial that are round about it. And that as often as thou shalt behold them, thou shalt still see the same: as the same things, so the same shortness of continuance of all those things. And, behold, these be the things that we are so proud and puffed up for.

XIX. Cast away from thee opinion, and thou art safe. And what is it that hinders thee from casting of it away? When thou art grieved at anything, hast thou forgotten that all things happen according to the nature of the universe; and that him only it concerns, who is in fault; and moreover, that what is now done, is that which from ever hath been done in the world, and will ever be done, and is now done everywhere: how nearly all men are allied one to another by a kindred not of blood, nor of seed, but of the same mind. Thou hast also forgotten that every man's mind partakes of the Deity, and issueth from thence; and that no man can properly call anything his own, no not his son, nor his body, nor his life; for that they all proceed from that One who is the giver of all things: that all things are but opinion; that no man lives properly, but that very instant of time which is now present. And therefore that no man whensoever he dieth can properly be said to lose any more, than an instant of time.

XX. Let thy thoughts ever run upon them, who once for some one thing or other, were moved with extraordinary indignation; who were once in the highest pitch of either honour, or calamity; or mutual hatred and enmity; or of any other fortune or condition whatsoever. Then consider what's now become of all those things. All is turned to smoke; all to ashes, and a mere fable; and perchance not so much as a fable. As also whatsoever is of this nature, as Fabius Catulinus in the field; Lucius Lupus, and Stertinius, at Baiae Tiberius at Caprem: and Velius Rufus, and all such examples of vehement prosecution in worldly matters; let these also run in thy mind at the same time; and how vile every object of such earnest and vehement prosecution is; and how much more agreeable to true philosophy it is, for a man to carry himself in every matter that offers itself; justly, and moderately, as one that followeth the Gods with all simplicity. For, for a man to be proud and high conceited, that he is not proud and high conceited, is of all kind of pride and presumption, the most intolerable.

XXI. To them that ask thee, Where hast thou seen the Gods, or how knowest thou certainly that there be Gods, that thou art so devout in their worship? I answer first of all, that even to the very eye, they are in some manner visible and apparent. Secondly, neither have I ever seen mine own soul, and yet I respect and honour it. So then for the Gods, by the daily experience that I have of their power and providence towards myself and others, I know certainly that they are, and therefore worship them.

XXII. Herein doth consist happiness of life, for a man to know thoroughly the true nature of everything; what is the matter, and what is the form of it: with all his heart and soul, ever to do that which is just, and to speak the truth. What then remaineth but to enjoy thy life in a course and coherence of good actions, one upon another immediately succeeding, and never interrupted, though for never so little a while?

XXIII. There is but one light of the sun, though it be intercepted by walls and mountains, and other thousand objects. There is but one common substance of the whole world, though it be concluded and restrained into several different bodies, in number infinite. There is but one common soul, though divided into innumerable particular essences and natures. So is there but one common intellectual soul, though it seem to be divided. And as for all other parts of those generals which we have mentioned, as either sensitive souls or subjects, these of themselves (as naturally irrational) have no common mutual reference one unto another, though many of them contain a mind, or reasonable faculty in them, whereby they are ruled and governed. But of every reasonable mind, this the particular nature, that it hath reference to whatsoever is of her own kind, and desireth to be united: neither can this common affection, or mutual unity and correspondency, be here intercepted or divided, or confined to particulars as those other common things are.

XXIV. What doest thou desire? To live long. What? To enjoy the operations of a sensitive soul; or of the appetitive faculty? or wouldst thou grow, and then decrease again? Wouldst thou long be able to talk, to think and reason with thyself? Which of all these seems unto thee a worthy object of thy desire? Now if of all these thou doest find that they be but little worth in themselves, proceed on unto the last, which is, in all things to follow God and reason. But for a man to grieve that by death he shall be deprived of any of these things, is both against God and reason.

XXV. What a small portion of vast and infinite eternity it is, that is allowed unto every one of us, and how soon it vanisheth into the general age of the world: of the common substance, and of the common soul also what a small portion is allotted unto us: and in what a little clod of the whole earth (as it were) it is that thou doest crawl. After thou shalt rightly have considered these things with thyself; fancy not anything else in the world any more to be of any weight and moment but this, to do that only which thine own nature doth require; and to conform thyself to that which the common nature doth afford.

XXVI. What is the present estate of my understanding? For herein lieth all indeed. As for all other things, they are without the compass of mine own will: and if without the compass of my will, then are they as dead things unto me, and as it were mere smoke.

XXVII. To stir up a man to the contempt of death this among other things, is of good power and efficacy, that even they who esteemed pleasure to be happiness, and pain misery, did nevertheless many of them contemn death as much as any. And can death be terrible to him, to whom that only seems good, which in the ordinary course of nature is seasonable? to him, to whom, whether his actions be many or few, so they be all good, is all one; and who whether he behold the things of the world being always the same either for many years, or for few years only, is altogether indifferent? O man! as a citizen thou hast lived, and conversed in this great city the world. Whether just for so many years, or no, what is it unto thee? Thou hast lived (thou mayest be sure) as long as the laws and orders of the city required; which may be the common comfort of all. Why then should it be grievous unto thee, if (not a tyrant, nor an unjust judge, but) the same nature that brought thee in, doth now send thee out of the world? As if the praetor should fairly dismiss him from the stage, whom he had taken in to act a while. Oh, but the play is not yet at an end, there are but three acts yet acted of it? Thou hast well said: for in matter of life, three acts is the whole play. Now to set a certain time to every man's acting, belongs unto him only, who as first he was of thy composition, so is now the cause of thy dissolution. As for thyself; thou hast to do with neither. Go thy ways then well pleased and contented: for so is He that dismisseth thee.

Notes

THIS being neither a critical edition of the text nor an emended edition of Casaubon's translation, it has not been thought necessary to add full notes. Casaubon's own notes have been omitted, because for the most part they are discursive, and not necessary to an understanding of what is written. In those which here follow, certain emendations of his are mentioned, which he proposes in his notes, and follows in the translation. In addition, one or two corrections are made where he has mistaken the Greek, and the translation might be misleading. Those which do not come under these two heads will explain themselves.

The text itself has been prepared by a comparison of the editions of 1634 and 1635. It should be borne in mind that Casaubon's is often rather a paraphrase than a close translation; and it did not seem worth while to notice every variation or amplification of the original. In the original editions all that Casauhon conceives as understood, but not expressed, is enclosed in square brackets. These brackets are here omitted, as they interfere with the comfort of the reader; and so have some of the alternative renderings suggested by the translator. In a few cases, Latin words in the text have been replaced by English.

Numbers in brackets refer to the Teubner text of Stich, but the divisions of the text are left unaltered. For some of the references identified I am indebted to Mr. G. H. Rendall's Marcus Aurelius.

BOOK II "Both to frequent" (4). Gr. to mh, C. conjectures to me. The text is probably right: "I did not frequent public lectures, and I was taught at home."

VI Idiots.... philosophers (9). The reading is doubtful, but the meaning seems to be: "simple and unlearned men"

XII "Claudius Maximus" (15). The reading of the Palatine MS. (now lost) was paraklhsiz Maximon, which C. supposes to conceal the letters kl as an abbreviation of Claudius.

XIII "Patient hearing... He would not" (16). C. translates his conjectural reading epimonon ollan. on proapsth Stich suggests a reading with much the same sense: .....epimonon all antoi "Strict and rigid dealing" (16). C. translates tonvn (Pal. MS.) as though from tonoz, in the sense of "strain." "rigour." The reading of other MSS. tonvn is preferable.

XIII "Congiaries" (13). dianomais, "doles."

XIV "Cajeta" (17). The passage is certainly corrupt. C. spies a reference to Chryses praying by the sea-shore in the Illiad, and supposes M. Aurelius to have done the like. None of the emendations suggested is satisfactory. At XV. Book II. is usually reckoned to begin. BOOK II III. "Do, soul" (6). If the received reading be right, it must be sarcastic; but there are several variants which show how unsatisfactory it is. C. translates "en gar o bioz ekasty so par eanty", which I do not understand. The sense required is: "Do not violence to thyself, for thou hast not long to use self-respect. Life is not (v. 1. so long for each, and this life for thee is all but done."

X. "honour and credit do proceed" (12). The verb has dropt out of the text, but C. has supplied one of the required meaning.

XI. "Consider," etc. (52). This verb is not in the Greek, which means: "(And reason also shows) how man, etc."

BOOK IV XV. "Agathos" (18): This is probably not a proper name, but the text seems to be unsound. The meaning may be "the good man ought"

XVI. oikonomian (16) is a "practical benefit," a secondary end. XXXIX. "For herein lieth all...." (~3). C. translates his conjecture olan for ola.

BOOK V XIV. katorqwseiz (15): Acts of "rightness" or "straightness." XXIII. "Roarer" (28): Gr. "tragedian." Ed. 1 has whoremonger,' ed. 2 corrects to "harlot," but omits to alter' the word at its second occurrence.

XXV. "Thou hast... them" (33): A quotation from Homer, Odyssey, iv. 690.

XXVII. "One of the poets" (33): Hesiod, Op. et Dies, 197.

XXIX and XXX. (36). The Greek appears to contain quotations from sources not known, and the translation is a paraphrase. (One or two alterations are here made on the authority of the second edition.) BOOK VI XIII. "Affected and qualified" (i4): exis, the power of cohesion shown in things inanimate; fusiz, power of growth seen in plants and the like.

XVII. "Wonder at them" (18): i.e. mankind.

XXXVII. "Chrysippus" (42): C. refers to a passage of Plutarch De Communibus Notitiis (c. xiv.), where Chrysippus is represented as saying that a coarse phrase may be vile in itself, yet have due place in a comedy as contributing to a certain effect.

XL. "Man or men..." There is no hiatus in the Greek, which means: "Whatever (is beneficial) for a man is so for other men also."

XLII. There is no hiatus in the Greek.

BOOK VII IX. C. translates his conjecture mh for h. The Greek means "straight, or rectified," with a play on the literal and metaphorical meaning of ortoz.

XIV. endaimonia. contains the word daimwn in composition. XXII. The text is corrupt, but the words "or if it be but few" should be "that is little enough."

XXIII. "Plato": Republic, vi. p. 486 A.

XXV. "It will," etc. Euripides, Belerophon, frag. 287 (Nauck).

"Lives," etc. Euripides, Hypsipyle, frag. 757 (Nauck). "As long," etc. Aristophanes, Acharne, 66 i.

"Plato" Apology, p. 28 B.

"For thus" Apology, p. 28 F.

XXVI. "But, O noble sir," etc. Plato, Gorgias, 512 D. XXVII. "And as for those parts," etc. A quotation from Euripides, Chryssipus, frag. 839 (Nauck).

"With meats," etc. From Euripides, Supplices, 1110. XXXIII. "They both," i.e. life and wrestling.

"Says he" (63): Plato, quoted by Epictetus, Arr. i. 28, 2 and 22.

XXXVII. "How know we," etc. The Greek means: "how know we whether Telauges were not nobler in character than Sophocles?" The allusion is unknown.

XXVII. "Frost" The word is written by Casaubon as a proper name, "Pagus.'

"The hardihood of Socrates was famous"; see Plato, Siymposium, p. 220.

BOOK X XXII. The Greek means, "paltry breath bearing up corpses, so that the tale of Dead Man's Land is clearer."

XXII. "The poet" (21): Euripides, frag. 898 (Nauck); compare Aeschylus, Danaides, frag. 44.

XXIV. "Plato" (23): Theaetetus, p. 174 D.

XXXIV. "The poet" (34): Homer, Iliad, vi. 147.

XXXIV. "Wood": A translation of ulh, "matter."

XXXVIII. "Rhetoric" (38): Rather "the gift of speech"; or perhaps the "decree" of the reasoning faculty.

BOOK XI V. "Cithaeron" (6): Oedipus utters this cry after discovering that he has fulfilled his awful doom, he was exposed on Cithaeron as an infant to die, and the cry implies that he wishes he had died there. Sophocles, Oedipus Tyrannus, 1391.

V. "New Comedy...," etc. C. has here strayed from the Greek rather widely. Translate: "and understand to what end the New Comedy was adopted, which by small degrees degenerated into a mere show of skill in mimicry." C. writes Comedia Vetus, Media, Nova. XII. "Phocion" (13): When about to be put to death he charged his son to bear no malice against the Athenians.

XXVIII. "My heart," etc. (31): From Homer, Odyssey ix. 413. "They will" From Hesiod, Opera et Dies, 184.

"Epictetus" Arr. i. II, 37.

XXX. "Cut down grapes" (35): Correct "ears of corn." "Epictetus"(36): Arr. 3, 22, 105.

ON THE SHORTNESS
OF LIFE

by

Seneca

On the Shortness of Life

I.

The majority of mortals, Paulinus,[1] complain bitterly of the spitefulness of Nature, because we are born for a brief span of life, because even this space that has been granted to us rushes by so speedily and so swiftly that all save a very few find life at an end just when they are getting ready to live. Nor is it merely the common herd and the unthinking crowd that bemoan what is, as men deem it, a universal ill; the same feeling has called forth complaint also from men who were famous. It was this that made the greatest of physicians exclaim that "life is short, art is long;"[2] it was this that led Aristotle,[3] while expostulating with Nature, to enter an indictment most unbecoming to a wise man—that, in point of age, she has shown such favour to animals that they drag out five or ten lifetimes,[4] but that a much shorter limit is fixed for man, though he is born for so many and such great achievements. It is not that we have a short space of time, but that we waste much of it. Life is long enough, and it has been given in sufficiently generous measure to allow the accomplishment of the very greatest things if the whole of it is well invested. But when it is squandered in luxury and carelessness, when it is devoted to no good end, forced at last by the ultimate necessity we perceive that it has passed away before we were aware that it was passing. So it is—the life we receive is not short, but we make it so, nor do we have any lack of it, but are wasteful of it. Just as great and princely wealth is scattered in a moment when it comes into the hands of a bad owner, while wealth however limited, if it is entrusted to a good guardian, increases by use, so our life is amply long for him who orders it properly.

II.

Why do we complain of Nature? She has shown herself kindly; life, if you know how to use it, is long. But one man is possessed by an avarice that is insatiable, another by a toilsome devotion to tasks that are useless; one man is besotted with wine, another is paralyzed by sloth; one man is exhausted by an ambition that always hangs upon the decision of others, another, driven on by the greed of the trader, is led over all lands and all seas by the hope of gain; some are tormented by a passion for war and are always either bent upon inflicting danger upon others or concerned about their own; some there are who are worn out by voluntary servitude in a thankless attendance upon the great; many are kept busy either in the pursuit of other men's fortune or in complaining of their own; many, following no fixed aim, shifting and inconstant and dissatisfied, are plunged by their fickleness into plans that are ever new; some have no fixed principle by which to direct their course, but Fate takes them unawares while they loll and yawn—so surely does it happen that I cannot doubt the truth of that utterance which the greatest of poets delivered with all the seeming of an oracle: "The part of life we really live is small."[5] For all the rest of existence is not life, but merely time. Vices beset us and surround us on every side, and they do not permit us to rise anew and lift up our eyes for the discernment of truth, but they keep us down when once they have overwhelmed us and we are chained to lust. Their victims are never allowed to return to their true selves; if ever they chance to find some release, like the waters of the deep sea which continue to heave even after the storm is past, they are tossed about, and no rest from their lusts abides. Think you that I am speaking of the wretches whose evils are admitted? Look at those whose prosperity men flock to behold; they are smothered by their blessings. To how many are riches a burden! From how many do eloquence and the daily straining to display their powers draw forth blood! How many are pale from constant pleasures! To how many does the throng of clients that crowd about them leave no freedom! In short, run through the list of all these men from the lowest to the highest—this man desires an advocate,[6] this one answers the call, that one is on trial, that one defends him, that one gives sentence; no one asserts his claim to himself, everyone is wasted for the sake of another. Ask about the men whose names are known by heart, and you will see that these are the marks that distinguish them: A cultivates B and B cultivates C; no one is his own master. And then certain men show the most senseless indignation—they complain of the insolence of their superiors, because they were too busy to see them when they wished an audience! But can anyone have the hardihood to complain of the pride of another when he himself has no time to attend to himself? After all, no matter who you are, the great man does sometimes look toward you even if his face is insolent, he does sometimes condescend to listen to your words, he permits you to appear at his side; but you never deign to look upon yourself, to give ear to yourself. There is no reason, therefore, to count anyone in debt for such services, seeing that, when you performed them, you had no wish for another's company, but could not endure your own.

III.

 Though all the brilliant intellects of the ages were to concentrate upon this one theme, never could they adequately express their wonder at this dense darkness of the human mind. Men do not suffer anyone to seize their estates, and they rush to stones and arms if there is even the slightest dispute about the limit of their lands, yet they allow others to trespass upon their life—nay, they themselves even lead in those who will eventually possess it. No one is to be found who is willing to distribute his money, yet among how many does each one of us distribute his life! In guarding their fortune men are often closefisted, yet, when it comes to the matter of wasting time, in the case of the one thing in which it is right to be miserly, they show themselves most prodigal. And so, I should like to lay hold upon someone from the company of older men and say: "I see that you have reached the farthest limit of human life, you are pressing hard upon your hundredth year, or are even beyond it; come now, recall your life and make a reckoning. Consider how much of your time was taken up with a moneylender, how much with a mistress, how much with a patron, how much with a client, how much in wrangling with your wife, how much in punishing your slaves, how much in rushing about the city on social duties. Add the diseases which we have caused by our own acts, add, too, the time that has lain idle and unused; you will see that you have fewer years to your credit than you count. Look back in memory and consider when you ever had a fixed plan, how few days have passed as you had intended, when you were ever at your own disposal, when your face ever wore its natural expression, when your mind was ever unperturbed, what work you have achieved in so long a life, how many have robbed you of life when you were not aware of what you were losing, how much was taken up in useless sorrow, in foolish joy, in greedy desire, in the allurements of society, how little of yourself was left to you; you will perceive that you are dying before your season!"[7] What, then, is the reason of this? You live as if you were destined to live forever, no thought of your frailty ever enters your head, of how much time has already gone by you take no heed. You squander time as if you drew from a full and abundant supply, though all the while that day which you bestow on some person or thing is perhaps your last. You have all the fears of mortals and all the desires of immortals. You will hear many men saying: "After my fiftieth year I shall retire into leisure, my sixtieth year shall release me from public duties." And what guarantee, pray, have you that your life will last longer? Who will suffer your course to be just as you plan it? Are you not ashamed to reserve for yourself only the remnant of life, and to set apart for wisdom only that time which cannot be devoted to any business? How late it is to begin to live just when we must cease to live! What foolish forgetfulness of mortality to postpone wholesome plans to the fiftieth and sixtieth year, and to intend to begin life at a point to which few have attained!

IV.

You will see that the most powerful and highly placed men let drop remarks in which they long for leisure, acclaim it, and prefer it to all their blessings. They desire at times, if it could be with safety, to descend from their high pinnacle; for, though nothing from without should assail or shatter, Fortune of its very self comes crashing down.[8]

The deified Augustus, to whom the gods vouchsafed more than to any other man, did not cease to pray for rest and to seek release from public affairs; all his conversation ever reverted to this subject—his hope of leisure. This was the sweet, even if vain, consolation with which he would gladden his labours—that he would one day live for himself. In a letter addressed to the senate, in which he had promised that his rest would not be devoid of dignity nor inconsistent with his former glory, I find these words: "But these matters can be shown better by deeds than by promises. Nevertheless, since the joyful reality is still far distant, my desire for that time most earnestly prayed for has led me to forestall some of its delight by the pleasure of words." So desirable a thing did leisure seem that he anticipated it in thought because he could not attain it in reality. He who saw everything depending upon himself alone, who determined the fortune of individuals and of nations, thought most happily of that future day on which he should lay aside his greatness. He had discovered how much sweat those blessings that shone throughout all lands drew forth, how many secret worries they concealed. Forced to pit arms first against his countrymen, then against his colleagues, and lastly against his relatives, he shed blood on land and sea.

Through Macedonia, Sicily, Egypt, Syria, and Asia, and almost all countries he followed the path of battle, and when his troops were weary of shedding Roman blood, he turned them to foreign wars. While he was pacifying the Alpine regions, and subduing the enemies planted in the midst of a peaceful empire, while he was extending its bounds even beyond the Rhine and the Euphrates and the Danube, in Rome itself the swords of Murena, Caepio, Lepidus, Egnatius, and others were being whetted to slay him. Not yet had he escaped their plots, when his daughter[9] and all the noble youths who were bound to her by adultery as by a sacred oath, oft alarmed his failing years—and there was Paulus, and a second time the need to fear a woman in league with an Antony.[10] When be had cut away these ulcers[11] together with the limbs themselves, others would grow in their place; just as in a body that was overburdened with blood, there was always a rupture somewhere. And so he longed for leisure, in the hope and thought of which he found relief for his labours. This was the prayer of one who was able to answer the prayers of mankind.

V.

Marcus Cicero, long flung among men like Catiline and Clodius and Pompey and Crassus, some open enemies, others doubtful friends, as he is tossed to and fro along with the state and seeks to keep it from destruction, to be at last swept away, unable as he was to be restful in prosperity or patient in adversity—how many times does he curse that very consulship of his, which he had lauded without end, though not without reason! How tearful the words he uses in a letter[12] written to Atticus, when Pompey the elder had been conquered, and the son was still trying to restore his shattered arms in Spain! "Do you ask," he said, "what I am doing here? I am lingering in my Tusculan villa half a prisoner." He then proceeds to other statements, in which he bewails his former life and complains of the present and despairs of the future. Cicero said that he was "half a prisoner." But, in very truth, never will the wise man resort to so lowly a term, never will he be half a prisoner—he who always possesses an undiminished and stable liberty, being free and his own master and towering over all others. For what can possibly be above him who is above Fortune?

VI.

When Livius Drusus,[13] a bold and energetic man, had with the support of a huge crowd drawn from all Italy proposed new laws and the evil measures of the Gracchi, seeing no way out for his policy, which he could neither carry through nor abandon when once started on, he is said to have complained bitterly against the life of unrest he had had from the cradle, and to have exclaimed that he was the only person who had never had a holiday even as a boy. For, while he was still a ward and wearing the dress of a boy, he had had the courage to commend to the favour of a jury those who were accused, and to make his influence felt in the law-courts, so powerfully, indeed, that it is very well known that in certain trials he forced a favourable verdict. To what lengths was not such premature ambition destined to go? One might have known that such precocious hardihood would result in great personal and public misfortune. And so it was too late for him to complain that he had never had a holiday when from boyhood he had been a trouble-maker and a nuisance in the forum. It is a question whether he died by his own hand; for he fell from a sudden wound received in his groin, some doubting whether his death was voluntary, no one, whether it was timely.

It would be superfluous to mention more who, though others deemed them the happiest of men, have expressed their loathing for every act of their years, and with their own lips have given true testimony against themselves; but by these complaints they changed neither themselves nor others. For when they have vented their feelings in words, they fall back into their usual round. Heaven knows! such lives as yours, though they should pass the limit of a thousand years, will shrink into the merest span; your vices will swallow up any amount of time. The space you have, which reason can prolong, although it naturally hurries away, of necessity escapes from you quickly; for you do not seize it, you neither hold it back, nor impose delay upon the swiftest thing in the world, but you allow it to slip away as if it were something superfluous and that could be re-placed.

VII.

But among the worst I count also those who have time for nothing but wine and lust; for none have more shameful engrossments.[14] The others, even if they are possessed by the empty dream of glory, nevertheless go astray in a seemly manner; though you should cite to me the men who are avaricious, the men who are wrathful, whether busied with unjust hatreds or with unjust wars, these all sin in more manly fashion. But those who are plunged into the pleasures of the belly and into lust bear a stain that is dishonourable. Search into the hours of all these people,[15] see how much time they give to accounts, how much to laying snares, how much to fearing them, how much to paying court, how much to being courted, how much is taken up in giving or receiving bail, how much by banquets—for even these have now become a matter of business—, and you will see how their interests, whether you call them evil or good, do not allow them time to breathe.

Finally, everybody agrees that no one pursuit can be successfully followed by a man who is busied with many things—eloquence cannot, nor the liberal stud-ies—since the mind, when its interests are divided, takes in nothing very deeply, but rejects everything that is, as it were, crammed into it. There is nothing the busy man is less busied with than living: there is nothing that is harder to learn. Of the other arts there are many teachers everywhere; some of them we have seen that mere boys have mastered so thoroughly that they could even play the master. It takes the whole of life to learn how to live, and—what will perhaps make you wonder more—it takes the whole of life to learn how to die. Many very great men, having laid aside all their encumbrances, having renounced riches, business, and pleasures, have made it their one aim up to the very end of life to know how to live; yet the greater number of them have departed from life confessing that they did not yet know—still less do those others know. Believe me, it takes a great man and one who has risen far above human weaknesses not to allow any of his time to be filched from him, and it follows that the life of such a man is very long because he has devoted wholly to himself whatever time he has had. None of it lay neglected and idle; none of it was under the control of another, for, guarding it most grudgingly, he found nothing that was worthy to be taken in exchange for his time. And so that man had time enough, but those who have been robbed of much of their life by the public, have necessarily had too little of it.

And there is no reason for you to suppose that these people are not sometimes aware of their loss. Indeed, you will hear many of those who are burdened by great prosperity cry out at times in the midst of their throngs of clients, or their pleadings in court, or their other glorious miseries: "I have no chance to live." Of course you have no chance! All those who summon you to themselves, turn you away from your own self. Of how many days has that defendant robbed you? Of how many that candidate? Of how many that old woman wearied with burying her heirs?[16] Of how many that man who is shamming sickness for the purpose of exciting the greed of the legacy-hunters? Of how many that very powerful friend who has you and your like on the list, not of his friends, but of his retinue? Check off, I say, and review the days of your life; you will see that very few, and those the refuse. have been left for you. That man who had prayed for the fasces,[17] when he attains them, desires to lay them aside and says over and over: "When will this year be over!" That man gives games,[18] and, after setting great value on gaining the chance to give them, now says: "When shall I be rid of them?" That advocate is lionized throughout the whole forum, and fills all the place with a great crowd that stretches farther than he can be heard, yet he says: "When will vacation time come?" Everyone hurries his life on and suffers from a yearning for the future and a weariness of the present. But he who bestows all of his time on his own needs, who plans out every day as if it were his last, neither longs for nor fears the morrow. For what new pleasure is there that any hour can now bring? They are all known, all have been enjoyed to the full. Mistress Fortune may deal out the rest as she likes; his life has already found safety. Something may be added to it, but nothing taken from it, and he will take any addition as the man who is satisfied and filled takes the food which he does not desire and yet can hold. And so there is no reason for you to think that any

man has lived long because he has grey hairs or wrinkles; he has not lived long—
he has existed long. For what if you should think that that man had had a long
voyage who had been caught by a fierce storm as soon as he left harbour, and,
swept hither and thither by a succession of winds that raged from different quarters, had been driven in a circle around the same course? Not much voyaging
did he have, but much tossing about.

VIII.

I am often filled with wonder when I see some men demanding the time of
others and those from whom they ask it most indulgent. Both of them fix their
eyes on the object of the request for time, neither of them on the time itself; just
as if what is asked were nothing, what is given, nothing. Men trifle with the most
precious thing in the world; but they are blind to it because it is an incorporeal
thing, because it does not come beneath the sight of the eyes, and for this reason
it is counted a very cheap thing—nay, of almost no value at all. Men set very
great store by pensions and doles, and for these they hire out their labour or
service or effort. But no one sets a value on time; all use it lavishly as if it cost
nothing. But see how these same people clasp the knees of physicians if they fall
ill and the danger of death draws nearer, see how ready they are, if threatened
with capital punishment, to spend all their possessions in order to live! So great
is the inconsistency of their feelings. But if each one could have the number of
his future years set before him as is possible in the case of the years that have
passed, how alarmed those would be who saw only a few remaining, how sparing
of them would they be! And yet it is easy to dispense an amount that is assured,
no matter how small it may be; but that must be guarded more carefully which
will fail you know not when

Yet there is no reason for you to suppose that these people do not know how
precious a thing time is; for to those whom they love most devotedly they have
a habit of saying that they are ready to give them a part of their own years. And
they do give it, without realizing it; but the result of their giving is that they
themselves suffer loss without adding to the years of their dear ones. But the
very thing they do not know is whether they are suffering loss; therefore, the
removal of something that is lost without being noticed they find is bearable.
Yet no one will bring back the years, no one will bestow you once more on
yourself. Life will follow the path it started upon, and will neither reverse nor
check its course; it will make no noise, it will not remind you of its swiftness.
Silent it will glide on; it will not prolong itself at the command of a king, or at
the applause of the populace. Just as it was started on its first day, so it will run;

nowhere will it turn aside, nowhere will it delay. And what will be the result? You have been engrossed, life hastens by; meanwhile death will be at hand, for which, willy nilly, you must find leisure.

IX.

Can anything be sillier than the point of view of certain people—I mean those who boast of their foresight? They keep themselves very busily engaged in order that they may be able to live better; they spend life in making ready to live! They form their purposes with a view to the distant future; yet postponement is the greatest waste of life; it deprives them of each day as it comes, it snatches from them the present by promising something hereafter. The greatest hindrance to living is expectancy, which depends upon the morrow and wastes to-day. You dispose of that which lies in the hands of Fortune, you let go that which lies in your own. Whither do you look? At what goal do you aim? All things that are still to come lie in uncertainty; live straightway! See how the greatest of bards cries out, and, as if inspired with divine utterance, sings the saving strain:

> The fairest day in hapless mortals' life
> Is ever first to flee.[19]

"Why do you delay," says he, "Why are you idle? Unless you seize the day, it flees." Even though you seize it, it still will flee; therefore you must vie with time's swiftness in the speed of using it, and, as from a torrent that rushes by and will not always flow, you must drink quickly. And, too, the utterance of the bard is most admirably worded to cast censure upon infinite delay, in that he says, not "the fairest age," but "the fairest day." Why, to whatever length your greed inclines, do you stretch before yourself months and years in long array, unconcerned and slow though time flies so fast? The poet speaks to you about the day, and about this very day that is flying. Is there, then, any doubt that for hapless mortals, that is, for men who are engrossed, the fairest day is ever the first to flee? Old age surprises them while their minds are still childish, and they come to it unprepared and unarmed, for they have made no provision for it; they have stumbled upon it suddenly and unexpectedly, they did not notice that it was drawing nearer day by day. Even as conversation or reading or deep meditation on some subject beguiles the traveller, and he finds that he has reached the end of his journey before he was aware that he was approaching it, just so with this unceasing and most swift journey of life, which we make at the same pace whether waking or sleeping; those who are engrossed become aware of it only at the end.

X.

Should I choose to divide my subject into heads with their separate proofs, many arguments will occur to me by which I could prove that busy men find life very short. But Fabianus,[20] who was none of your lecture-room philosophers of to-day, but one of the genuine and old-fashioned kind, used to say that we must fight against the passions with main force, not with artifice, and that the battle-line must be turned by a bold attack, not by inflicting pinpricks; that sophistry is not serviceable, for the passions must be, not nipped, but crushed. Yet, in order that the victims of them nay be censured, each for his own particular fault, I say that they must be instructed, not merely wept over.

Life is divided into three periods—that which has been, that which is, that which will be. Of these the present time is short, the future is doubtful, the past is certain. For the last is the one over which Fortune has lost control, is the one which cannot be brought back under any man's power. But men who are engrossed lose this; for they have no time to look back upon the past, and even if they should have, it is not pleasant to recall something they must view with regret. They are, therefore, unwilling to direct their thoughts backward to ill-spent hours, and those whose vices become obvious if they review the past, even the vices which were disguised under some allurement of momentary pleasure, do not have the courage to revert to those hours. No one willingly turns his thought back to the past, unless all his acts have been submitted to the censorship of his conscience, which is never deceived; he who has ambitiously coveted, proudly scorned, recklessly conquered, treacherously betrayed, greedily seized, or lavishly squandered, must needs fear his own memory. And yet this is the part of our time that is sacred and set apart, put beyond the reach of all human mishaps, and removed from the dominion of Fortune, the part which is disquieted by no want, by no fear, by no attacks of disease; this can neither be troubled nor be snatched away—it is an everlasting and unanxious possession. The present offers only one day at a time, and each by minutes; but all the days of past time will appear when you bid them, they will suffer you to behold them and keep them at your will— a thing which those who are engrossed have no time to do. The mind that is untroubled and tranquil has the power to roam into all the parts of its life; but the minds of the engrossed, just as if weighted by a yoke, cannot turn and look behind. And so their life vanishes into an abyss; and as it does no good, no matter how much water you pour into a vessel, if there is no bottom[21] to receive and hold it, so with time—it makes no difference how much is given; if there is nothing for it to settle upon, it passes out through the chinks and holes of the mind. Present time is very brief, so brief, indeed, that to some there seems to be none; for it is always in motion, it ever flows and hurries on; it ceases to be before it has come, and can no more brook delay than the firmament or the stars, whose ever unresting movement never lets them abide in the same track. The engrossed, therefore, are concerned with present time alone, and it is so brief that it cannot be grasped, and even this is filched away from them, distracted as they are among many things.

XI.

In a word, do you want to know how they do not "live long"? See how eager they are to live long! Decrepit old men beg in their prayers for the addition of a few more years; they pretend that they are younger than they are; they comfort themselves with a falsehood, and are as pleased to deceive themselves as if they deceived Fate at the same time. But when at last some infirmity has reminded them of their mortality, in what terror do they die, feeling that they are being dragged out of life, and not merely leaving it. They cry out that they have been fools, because they have not really lived, and that they will live henceforth in leisure if only they escape from this illness; then at last they reflect how uselessly they have striven for things which they did not enjoy, and how all their toil has gone for nothing. But for those whose life is passed remote from all business, why should it not be ample? None of it is assigned to another, none of it is scattered in this direction and that, none of it is committed to Fortune, none of it perishes from neglect, none is subtracted by wasteful giving, none of it is unused; the whole of it, so to speak, yields income. And so, however small the amount of it, it is abundantly sufficient, and therefore, whenever his last day shall come, the wise man will not hesitate to go to meet death with steady step.

XII.

Perhaps you ask whom I would call "the engrossed "? There is no reason for you to suppose that I mean only those whom the dogs[22] that have at length been let in drive out from the law-court, those whom you see either gloriously crushed in their own crowd of followers, or scornfully in someone else's, those whom social duties call forth from their own homes to bump them against someone else's doors, or whom the praetor's hammer[23] keeps busy in seeking gain that is disreputable and that will one day fester. Even the leisure of some men is engrossed; in their villa or on their couch, in the midst of solitude, although they have withdrawn from all others, they are themselves the source of their own worry; we should say that these are living, not in leisure, but in busy idleness.[24] Would you say that that man is at leisure[25] who arranges with finical care his Corinthian bronzes, that the mania of a few makes costly, and spends the greater part of each day upon rusty bits of copper? Who sits in a public wrestling-place (for, to our shame I we labour with vices that are not even Roman) watching the wrangling of lads? Who sorts out the herds of his pack-mules into pairs of the same age and colour? Who feeds all the newest athletes? Tell me, would you say that those men are at leisure who pass many hours at the barber's while they are being stripped of whatever grew out the night before? while a solemn debate is held over each separate hair? while either disarranged locks are restored to their place or thinning ones drawn from this side and that toward the forehead? How angry they get if the barber has been a bit too careless, just as if he were shearing a real man! How they flare up if any of their mane is lopped off, if any of it lies out of order, if it does not all fall into its proper ringlets! Who of these would not rather have the state disordered than his hair? Who is not more concerned to have his head trim rather than safe? Who would not rather be well barbered than upright? Would you say that these are at leisure who are occupied with the comb and the mirror? And what of those who are engaged in composing, hearing, and learning songs, while they twist the voice, whose best and simplest movement Nature designed to be straightforward, into the meanderings of some indolent tune, who are always snapping their fingers as they beat time to some song they have in their head, who are overheard humming a tune when they have been summoned to serious, often even melancholy, matters? These have not leisure, but idle occupation. And their banquets, Heaven knows! I cannot reckon among their unoccupied hours, since I see how anxiously they set out their silver plate, how diligently they tie up the tunics of their pretty slave-boys, how breathlessly they watch to see in what style the wild boar issues from the hands of the cook, with what speed at a given signal smooth-faced boys hurry to perform their duties, with what skill the birds are carved into portions all according to rule, how carefully unhappy little lads wipe up the spittle of drunkards. By such means they seek the reputation of being fastidious and elegant, and to such an extent do their evils follow them into all the privacies of life that they can neither eat nor drink without ostentation. And I would not count these among the leisured class either—the men who have themselves borne hither and thither in a sedan-chair and a litter, and are punctual at the hours for their rides as if it were unlawful to omit them, who are reminded by someone else when they must bathe, when they must swim, when they must dine; so enfeebled are they by the excessive lassitude of a pampered mind that they cannot find out by themselves whether they are hungry! I hear that one of these pampered people—provided that you can call it pampering to unlearn the habits of human life—when he had been lifted by hands from the bath and placed in his sedan-chair, said questioningly: "Am I now seated?" Do you think that this man, who does not know whether he is sitting, knows whether he is alive, whether he sees, whether he is at leisure? I find it hard to say whether I pity him more if he really did not know, or if he pretended not to know this. They really are subject to forgetfulness of many things, but they also pretend forgetfulness of many. Some vices delight them as being proofs of their prosperity; it seems the part of a man who is very lowly and despicable to know what he is doing. After this imagine that the mimes[26] fabricate many things to make a mock of luxury! In very truth, they pass over more than they invent, and such a multitude of unbelievable vices has come forth in this age, so clever in this one direction, that by now we can charge the mimes with neglect. To think that there is anyone who is so lost in luxury that he takes another's word as to whether he is sitting down! This man, then, is not at leisure, you must apply to him a different term—he is sick, nay, he is dead; that man is at leisure, who has also a perception of his leisure. But this other who is half alive, who, in order that he may know the postures of his own body, needs someone to tell him—how can he be the master of any of his time?

XIII.

It would be tedious to mention all the different men who have spent the whole of their life over chess or ball or the practice of baking their bodies in the sun. They are not unoccupied whose pleasures are made a busy occupation. For instance, no one will have any doubt that those are laborious triflers who spend their time on useless literary problems, of whom even among the Romans there is now a great number. It was once a foible confined to the Greeks to inquire into what number of rowers Ulysses had, whether the Iliad or the Odyssey was written first, whether moreover they belong to the same author, and various other matters of this stamp, which, if you keep them to yourself, in no way pleasure your secret soul, and, if you publish them, make you seem more of a bore than a scholar. But now this vain passion for learning useless things has assailed the Romans also. In the last few days I heard someone telling who was the first Roman general to do this or that; Duilius was the first who won a naval battle, Curius Dentatus was the first who had elephants led in his triumph. Still, these matters, even if they add nothing to real glory, are nevertheless concerned with signal services to the state; there will be no profit in such knowledge, nevertheless it wins our attention by reason of the attractiveness of an empty subject. We may excuse also those who inquire into this—who first induced the Romans to go on board ship. It was Claudius, and this was the very reason he was surnamed Caudex, because among the ancients a structure formed by joining together several boards was called a *caudex*, whence also the Tables of the Law are called *codices*,[27] and, in the ancient fashion, boats that carry provisions up the Tiber are even to-day called *codicariae*. Doubtless this too may have some point—the fact that Valerius Corvinus was the first to conquer Messana, and was the first of the family of the Valerii to bear the surname Messana because be had transferred the name of the conquered city to himself, and was later called Messala after the gradual corruption of the name in the popular speech. Perhaps you will permit someone to be interested also in this—the fact that Lucius Sulla was the first to exhibit loosed lions in the Circus, though at other times they were exhibited in chains, and that javelin-throwers were sent by King Bocchus to despatch them? And, doubtless, this too may find some excuse—but does it serve any useful purpose to know that Pompey was the first to exhibit the slaughter of eighteen elephants in the Circus, pitting criminals against them in a mimic battle? He, a leader of the state and one who, according to report, was conspicuous among the leaders[28] of old for the kindness of his heart, thought it a notable kind of spectacle to kill human beings after a new fashion. Do they fight to the death? That is not enough! Are they torn to pieces? That is not enough! Let them be crushed by animals of monstrous bulk! Better would it be that these things pass into oblivion lest hereafter some all-powerful man should learn them and be jealous of an act that was nowise human.[29] O, what blindness does great prosperity cast upon our minds! When he was casting so many troops of wretched human beings to wild beasts born under a different sky, when he was proclaiming war between creatures so ill matched, when he was shedding so much blood before the eyes of the Roman people, who itself was soon to be forced to shed more. he then believed that he was beyond the power of Nature. But later this same man, betrayed by Alexandrine treachery, offered himself to the dagger of the vilest slave, and then at last discovered what an empty boast his surname[30] was.

But to return to the point from which I have digressed, and to show that some people bestow useless pains upon these same matters—the man I mentioned related that Metellus, when he triumphed after his victory over the Carthaginians in Sicily, was the only one of all the Romans who had caused a hundred and twenty captured elephants to be led before his car; that Sulla was the last of the Roman's who extended the *pomerium*,[31] which in old times it was customary to extend after the acquisition of Italian but never of provincial, territory. Is it more profitable to know this than that Mount Aventine, according to him, is outside the *pomerium* for one of two reasons, either because that was the place to which the plebeians had seceded, or because the birds had not been favourable when Remus took his auspices on that spot—and, in turn, countless other reports that are either crammed with falsehood or are of the same sort? For though you grant that they tell these things in good faith, though they pledge themselves for the truth of what they write, still whose mistakes will be made fewer by such stories? Whose passions will they restrain? Whom will they make more brave, whom more just, whom more noble-minded? My friend Fabianus used to say that at times he was doubtful whether it was not better not to apply oneself to any studies than to become entangled in these.

XIV.

Of all men they alone are at leisure who take time for philosophy, they alone really live; for they are not content to be good guardians of their own lifetime only. They annex ever age to their own; all the years that have gone ore them are an addition to their store. Unless we are most ungrateful, all those men, glorious fashioners of holy thoughts, were born for us; for us they have prepared a way of life. By other men's labours we are led to the sight of things most beautiful that have been wrested from darkness and brought into light; from no age are we shut out, we have access to all ages, and if it is our wish, by greatness of mind, to pass beyond the narrow limits of human weakness, there is a great stretch of time through which we may roam. We may argue with Socrates, we may doubt[32] with Carneades, find peace with Epicurus, overcome human nature with the Stoics, exceed it with the Cynics. Since Nature allows us to enter into fellowship with every age, why should we not turn from this paltry and fleeting span of time and surrender ourselves with all our soul to the past, which is boundless, which is eternal, which we share with our betters?

Those who rush about in the performance of social duties, who give themselves and others no rest, when they have fully indulged their madness, when they have every day crossed everybody's threshold, and have left no open door unvisited, when they have carried around their venal greeting to houses that are very far apart—out of a city so huge and torn by such varied desires, how few will they be able to see? How many will there be who either from sleep or self-indulgence or rudeness will keep them out! How many who, when they have tortured them with long waiting, will rush by, pretending to be in a hurry! How many will avoid passing out through a hall that is crowded with clients, and will make their escape through some concealed door as if it were not more discourteous to deceive than to exclude. How many, still half asleep and sluggish from last night's debauch, scarcely lifting their lips in the midst of a most insolent yawn, manage to bestow on yonder poor wretches, who break their own slumber[33] in order to wait on that of another, the right name only after it has been whispered to them a thousand times!

But we may fairly say that they alone are engaged in the true duties of life who shall wish to have Zeno, Pythagoras, Democritus, and all the other high priests of liberal studies, and Aristotle and Theophrastus, as their most intimate friends every day. No one of these will be "not at home," no one of these will fail to have his visitor leave more happy and more devoted to himself than when he came, no one of these will allow anyone to leave him with empty hands; all mortals can meet with them by night or by day.

XV.

No one of these will force you to die, but all will teach you how to die; no one of these will wear out your years, but each will add his own years to yours; conversations with no one of these will bring you peril, the friendship of none will endanger your life, the courting of none will tax your purse. From them you will take whatever you wish; it will be no fault of theirs if you do not draw the utmost that you can desire. What happiness, what a fair old age awaits him who has offered himself as a client to these! He will have friends from whom he may seek counsel on matters great and small, whom he may consult every day about himself, from whom he may hear truth without insult, praise without flattery, and after whose likeness he may fashion himself.

We are wont to say that it was not in our power to choose the parents who fell to our lot, that they have been given to men by chance; yet *we* may be the sons of whomsoever we will. Households there are of noblest intellects; choose the one into which you wish to be adopted; you will inherit not merely their name, but even their property, which there will be no need to guard in a mean or niggardly spirit; the more persons you share it with, the greater it will become. These will open to you the path to immortality, and will raise you to a height from which no one is cast down. This is the only way of prolonging mortality—nay, of turning it into immortality. Honours, monuments, all that ambition has commanded by decrees or reared in works of stone, quickly sink to ruin; there is nothing that the lapse of time does not tear down and remove. But the works which philosophy has consecrated cannot be harmed; no age will destroy them, no age reduce them; the following and each succeeding age will but increase the reverence for them, since envy works upon what is close at hand, and things that are far off we are more free to admire. The life of the philosopher, therefore, has wide range, and he is not confined by the same bounds that shut others in. He alone is freed from the limitations of the human race; all ages serve him as if a god. Has some time passed by? This he embraces by recollection. Is time present? This he uses. Is it still to come? This he anticipates. He makes his life long by combining all times into one.

XVI.

 But those who forget the past, neglect the present, and fear for the future have a life that is very brief and troubled; when they have reached the end of it, the poor wretches perceive too late that for such a long while they have been busied in doing nothing. Nor because they sometimes invoke death, have you any reason to think it any proof that they find life long. In their folly they are harassed by shifting emotions which rush them into the very things they dread; they often pray for death because they fear it. And, too, you have no reason to think that this is any proof that they are living a long time—the fact that the day often seems to them long, the fact that they complain that the hours pass slowly until the time set for dinner arrives; for, whenever their engrossments fail them, they are restless because they are left with nothing to do, and they do not know how to dispose of their leisure or to drag out the time. And so they strive for something else to occupy them, and all the intervening time is irksome; exactly as they do when a gladiatorial exhibition\b is been announced, or when they are waiting for the appointed time of some other show or amusement, they want to skip over the days that lie between. All postponement of something they hope for seems long to them. Yet the time which they enjoy is short and swift, and it is made much shorter by their own fault; for they flee from one pleasure to another and cannot remain fixed in one desire. Their days are not long to them, but hateful; yet, on the other hand, how scanty seem the nights which they spend in the arms of a harlot or in wine! It is this also that accounts for the madness of poets in fostering human frailties by the tales in which they represent that Jupiter under the enticement of the pleasures of a lover doubled the length of the night. For what is it but to inflame our vices to inscribe the name of the gods as their sponsors, and to present the excused indulgence of divinity as an example to our own weakness? Can the nights which they pay for so dearly fail to seem all too short to these men? They lose the day in expectation of the night, and the night in fear of the dawn.

XVII.

 The very pleasures of such men are uneasy and disquieted by alarms of various sorts, and at the very moment of rejoicing the anxious thought comes over them: How long will these things last?" This feeling has led kings to weep over the power they possessed, and they have not so much delighted in the greatness of their fortune, as they have viewed with terror the end to which it must some time come. When the King of Persia,[34] in all the insolence of his pride, spread his army over the vast plains and could not grasp its number but simply its measure,[35] he shed copious tears because inside of a hundred years not a man of such a mighty army would be alive.[36] But he who wept was to bring upon them their fate, was to give some to their doom on the sea, some on the land, some in battle, some in flight, and within a short time was to destroy all those for whose hundredth year he had such fear. And why is it that even their joys are uneasy from fear? Because they do not rest on stable causes, but are perturbed as groundlessly as they are born. But of what sort do you think those times are which even by their own confession are wretched, since even the joys by which they are exalted and lifted above mankind are by no means pure? All the greatest blessings are a source of anxiety, and at no time is fortune less wisely trusted than when it is best; to maintain prosperity there is need of other prosperity, and in behalf of the prayers that have turned out well we must make still other prayers. For everything that comes to us from chance is unstable, and the higher it rises, the more liable it is to fall. Moreover, what is doomed to perish brings pleasure to no one; very wretched, therefore, and not merely short, must the life of those be who work hard to gain what they must work harder to keep. By great toil they attain what they wish, and with anxiety hold what they have attained; meanwhile they take no account of time that will never more return. New engrossments take the place of the old, hope leads to new hope, ambition to new ambition. They do not seek an end of their wretchedness, but change the cause. Have we been tormented by our own public honours? Those of others take more of our time. Have we ceased to labour as candidates? We begin to canvass for others. Have we got rid of the troubles of a prosecutor? We find those of a judge. Has a man ceased to be a judge? He becomes president of a court. Has he become infirm in managing the property of others at a salary? He is perplexed by caring for his own wealth. Have the barracks[37] set Marius free? The consulship keeps him busy. Does Quintius[38] hasten to get to the end of his dictatorship? He will be called back to it from the plough. Scipio will go against the Carthaginians before he is ripe for so great an undertaking; victorious over Hannibal, victorious over Antiochus, the glory of his own consulship, the surety for his brother's, did he not stand in his own way, he would be set beside Jove[39]; but the discord of civilians will vex their preserver, and, when as a young man he had scorned honours that rivalled those of the gods, at length, when he is old, his ambition will take delight in stubborn exile.[40] Reasons for anxiety will never be lacking, whether born of prosperity or of wretchedness; life pushes on in a succession of engrossments. We shall always pray for leisure, but never enjoy it.

XVIII.

And so, my dearest Paulinus, tear yourself away from the crowd, and, too much storm-tossed for the time you have lived, at length withdraw into a peaceful harbour. Think of how many waves you have encountered, how many storms, on the one hand, you have sustained in private life, how many, on the other, you have brought upon yourself in public life; long enough has your virtue been displayed in laborious and unceasing proofs—try how it will behave in leisure. The greater part of your life, certainly the better part of it, has been given to the state; take now some part of your time for yourself as well. And I do not summon you to slothful or idle inaction, or to drown all your native energy in slumbers and the pleasures that are dear to the crowd. That is not to rest; you will find far greater works than all those you have hitherto performed so energetically, to occupy you in the midst of your release and retirement. You, I know, manage the accounts of the whole world as honestly as you would a stranger's, as carefully as you would your own, as conscientiously as you would the state's. You win love in an office in which it is difficult to avoid hatred; but nevertheless believe me, it is better to have knowledge of the ledger of one's own life than of the corn-market. Recall that keen mind of yours, which is most competent to cope with the greatest subjects, from a service that is indeed honourable but hardly adapted to the happy life, and reflect that in all your training in the liberal studies, extending from your earliest years, you were not aiming at this—that it might be safe to entrust many thousand pecks of corn to your charge; you gave hope of something greater and more lofty. There will be no lack of men of tested worth and painstaking industry. But plodding oxen are much more suited to carrying heavy loads than thoroughbred horses, and who ever hampers the fleetness of such high-born creatures with a heavy pack? Reflect, besides, how much worry you have in subjecting yourself to such a great burden; your dealings are with the belly of man. A hungry people neither listens to reason, nor is appeased by justice, nor is bent by any entreaty. Very recently within those few day's after Gaius Caesar died—still grieving most deeply (if the dead have any feeling) because he knew that the Roman people were alive[41] and had enough food left for at any rate seven or eight days while he was building his bridges of boats[42] and playing with the resources of the empire, we were threatened with the worst evil that can befall men even during a siege—the lack of provisions; his imitation of a mad and foreign and misproud king[43] was very nearly at the cost of the city's destruction and famine and the general revolution that follows famine. What then must have been the feeling of those who had charge of the corn-market, and had to face stones, the sword, fire—and a Caligula? By the greatest subterfuge they concealed the great evil that lurked in the vitals of the state—with good reason, you may be sure. For certain maladies must be treated while the patient is kept in ignorance; knowledge of their disease has caused the death of many.

XIX.

Do you retire to these quieter, safer, greater things! Think you that it is just the same whether you are concerned in having corn from oversea poured into the granaries, unhurt either by the dishonesty or the neglect of those who transport it, in seeing that it does not become heated and spoiled by collecting moisture and tallies in weight and measure, or whether you enter upon these sacred and lofty studies with the purpose of discovering what substance, what pleasure, what mode of life, what shape God has; what fate awaits your soul; where Nature lays us to rest When we are freed from the body; what the principle is that upholds all the heaviest matter in the centre of this world, suspends the light on high, carries fire to the topmost part, summons the stars to their proper changes—and ether matters, in turn, full of mighty wonders? You really must leave the ground and turn your mind's eye upon these things! Now while the blood is hot, we must enter with brisk step upon the better course. In this kind of life there awaits much that is good to know—the love and practice of the virtues, forgetfulness of the passions, knowledge of living and dying, and a life of deep repose.

The condition of all who are engrossed is wretched, but most wretched is the condition of those who labour at engrossments that are not even their own, who regulate their sleep by that of another, their walk by the pace of another, who are under orders in case of the freest things in the world—loving and hating. If these wish to know how short their life is, let them reflect how small a part of it is their own.

XX.

And so when you see a man often wearing the robe of office, when you see one whose name is famous in the Forum, do not envy him; those things are bought at the price of life. They will waste all their years, in order that they may have one year reckoned by their name.[44] Life has left some in the midst of their first struggles, before they could climb up to the height of their ambition; some, when they have crawled up through a thousand indignities to the crowning dignity, have been possessed by the unhappy thought that they have but toiled for an inscription on a tomb; some who have come to extreme old age, while they adjusted it to new hopes as if it were youth, have had it fail from sheer weakness in the midst of their great and shameless endeavours. Shameful is he whose breath leaves him in the midst of a trial when, advanced in years and still courting the applause of an ignorant circle, he is pleading for some litigant who is the veriest stranger; disgraceful is he who, exhausted more quickly by his mode of living than by his labour, collapses in the very midst of his duties; disgraceful is he who dies in the act of receiving payments on account, and draws a smile from his long delayed[45] heir. I cannot pass over an instance which occurs to me. Sextus[46] Turannius was an old man of long tested diligence, who, after his ninetieth year, having received release from the duties of his office by Gaius Caesar's own act, ordered himself to be laid out on his bed and to be mourned by the assembled household as if he were dead. The whole house bemoaned the leisure of its old master, and did not end its sorrow until his accustomed work was restored to him. Is it really such pleasure for a man to die in harness? Yet very many have the same feeling; their desire for their labour lasts longer than their ability; they fight against the weakness of the body, they judge old age to be a hardship on no other score than because it puts them aside. The law does not draft a soldier after his fiftieth year, it does not call a senator after his sixtieth; it is more difficult for men to obtain leisure from themselves than from the law. Meantime, while they rob and are being robbed, while they break up each other's repose, while they make each other wretched, their life is without profit, without pleasure, without any improvement of the mind. No one keeps death in view, no one refrains from far-reaching hopes; some men, indeed, even arrange for things that lie beyond life—huge masses of tombs and dedications of public works and gifts for their funeral-pyres and ostentatious funerals. But, in very truth, the funerals of such men ought to be conducted by the light of torches and wax tapers,[47] as though they had lived but the tiniest span.

Footnotes

[1] It is clear from chapters 18 and 19 that, when this essay was written (in or about A.D. 49), Paulinus was *praefectus annonae*, the official who superintended the grain supply of Rome, and was, therefore, a man of importance. He was, believably, a near relative of Seneca's wife, Pompeia Paulina, and is usually identified with the father of a certain Pompeius Paulinus, who held high public posts under Nero (Pliny, *Nat. Hist.* xxxiii. 143; Tacitus, *Annals*, xiii. 53. 2; xv.

[2] The famous aphorism of Hippocrates of Cos: ὁ βίος βραχύς, ἡ δὲ τέχνη μακρή.

[3] An error for Theophrastus, as shown by Cicero, Tusc. Disp. iii. 69: "Theophrastus autem moriens accusasse naturam dicitur, quod cervis et cornicibus vitam diuturnam, quorum id nihil interesset, hominibus, quorum maxime interfuisset, tam exiguam vitam dedisset; quorum si aetas potuisset esse longinquior, futurum fuisse ut omnibus perfectis artibus omni doctrina hominum vita erudiretur."

[4] *i.e.*, of man. *Cf.* Hesiod, *Frag.* 183 (Rzach):

Ἐννέα τοι ζώει γενεὰς λακέρυζα κορώνη
ἀνδρῶν γηράντω· ἔλαφος δέ τε τετρακόρωνος.

[5] A prose rendering of an unknown poet. *Cf.* the epitaph quoted by Cassius Dio, lxix. 19: Σίμιλις ἐνταῦθα κεῖται βιοὺς μὲν ἔτη τόσα, ζήσας δὲ ἔτη ἑπτά.

[6] Not one who undertook the actual defense, but one who by his presence and advice lent support in court.

[7] Literally, "unripe." At 100 he should "come to his grave in a full age, like as a shock of corn cometh in in his season" (Job v. 26); but he is still unripe.

[8] The idea is that greatness sinks beneath its own weight. *Cf.* Seneca, *Agamemnon*, 88 *sq.*:

Sidunt ipso pondere magna
ceditque oneri Fortuna suo.

[9] The notorious Julia, who was banished by Augustus to the island of Pandataria.

[10] In 31 B.C. Augustus had been pitted against Mark Antony and Cleopatra; in 2 B.C. Iullus Antonius, younger son of the triumvir, was sentenced to death by reason of his intrigue with the elder Julia.

[11] The language is reminiscent of Augustus's own characterization of Julia and his two grandchildren in Suetonius (*Aug.* 65. 5): "nec (solebat) aliter eos appellare quam tris vomicas ac tria carcinomata sua" ("his trio of boils and trio of ulcers").

[12] Not extant.

[13] As tribune in 91 B.C. he proposed a corn law and the granting of citizenship to the Italians.

[14] Throughout the essay *occupati*, "the engrossed," is a technical term designating those who are so absorbed in the interests of life that they take no time for philosophy.

[15] *i.e.*, the various types of *occupati* that have been sketchily presented. The looseness of the structure has led some editors to doubt the integrity of the passage.

[16] *i.e.*, she has become the prey of legacy-hunters.

[17] The rods that were the symbol of high office.

[18] At this time the management of the public games was committed to the praetors.

[19] Virgil, *Georgics*, iii. 66 *sq.*

[20] A much admired teacher of Seneca.

[21] An allusion to the fate of the Danaids, who in Hades forever poured water into a vessel with a perforated bottom.

[22] Apparently watch-dogs that were let in at nightfall, and caught the engrossed lawyer still at his task.

[23] Literally, "spear," which was stuck in the ground as the sign of a public auction where captured or confiscated goods were put up for sale.

[24] *Cf.* Pliny, *Epistles*, i. 9. 8: "satius est enim, ut Atilius noster eruditissime simul et facetissime dixit, otiosum esse quam nihil agere."

[25] For the technical meaning of *otiosi*, "the leisured," see Seneca's definition at the beginning of chap. 14.

[26] Actors in the popular mimes, or low farces, that were often censured for their indecencies.

[27] The ancient codex was made of tablets of wood fastened together.

[28] Such, doubtless, as Marius, Sulla, Caesar, Crassus.

[29] Pliny (*Nat. Hist.* viii. 21) reports that the people were so moved by pity that they rose in a body and called down curses upon Pompey. Cicero's impressions of the occasion are recorded in *Ad Fam.* vii. 1. 3: "extremus elephantorum dies fuit, in quo admiratio magna vulgi atque turbae, delectatio nulla exstitit; quin etiam misericordia quaedam consecuta est atque opinio eiusmodi, esse quandam illi beluae cum genere humana societatem."

[30] *i.e.*, *Magnus.*

[31] A name applied to a consecrated space kept vacant within and (according to Livy, i. 44) without the city wall. The right of extending it belonged originally to the king who had added territory to Rome.

[32] The New Academy taught that certainty of knowledge was unattainable.

[33] The *salutatio* was held in the early morning.

[34] Xerxes, who invaded Greece in 480 B.C.

[35] On the plain of Doriscus in Thrace the huge land force was estimated by counting the number of times a space capable of holding 10,000 men was filled (Herodotus, vii. 60).

[36] Herodotus, vii. 45, 46 tells the story.

[37] *Caliga*, the boot of the common soldier, is here synonymous with service in the army.

[38] His first appointment was announced to him while he was ploughing his own fields.

[39] He did not allow his statue to be placed in the Capitol.

[40] Disgusted with politics, he died in exile at Liternum.

[41] Probably an allusion to the mad wish of Caligula: "utinam populus Romanus unam cervicem haberet!" (Suetonius, *Calig.* 30), cited in *De Ira*, iii. 19. 2. The logic of the whole passage suffers from the uncertainty of the text.

[42] Three and a half miles long, reaching from Baiae to the mole of Puteoli (Suetonius, *Calig.* 19).

[43] Xerxes, who laid a bridge over the Hellespont.

[44] The Roman year was dated by the names of the two annual consuls.

[45] *i.e.*, long kept out of his inheritance.

[46] Tacitus (*Annals*, i. 7) gives the *praenomen* as Gaius.

[47] *i.e.*, as if they were children, whose funerals took place by night (Servius, *Aeneid*, xi. 143).

SELECTED DISCOURSES

by
Epictetus

SELECTED DISCOURSES OF EPICTETUS

OF THE THINGS WHICH ARE IN OUR POWER AND NOT IN OUR POWER.

Of all the faculties (except that which I shall soon mention), you will find not one which is capable of contemplating itself, and, consequently, not capable either of approving or disapproving. How far does the grammatic art possess the contemplating power? As far as forming a judgment about what is written and spoken. And how far music? As far as judging about melody. Does either of them then contemplate itself? By no means. But when you must write something to your friend, grammar will tell you what words you should write; but whether you should write or not, grammar will not tell you. And so it is with music as to musical sounds; but whether you should sing at the present time and play on the lute, or do neither, music will not tell you. What faculty then will tell you? That which contemplates both itself and all other things. And what is this faculty? The rational faculty; for this is the only faculty that we have received which examines itself, what it is, and what power it has, and what is the value of this gift, and examines all other faculties: for what else is there which tells us that golden things are beautiful, for they do not say so themselves? Evidently it is the faculty which is capable of judging of appearances. What else judges of music, grammar, and the other faculties, proves their uses, and points out the occasions for using them? Nothing else.

What then should a man have in readiness in such circumstances? What else than this? What is mine, and what is not mine; and what is permitted to me, and what is not permitted to me. I must die. Must I then die lamenting? I must be put in chains. Must I then also lament? I must go into exile. Does any man then hinder me from going with smiles and cheerfulness and contentment? Tell me the secret which you possess. I will not, for this is in my power. But I will put you in chains. Man, what are you talking about? Me, in chains? You may fetter my leg, but my will not even Zeus himself can overpower. I will throw you into prison. My poor body, you mean. I will cut your head off. When then have I told you that my head alone cannot be cut off? These are the things which philosophers should meditate on, which they should write daily, in which they should exercise themselves.

What then did Agrippinus say? He said, "I am not a hindrance to myself." When it was reported to him that his trial was going on in the Senate, he said: "I hope it may turn out well; but it is the fifth hour of the day" this was the time when he was used to exercise himself and then take the cold bath," let us go and take our exercise." After he had taken his exercise, one comes and tells him, "You have been condemned." "To banishment," he replies, "or to death?" "To banishment." "What about my property?" "It is not taken from you." "Let us go to Aricia then," he said, "and dine."

HOW A MAN ON EVERY OCCASION CAN MAINTAIN HIS PROPER CHARACTER.

To the rational animal only is the irrational intolerable; but that which is rational is tolerable. Blows are not naturally intolerable. How is that? See how the Lacedaemonians endure whipping when they have learned that whipping is consistent with reason. To hang yourself is not intolerable. When then you have the opinion that it is rational, you go and hang yourself. In short, if we observe, we shall find that the animal man is pained by nothing so much as by that which is irrational; and, on the contrary, attracted to nothing so much as to that which is rational.

Only consider at what price you sell your own will: if for no other reason, at least for this, that you sell it not for a small sum. But that which is great and superior perhaps belongs to Socrates and such as are like him. Why then, if we are naturally such, are not a very great number of us like him? Is it true then that all horses become swift, that all dogs are skilled in tracking footprints? What then, since I am naturally dull, shall I, for this reason, take no pains? I hope not. Epictetus is not superior to Socrates; but if he is not inferior, this is enough for me; for I shall never be a Milo, and yet I do not neglect my body; nor shall I be a Croesus, and yet I do not neglect my property; nor, in a word, do we neglect looking after anything because we despair of reaching the highest degree.

HOW A MAN SHOULD PROCEED FROM THE PRINCIPLE OF GOD BEING THE FATHER OF ALL MEN TO THE REST.

If a man should be able to assent to this doctrine as he ought, that we are all sprung from God in an especial manner, and that God is the father both of men and of gods, I suppose that he would never have any ignoble or mean thoughts about himself. But if Cæsar (the emperor) should adopt you, no one could endure your arrogance; and if you know that you are the son of Zeus, will you not be elated? Yet we do not so; but since these two things are mingled in the generation of man, body in common with the animals, and reason and intelligence in common with the gods, many incline to this kinship, which is miserable and mortal; and some few to that which is divine and happy. Since then it is of necessity that every man uses everything according to the opinion which he has about it, those, the few, who think that they are formed for fidelity and modesty and a sure use of appearances have no mean or ignoble thoughts about themselves; but with the many it is quite the contrary. For they say, What am I? A poor, miserable man, with my wretched bit of flesh. Wretched, indeed; but you possess something better than your bit of flesh. Why then do you neglect that which is better, and why do you attach yourself to this?

Through this kinship with the flesh, some of us inclining to it become like wolves, faithless and treacherous and mischievous; some become like lions, savage and bestial and untamed; but the greater part of us become foxes, and other worse animals. For what else is a slanderer and malignant man than a fox, or some other more wretched and meaner animal? See then and take care that you do not become some one of these miserable things.

OF PROGRESS OR IMPROVEMENT.

He who is making progress, having learned from philosophers that desire means the desire of good things, and aversion means aversion from bad things; having learned too that happiness and tranquillity are not attainable by man otherwise than by not failing to obtain what he desires, and not falling into that which he would avoid; such a man takes from himself desire altogether and confers it, but he employs his aversion only on things which are dependent on his will. For if he attempts to avoid anything independent of his will, he knows that sometimes he will fall in with something which he wishes to avoid, and he will be unhappy. Now if virtue promises good fortune and tranquillity and happiness, certainly also the progress towards virtue is progress towards each of these things. For it is always true that to whatever point the perfecting of anything leads us, progress is an approach towards this point.

How then do we admit that virtue is such as I have said, and yet seek progress in other things and make a display of it? What is the product of virtue? Tranquillity. Who then makes improvement? Is it he who has read many books of Chrysippus? But does virtue consist in having understood Chrysippus? If this is so, progress is clearly nothing else than knowing a great deal of Chrysippus. But now we admit that virtue produces one thing, and we declare that approaching near to it is another thing, namely, progress or improvement. Such a person, says one, is already able to read Chrysippus by himself. Indeed, sir, you are making great progress. What kind of progress? But why do you mock the man? Why do you draw him away from the perception of his own misfortunes? Will you not show him the effect of virtue that he may learn where to look for improvement? Seek it there, wretch, where your work lies. And where is your work? In desire and in aversion, that you may not be disappointed in your desire, and that you may not fall into that which you would avoid; in your pursuit and avoiding, that you commit no error; in assent and suspension of assent, that you be not deceived. The first things, and the most necessary are those which I have named. But if with trembling and lamentation you seek not to fall into that which you avoid, tell me how you are improving.

Do you then show me your improvement in these things? If I were talking to an athlete, I should say, Show me your shoulders; and then he might say, Here are my Halteres. You and your Halteres look to that. I should reply, I wish to see the effect of the Halteres. So, when you say: Take the treatise on the active powers, and see how I have studied it, I reply: Slave, I am not inquiring about this, but how you exercise pursuit and avoidance, desire and aversion, how you design and purpose and prepare yourself, whether conformably to nature or not. If conformably, give me evidence of it, and I will say that you are making progress; but if not conformably, be gone, and not only expound your books, but write such books yourself; and what will you gain by it? Do you not know that the whole book costs only five denarii? Does then the expounder seem to be worth more than five denarii? Never then look for the matter itself in one place, and progress towards it in another. Where then is progress? If any of you, withdrawing himself from externals, turns to his own will to exercise it and to improve it by labor, so as to make it conformable to nature, elevated, free, unrestrained, unimpeded, faithful, modest; and if he has learned that he who desires or avoids the things which are not in his power can neither be faithful nor free, but of necessity he must change with them and be tossed about with them as in a tempest, and of necessity must subject himself to others who have the power to procure or prevent what he desires or would avoid; finally, when he rises in the morning, if he observes and keeps these rules, bathes as a man of fidelity, eats as a modest man; in like manner, if in every matter that occurs he works out his chief principles as the runner does with reference to running, and the trainer of the voice with reference to the voice—this is the man who truly makes progress, and this is the man who has not travelled in vain. But if he has strained his efforts to the practice of reading books, and labors only at this, and has travelled for this, I tell him to return home immediately, and not to neglect his affairs there; for this for which he has travelled is nothing. But the other thing is something, to study how a man can rid his life of lamentation and groaning, and saying, Woe to me, and wretched that I am, and to rid it also of misfortune and disappointment, and to learn what death is, and exile, and prison, and poison, that he may be able to say when he is in fetters, Dear Crito, if it is the will of the gods that it be so, let it be so; and not to say, Wretched am I, an old man: have I kept my gray hairs for this? Who is it that speaks thus? Do you think that I shall name some man of no repute and of low condition? Does not Priam say this? Does not Oedipus say this? Nay, all kings say it! For what else is tragedy than the perturbations of men who value externals exhibited in this kind of poetry? But if a man must learn by fiction that no external things which are independent of the will concern us, for my part I should like this fiction, by the aid of which I should live happily and undisturbed. But you must consider for yourselves what you wish.

What then does Chrysippus teach us? The reply is, to know that these things are not false, from which happiness comes and tranquillity arises. Take my books, and you will learn how true and conformable to nature are the things which make me free from perturbations. O great good fortune! O the great benefactor who points out the way! To Triptolemus all men have erected temples and altars, because he gave us food by cultivation; but to him who discovered truth and brought it to light and communicated it to all, not the truth which shows us how to live, but how to live well, who of you for this reason has built an altar, or a temple, or has dedicated a statue, or who worships God for this? Because the gods have given the vine, or wheat, we sacrifice to them; but because they have produced in the human mind that fruit by which they designed to show us the truth which relates to happiness, shall we not thank God for this?

AGAINST THE ACADEMICS.

If a man, said Epictetus, opposes evident truths, it is not easy to find arguments by which we shall make him change his opinion. But this does not arise either from the man's strength or the teacher's weakness; for when the man, though he has been confuted, is hardened like a stone, how shall we then be able to deal with him by argument?

Now there are two kinds of hardening, one of the understanding, the other of the sense of shame, when a man is resolved not to assent to what is manifest nor to desist from contradictions. Most of us are afraid of mortification of the body, and would contrive all means to avoid such a thing, but we care not about the soul's mortification. And indeed with regard to the soul, if a man be in such a state as not to apprehend anything, or understand at all, we think that he is in a bad condition; but if the sense of shame and modesty are deadened, this we call even power (or strength).

OF PROVIDENCE.

From everything, which is or happens in the world, it is easy to praise Providence, if a man possesses these two qualities: the faculty of seeing what belongs and happens to all persons and things, and a grateful disposition. If he does not possess these two qualities, one man will not see the use of things which are and which happen: another will not be thankful for them, even if he does know them. If God had made colors, but had not made the faculty of seeing them, what would have been their use? None at all. On the other hand, if he had made the faculty of vision, but had not made objects such as to fall under the faculty, what in that case also would have been the use of it? None at all. Well, suppose that he had made both, but had not made light? In that case, also, they would have been of no use. Who is it then who has fitted this to that and that to this?

What, then, are these things done in us only? Many, indeed, in us only, of which the rational animal had peculiar need; but you will find many common to us with irrational animals. Do they then understand what is done? By no means. For use is one thing, and understanding is another; God had need of irrational animals to make use of appearances, but of us to understand the use of appearances. It is therefore enough for them to eat and to drink, and to copulate, and to do all the other things which they severally do. But for us, to whom he has given also the intellectual faculty, these things are not sufficient; for unless we act in a proper and orderly manner, and conformably to the nature and constitution of each thing, we shall never attain our true end. For where the constitutions of living beings are different, there also the acts and the ends are different. In those animals then whose constitution is adapted only to use, use alone is enough; but in an animal (man), which has also the power of understanding the use, unless there be the due exercise of the understanding, he will never attain his proper end. Well then God constitutes every animal, one to be eaten, another to serve for agriculture, another to supply cheese, and another for some like use; for which purposes what need is there to understand appearances and to be able to distinguish them? But God has introduced man to be a spectator of God and of his works; and not only a spectator of them, but an interpreter. For this reason it is shameful for man to begin and to end where irrational animals do; but rather he ought to begin where they begin, and to end where nature ends in us; and nature ends in contemplation and understanding, and in a way of life conformable to nature. Take care then not to die without having been spectators of these things.

But you take a journey to Olympia to see the work of Phidias, and all of you think it a misfortune to die without having seen such things. But when there is no need to take a journey, and where a man is, there he has the works (of God) before him, will you not desire to see and understand them? Will you not perceive either what you are, or what you were born for, or what this is for which you have received the faculty of sight? But you may say, There are some things disagreeable and troublesome in life. And are there none at Olympia? Are you not scorched? Are you not pressed by a crowd? Are you not without comfortable means of bathing? Are you not wet when it rains? Have you not abundance of noise, clamor, and other disagreeable things? But I suppose that setting all these things off against the magnificence of the spectacle, you bear and endure. Well then and have you not received faculties by which you will be able to bear all that happens? Have you not received greatness of soul? Have you not received manliness? Have you not received endurance? And why do I trouble myself about anything that can happen if I possess greatness of soul? What shall distract my mind, or disturb me, or appear painful? Shall I not use the power for the purposes for which I received it, and shall I grieve and lament over what happens?

Come, then, do you also having observed these things look to the faculties which you have, and when you have looked at them, say: Bring now, O Zeus, any difficulty that thou pleasest, for I have means given to me by thee and powers for honoring myself through the things which happen. You do not so; but you sit still, trembling for fear that some things will happen, and weeping, and lamenting, and groaning for what does happen; and then you blame the gods. For what is the consequence of such meanness of spirit but impiety? And yet God has not only given us these faculties, by which we shall be able to bear everything that happens without being depressed or broken by it; but, like a good king and a true father, He has given us these faculties free from hindrance, subject to no compulsion, unimpeded, and has put them entirely in our own power, without even having reserved to Himself any power of hindering or impeding. You, who have received these powers free and as your own, use them not; you do not even see what you have received, and from whom; some of you being blinded to the giver, and not even acknowledging your benefactor, and others, through meanness of spirit, betaking yourselves to fault-finding and making charges against God. Yet I will show to you that you have powers and means for greatness of soul and manliness; but what powers you have for finding fault making accusations, do you show me.

HOW FROM THE FACT THAT WE ARE AKIN TO GOD A MAN MAY PROCEED TO THE CONSEQUENCES.

I indeed think that the old man ought to be sitting here, not to contrive how you may have no mean thoughts nor mean and ignoble talk about yourselves, but to take care that there be not among us any young men of such a mind, that when they have recognized their kinship to God, and that we are fettered by these bonds, the body, I mean, and its possessions, and whatever else on account of them is necessary to us for the economy and commerce of life, they should intend to throw off these things as if they were burdens painful and intolerable, and to depart to their kinsmen. But this is the labor that your teacher and instructor ought to be employed upon, if he really were what he should be. You should come to him and say: Epictetus, we can no longer endure being bound to this poor body, and feeding it, and giving it drink and rest, and cleaning it, and for the sake of the body complying with the wishes of these and of those. Are not these things indifferent and nothing to us; and is not death no evil? And are we not in a manner kinsmen of God, and did we not come from him? Allow us to depart to the place from which we came; allow us to be released at last from these bonds by which we are bound and weighed down. Here there are robbers and thieves and courts of justice, and those who are named tyrants, and think that they have some power over us by means of the body and its possessions. Permit us to show them that they have no power over any man. And I on my part would say: Friends, wait for God: when he shall give the signal and release you from this service, then go to him; but for the present endure to dwell in this place where he has put you. Short indeed is this time of your dwelling here, and easy to bear for those who are so disposed; for what tyrant, or what thief, or what courts of justice are formidable to those who have thus considered as things of no value the body and the possessions of the body? Wait then, do not depart without a reason.

OF CONTENTMENT.

With respect to gods, there are some who say that a divine being does not exist; others say that it exists, but is inactive and careless, and takes no forethought about anything; a third class say that such a being exists and exercises forethought, but only about great things and heavenly things, and about nothing on the earth; a fourth class say that a divine being exercises forethought both about things on the earth and heavenly things, but in a general way only, and not about things severally. There is a fifth class to whom Ulysses and Socrates belong, who say:

I move not without thy knowledge.Iliad, x., 278.

Before all other things then it is necessary to inquire about each of these opinions, whether it is affirmed truly or not truly. For if there are no gods, how is it our proper end to follow them? And if they exist, but take no care of anything, in this case also how will it be right to follow them? But if indeed they do exist and look after things, still if there is nothing communicated from them to men, nor in fact to myself, how even so is it right (to follow them)? The wise and good man then, after considering all these things, submits his own mind to him who administers the whole, as good citizens do to the law of the state. He who is receiving instruction ought to come to be instructed with this intention, How shall I follow the gods in all things, how shall I be contented with the divine administration, and how can I become free? For he is free to whom everything happens according to his will, and whom no man can hinder. What then, is freedom madness? Certainly not; for madness and freedom do not consist. But, you say, I would have everything result just as I like, and in whatever way I like. You are mad, you are beside yourself. Do you not know that freedom is a noble and valuable thing? But for me inconsiderately to wish for things to happen as I inconsiderately like, this appears to be not only not noble, but even most base. For how do we proceed in the matter of writing? Do I wish to write the name of Dion as I choose? No, but I am taught to choose to write it as it ought to be written. And how with respect to music? In the same manner. And what universally in every art or science? Just the same. If it were not so, it would be of no value to know anything, if knowledge were adapted to every man's whim. Is it then in this alone, in this which is the greatest and the chief thing, I mean freedom, that I am permitted to will inconsiderately? By no means; but to be instructed is this, to learn to wish that everything may happen as it does. And how do things happen? As the disposer has disposed them? And he has appointed summer and winter, and abundance and scarcity, and virtue and vice, and all such opposites for the harmony of the whole; and to each of us he has given a body, and parts of the body, and possessions, and companions.

What then remains, or what method is discovered of holding commerce with them? Is there such a method by which they shall do what seems fit to them, and we not the less shall be in a mood which is conformable to nature? But you are unwilling to endure, and are discontented; and if you are alone, you call it solitude; and if you are with men, you call them knaves and robbers; and you find fault with your own parents and children, and brothers and neighbors. But you ought when you are alone to call this condition by the name of tranquillity and freedom, and to think yourself like to the gods; and when you are with many, you ought not to call it crowd, nor trouble, nor uneasiness, but festival and assembly, and so accept all contentedly.

What then is the punishment of those who do not accept? It is to be what they are. Is any person dissatisfied with being alone? Let him be alone. Is a man dissatisfied with his parents? Let him be a bad son, and lament. Is he dissatisfied with his children? Let him be a bad father. Cast him into prison. What prison? Where he is already, for he is there against his will; and where a man is against his will, there he is in prison. So Socrates was not in prison, for he was there willingly. Must my leg then be lamed? Wretch, do you then on account of one poor leg find fault with the world? Will you not willingly surrender it for the whole? Will you not withdraw from it? Will you not gladly part with it to him who gave it? And will you be vexed and discontented with the things established by Zeus, which he, with the Moirae (fates) who were present and spinning the thread of your generation, defined and put in order? Know you not how small a part you are compared with the whole. I mean with respect to the body, for as to intelligence you are not inferior to the gods nor less; for the magnitude of intelligence is not measured by length nor yet by height, but by thoughts.

HOW EVERYTHING MAY BE DONE ACCEPTABLY TO THE GODS.

When some one asked, How may a man eat acceptably to the gods, he answered: If he can eat justly and contentedly, and with equanimity, and temperately, and orderly, will it not be also acceptable to the gods? But when you have asked for warm water and the slave has not heard, or if he did hear has brought only tepid water, or he is not even found to be in the house, then not to be vexed or to burst with passion, is not this acceptable to the gods? How then shall a man endure such persons as this slave? Slave yourself, will you not bear with your own brother, who has Zeus for his progenitor, and is like a son from the same seeds and of the same descent from above? But if you have been put in any such higher place, will you immediately make yourself a tyrant? Will you not remember who you are, and whom you rule? That they are kinsmen, that they are brethren by nature, that they are the offspring of Zeus? But I have purchased them, and they have not purchased me. Do you see in what direction you are looking, that it is towards the earth, towards the pit, that it is towards these wretched laws of dead men? but towards the laws of the gods you are not looking.

WHAT PHILOSOPHY PROMISES.

When a man was consulting him how he should persuade his brother to cease being angry with him, Epictetus replied: Philosophy does not propose to secure for a man any external thing. If it did (or if it were not, as I say), philosophy would be allowing something which is not within its province. For as the carpenter's material is wood, and that of the statuary is copper, so the matter of the art of living is each man's life. When then is my brother's? That again belongs to his own art; but with respect to yours, it is one of the external things, like a piece of land, like health, like reputation. But Philosophy promises none of these. In every circumstance I will maintain, she says, the governing part conformable to nature. Whose governing part? His in whom I am, she says.

How then shall my brother cease to be angry with me? Bring him to me and I will tell him. But I have nothing to say to you about his anger.

When the man who was consulting him said, I seek to know this, How, even if my brother is not reconciled to me, shall I maintain myself in a state conformable to nature? Nothing great, said Epictetus, is produced suddenly, since not even the grape or the fig is. If you say to me now that you want a fig, I will answer to you that it requires time: let it flower first, then put forth fruit, and then ripen. Is then the fruit of a fig-tree not perfected suddenly and in one hour, and would you possess the fruit of a man's mind in so short a time and so easily? Do not expect it, even if I tell you.

THAT WE OUGHT NOT TO BE ANGRY WITH THE ERRORS (FAULTS) OF OTHERS.

Ought not then this robber and this adulterer to be destroyed? By no means say so, but speak rather in this way: This man who has been mistaken and deceived about the most important things, and blinded, not in the faculty of vision which distinguishes white and black, but in the faculty which distinguishes good and bad, should we not destroy him? If you speak thus you will see how inhuman this is which you say, and that it is just as if you would say, Ought we not to destroy this blind and deaf man? But if the greatest harm is the privation of the greatest things, and the greatest thing in every man is the will or choice such as it ought to be, and a man is deprived of this will, why are you also angry with him? Man, you ought not to be affected contrary to nature by the bad things of another. Pity him rather; drop this readiness to be offended and to hate, and these words which the many utter: "These accursed and odious fellows." How have you been made so wise at once? and how are you so peevish? Why then are we angry? Is it because we value so much the things of which these men rob us? Do not admire your clothes, and then you will not be angry with the thief. Consider this matter thus: you have fine clothes; your neighbor has not; you have a window; you wish to air the clothes. The thief does not know wherein man's good consists, but he thinks that it consist in having fine clothes, the very thing which you also think. Must he not then come and take them away? When you show a cake to greedy persons, and swallow it all yourself, do you expect them not to snatch it from you? Do not provoke them; do not have a window; do not air your clothes. I also lately had an iron lamp placed by the side of my household gods; hearing a noise at the door, I ran down, and found that the lamp had been carried off. I reflected that he who had taken the lamp had done nothing strange. What then? To-morrow, I said, you will find an earthen lamp; for a man only loses that which he has. I have lost my garment. The reason is that you had a garment. I have a pain in my head. Have you any pain in your horns? Why then are you troubled? For we only lose those things, we have only pains about those things, which we possess.

But the tyrant will chainwhat? The leg. He will take awaywhat? The neck. What then will he not chain and not take away? The will. This is why the ancients taught the maxim, Know thyself. Therefore we ought to exercise ourselves in small things, and beginning with them to proceed to the greater. I have pain in the head. Do not say, Alas! I have pain in the ear. Do not say alas! And I do not say that you are not allowed to groan, but do not groan inwardly; and if your slave is slow in bringing a bandage, do not cry out and torment yourself, and say, Every body hates me; for who would not hate such a man? For the future, relying on these opinions, walk about upright, free; not trusting to the size of your body, as an athlete, for a man ought not to be invincible in the way that an ass is.

HOW WE SHOULD BEHAVE TO TYRANTS.

If a man possesses any superiority, or thinks that he does when he does not, such a man, if he is uninstructed, will of necessity be puffed up through it. For instance, the tyrant says, I am master of all! And what can you do for me? Can you give me desire which shall have no hindrance? How can you? Have you the infallible power of avoiding what you would avoid? Have you the power of moving towards an object without error? And how do you possess this power? Come, when you are in a ship, do you trust to yourself or to the helmsman? And when you are in a chariot, to whom do you trust but to the driver? And how is it in all other arts? Just the same. In what, then, lies your power? All men pay respect to me. Well, I also pay respect to my platter, and I wash it and wipe it; and for the sake of my oil-flask, I drive a peg into the wall. Well, then, are these things superior to me? No, but they supply some of my wants, and for this reason I take care of them. Well, do I not attend to my ass? Do I not wash his feet? Do I not clean him? Do you not know that every man has regard to himself, and to you just the same as he has regard to his ass? For who has regard to you as a man? Show me. Who wishes to become like you? Who imitates you, as he imitates Socrates? But I can cut off your head. You say right. I had forgotten that I must have regard to you, as I would to a fever and the bile, and raise an altar to you, as there is at Rome an altar to fever.

What is it then that disturbs and terrifies the multitude? Is it the tyrant and his guards? (By no means.) I hope that it is not so. It is not possible that what is by nature free can be disturbed by anything else, or hindered by any other thing than by itself. But it is a man's own opinions which disturb him. For when the tyrant says to a man, I will chain your leg, he who values his leg says, Do not; have pity. But he who values his own will says, If it appears more advantageous to you, chain it. Do you not care? I do not care. I will show you that I am master. You cannot do that. Zeus has set me free; do you think that he intended to allow his own son to be enslaved? But you are master of my carcase; take it. So when you approach me, you have no regard to me? No, but I have regard to myself; and if you wish me to say that I have regard to you also, I tell you that I have the same regard to you that I have to my pipkin.

What then? When absurd notions about things independent of our will, as if they were good and (or) bad, lie at the bottom of our opinions, we must of necessity pay regard to tyrants: for I wish that men would pay regard to tyrants only, and not also to the bedchamber men. How is it that the man becomes all at once wise, when Cæsar has made him superintendent of the close stool? How is it that we say immediately, Felicion spoke sensibly to me? I wish he were ejected from the bedchamber, that he might again appear to you to be a fool.

Has a man been exalted to the tribuneship? All who meet him offer their congratulations; one kisses his eyes, another the neck, and the slaves kiss his hands. He goes to his house, he finds torches lighted. He ascends the Capitol;

he offers a sacrifice on the occasion. Now who ever sacrificed for having had good desires? for having acted conformably to nature? For in fact we thank the gods for those things in which we place our good.

A person was talking to me to-day about the priesthood of Augustus. I say to him: Man, let the thing alone; you will spend much for no purpose. But he replies, Those who draw up agreements will write my name. Do you then stand by those who read them, and say to such persons, It is I whose name is written there? And if you can now be present on all such occasions, what will you do when you are dead? My name will remain. Write it on a stone, and it will remain. But come, what remembrance of you will there be beyond Nicopolis? But I shall wear a crown of gold. If you desire a crown at all, take a crown of roses and put it on, for it will be more elegant in appearance.

AGAINST THOSE WHO WISH TO BE ADMIRED.

When a man holds his proper station in life, he does not gape after things beyond it. Man, what do you wish to happen to you? I am satisfied if I desire and avoid conformably to nature, if I employ movements towards and from an object as I am by nature formed to do, and purpose and design and assent. Why then do you strut before us as if you had swallowed a spit? My wish has always been that those who meet me should admire me, and those who follow me should exclaim, O the great philosopher! Who are they by whom you wish to be admired? Are they not those of whom you are used to say that they are mad? Well, then, do you wish to be admired by madmen?

ON PRÆCOGNITIONS.

Præcognitions are common to all men, and præcognition is not contradictory to præcognition. For who of us does not assume that Good is useful and eligible, and in all circumstances that we ought to follow and pursue it? And who of us does not assume that Justice is beautiful and becoming? When then does the contradiction arise? It arises in the adaptation of the præcognitions to the particular cases. When one man says, "He has done well; he is a brave man," and another says, "Not so; but he has acted foolishly," then the disputes arise among men. This is the dispute among the Jews and the Syrians and the Egyptians and the Romans; not whether holiness should be preferred to all things and in all cases should be pursued, but whether it is holy to eat pig's flesh or not holy. You will find this dispute also between Agamemnon and Achilles; for call them forth. What do you say, Agamemnon? ought not that to be done which is proper and right? "Certainly." Well, what do you say, Achilles? do you not admit that what is good ought to be done? "I do most certainly." Adapt your præcognitions then to the present matter. Here the dispute begins. Agamemnon says, "I ought not to give up Chryseis to her father." Achilles says, "You ought." It is certain that one of the two makes a wrong adaptation of the præcognition of "ought" or "duty." Further, Agamemnon says, "Then if I ought to restore Chryseis, it is fit that I take his prize from some of you." Achilles replies, "Would you then take her whom I love?" "Yes, her whom you love." "Must I then be the only man who goes without a prize? and must I be the only man who has no prize?" Thus the dispute begins.

What then is education? Education is the learning how to adapt the natural præcognitions to the particular things conformably to nature; and then to distinguish that of things some are in our power, but others are not. In our power are will and all acts which depend on the will; things not in our power are the body, the parts of the body, possessions, parents, brothers, children, country, and, generally, all with whom we live in society. In what then should we place the good? To what kind of things shall we adapt it? To the things which are in our power? Is not health then a good thing, and soundness of limb, and life, and are not children and parents and country? Who will tolerate you if you deny this?

Let us then transfer the notion of good to these things. Is it possible, then, when a man sustains damage and does not obtain good things, that he can be happy? It is not possible. And can he maintain towards society a proper behavior? He can not. For I am naturally formed to look after my own interest. If it is my interest to have an estate in land, it is my interest also to take it from my neighbor. If it is my interest to have a garment, it is my interest also to steal it from the bath. This is the origin of wars, civil commotions, tyrannies, conspiracies. And how shall I be still able to maintain my duty towards Zeus? For if I sustain damage and am unlucky, he takes no care of me. And what is he to me if he cannot help me? And further, what is he to me if he allows me to be in the condition in which I am? I now begin to hate him. Why then do we build temples, why setup statues to Zeus, as well as to evil demons, such as to Fever; and how is Zeus the Saviour, and how the giver of rain, and the giver of fruits? And in truth if we place the nature of Good in any such things, all this follows.

What should we do then? This is the inquiry of the true philosopher who is in labor. Now I do not see what the good is nor the bad. Am I not mad? Yes. But suppose that I place the good somewhere among the things which depend on the will; all will laugh at me. There will come some greyhead wearing many gold rings on his fingers, and he will shake his head and say: "Hear, my child. It is right that you should philosophize; but you ought to have some brains also; all this that you are doing is silly. You learn the syllogism from philosophers; but you know how to act better than philosophers do." Man why then do you blame me, if I know? What shall I say to this slave? If I am silent, he will burst. I must speak in this way: "Excuse me, as you would excuse lovers; I am not my own master; I am mad."

HOW WE SHOULD STRUGGLE WITH CIRCUMSTANCES.

It is circumstances (difficulties) which show what men are. Therefore when a difficulty falls upon you, remember that God, like a trainer of wrestlers, has matched you with a rough young man. For what purpose? you may say. Why, that you may become an Olympic conqueror; but it is not accomplished without sweat. In my opinion no man has had a more profitable difficulty than you have had, if you choose to make use of it as an athlete would deal with a young antagonist. We are now sending a scout to Rome; but no man sends a cowardly scout, who, if he only hears a noise and sees a shadow anywhere, comes running back in terror and reports that the enemy is close at hand. So now if you should come and tell us: "Fearful is the state of affairs at Rome; terrible is death; terrible is exile; terrible is calumny; terrible is poverty; fly, my friends, the enemy is near," we shall answer: "Begone, prophesy for yourself; we have committed only one fault, that we sent such a scout."

Diogenes, who was sent as a scout before you, made a different report to us. He says that death is no evil, for neither is it base; he says that fame (reputation) is the noise of madmen. And what has this spy said about pain, about pleasure, and about poverty? He says that to be naked is better than any purple robe, and to sleep on the bare ground is the softest bed; and he gives as a proof of each thing that he affirms his own courage, his tranquillity, his freedom, and the healthy appearance and compactness of his body. There is no enemy near, he says; all is peace. How so, Diogenes? "See," he replies, "if I am struck, if I have been wounded, if I have fled from any man." This is what a scout ought to be. But you come to us and tell us one thing after another. Will you not go back, and you will see clearer when you have laid aside fear?

ON THE SAME.

If these things are true, and if we are not silly, and are not acting hypocritically when we say that the good of man is in the will, and the evil too, and that everything else does not concern us, why are we still disturbed, why are we still afraid? The things about which we have been busied are in no man's power; and the things which are in the power of others, we care not for. What kind of trouble have we still?

But give me directions. Why should I give you directions? Has not Zeus given you directions? Has he not given to you what is your own free from hindrance and free from impediment, and what is not your own subject to hindrance and impediment? What directions then, what kind of orders did you bring when you came from him? Keep by every means what is your own; do not desire what belongs to others. Fidelity (integrity) is your own, virtuous shame is your own; who then can take these things from you? who else than yourself will hinder you from using them? But how do you act? When you seek what is not your own, you lose that which is your own. Having such promptings and commands from Zeus, what kind do you still ask from me? Am I more powerful than he, am I more worthy of confidence? But if you observe these, do you want any others besides? "Well, but he has not given these orders," you will say. Produce your præcognitions, produce these proofs of philosophers, produce what you have often heard, and produce what you have said yourself, produce what you have read, produce what you have meditated on; and you will then see that all these things are from God.

If I have set my admiration on the poor body, I have given myself up to be a slave; if on my poor possessions, I also make myself a slave. For I immediately make it plain with what I may be caught; as if the snake draws in his head, I tell you to strike that part of him which he guards; and do you be assured that whatever part you choose to guard, that part your master will attack. Remembering this, whom will you still flatter or fear?

But I should like to sit where the Senators sit. Do you see that you are putting yourself in straits, you are squeezing yourself? How then shall I see well in any other way in the amphitheatre? Man, do not be a spectator at all, and you will not be squeezed. Why do you give yourself trouble? Or wait a little, and when the spectacle is over, seat yourself in the place reserved for the Senators and sun yourself. For remember this general truth, that it is we who squeeze ourselves, who put ourselves in straits; that is, our opinions squeeze us and put us in straits. For what is it to be reviled? Stand by a stone and revile it, and what will you gain? If then a man listens like a stone, what profit is there to the reviler? But if the reviler has as a stepping-stone (or ladder) the weakness of him who is reviled, then he accomplishes something. Strip him. What do you mean by him? Lay hold of his garment, strip it off. I have insulted you. Much good may it do you.

This was the practice of Socrates; this was the reason why he always had one face. But we choose to practise and study anything rather than the means by which we shall be unimpeded and free. You say: "Philosophers talk paradoxes." But are there no paradoxes in the other arts? And what is more paradoxical than to puncture a man's eye in order that he may see? If any one said this to a man ignorant of the surgical art, would he not ridicule the speaker? Where is the wonder, then, if in philosophy also many things which are true appear paradoxical to the inexperienced?

IN HOW MANY WAYS APPEARANCES EXIST, AND WHAT AIDS WE SHOULD PROVIDE AGAINST THEM.

Appearances are to us in four ways. For either things appear as they are; or they are not, and do not even appear to be; or they are, and do not appear to be; or they are not, and yet appear to be. Further, in all these cases to form a right judgment (to hit the mark) is the office of an educated man. But whatever it is that annoys (troubles) us, to that we ought to apply a remedy. If the sophisms of Pyrrho and of the Academics are what annoys (troubles), we must apply the remedy to them. If it is the persuasion of appearances, by which some things appear to be good, when they are not good, let us seek a remedy for this. If it is habit which annoys us, we must try to seek aid against habit. What aid, then, can we find against habit? The contrary habit. You hear the ignorant say: "That unfortunate person is dead; his father and mother are overpowered with sorrow; he was cut off by an untimely death and in a foreign land." Hear the contrary way of speaking. Tear yourself from these expressions; oppose to one habit the contrary habit; to sophistry oppose reason, and the exercise and discipline of reason; against persuasive (deceitful) appearances we ought to have manifest præcognitions, cleared of all impurities and ready to hand.

When death appears an evil, we ought to have this rule in readiness, that it is fit to avoid evil things, and that death is a necessary thing. For what shall I do, and where shall I escape it? Suppose that I am not Sarpedon, the son of Zeus, nor able to speak in this noble way. I will go and I am resolved either to behave bravely myself or to give to another the opportunity of doing so; if I cannot succeed in doing anything myself, I will not grudge another the doing of something noble. Suppose that it is above our power to act thus; is it not in our power to reason thus? Tell me where I can escape death; discover for me the country, show me the men to whom I must go, whom death does not visit. Discover to me a charm against death. If I have not one, what do you wish me to do? I cannot escape from death. Shall I not escape from the fear of death, but shall I die lamenting and trembling? For the origin of perturbation is this, to wish for something, and that this should not happen. Therefore if I am able to change externals according to my wish, I change them; but if I cannot, I am ready to tear out the eyes of him who hinders me. For the nature of man is not to endure to be deprived of the good, and not to endure the falling into the evil. Then at last, when I am neither able to change circumstances nor to tear out the eyes of him who hinders me, I sit down and groan, and abuse whom I can, Zeus and the rest of the gods. For if they do not care for me, what are they to me? Yes, but you will be an impious man. In what respect, then, will it be worse for me than it is now? To sum up, remember that unless piety and your interest be in the same thing, piety cannot be maintained in any man. Do not these things seem necessary (true)?

THAT WE OUGHT NOT TO BE ANGRY WITH MEN; AND WHAT ARE THE SMALL AND THE GREAT THINGS AMONG MEN.

What is the cause of assenting to anything? The fact that it appears to be true. It is not possible then to assent to that which appears not to be true. Why? Because this is the nature of the understanding, to incline to the true, to be dissatisfied with the false, and in matters uncertain to withhold assent. What is the proof of this? Imagine (persuade yourself), if you can, that it is now night. It is not possible. Take away your persuasion that it is day. It is not possible. Persuade yourself or take away your persuasion that the stars are even in number. It is impossible. When then any man assents to that which is false, be assured that he did not intend to assent to it as false, for every soul is unwillingly deprived of the truth, as Plato says; but the falsity seemed to him to be true. Well, in acts what have we of the like kind as we have here truth or falsehood? We have the fit and the not fit (duty and not duty), the profitable and the unprofitable, that which is suitable to a person and that which is not, and whatever is like these. Can then a man think that a thing is useful to him and not choose it? He cannot. How says Medea?

> "'Tis true I know what evil I shall do,
> But passion overpowers the better counsel."

She thought that to indulge her passion and take vengeance on her husband was more profitable than to spare her children. It was so; but she was deceived. Show her plainly that she is deceived, and she will not do it; but so long as you do not show it, what can she follow except that which appears to herself (her opinion)? Nothing else. Why then are you angry with the unhappy woman that she has been bewildered about the most important things, and is become a viper instead of a human creature? And why not, if it is possible, rather pity, as we pity the blind and the lame, so those who are blinded and maimed in the faculties which are supreme?

Whoever then clearly remembers this, that to man the measure of every act is the appearance (the opinion), whether the thing appears good or bad. If good, he is free from blame; if bad, himself suffers the penalty, for it is impossible that he who is deceived can be one person, and he who suffers another person—whoever remembers this will not be angry with any man, will not be vexed at any man, will not revile or blame any man, nor hate, nor quarrel with any man.

So then all these great and dreadful deeds have this origin, in the appearance (opinion)? Yes, this origin and no other. The Iliad is nothing else than appearance and the use of appearances. It appeared to Alexander to carry off the wife of Menelaus. It appeared to Helene to follow him. If then it had appeared to Menelaus to feel that it was a gain to be deprived of such a wife, what would have happened? Not only would the Iliad have been lost, but the Odyssey also.

On so small a matter then did such great things depend? But what do you mean by such great things? Wars and civil commotions, and the destruction of many men and cities. And what great matter is this? Is it nothing? But what great matter is the death of many oxen, and many sheep, and many nests of swallows or storks being burnt or destroyed? Are these things then like those? Very like. Bodies of men are destroyed, and the bodies of oxen and sheep; the dwellings of men are burnt, and the nests of storks. What is there in this great or dreadful? Or show me what is the difference between a man's house and a stork's nest, as far as each is a dwelling; except that man builds his little houses of beams and tiles and bricks, and the stork builds them of sticks and mud. Are a stork and a man then like things? What say you? In body they are very much alike.

Does a man then differ in no respect from a stork? Don't suppose that I say so; but there is no difference in these matters (which I have mentioned). In what then is the difference? Seek and you will find that there is a difference in another matter. See whether it is not in a man the understanding of what he does, see if it is not in social community, in fidelity, in modesty, in steadfastness, in intelligence. Where then is the great good and evil in men? It is where the difference is. If the difference is preserved and remains fenced round, and neither modesty is destroyed, nor fidelity, nor intelligence, then the man also is preserved; but if any of these things is destroyed and stormed like a city, then the man too perishes: and in this consist the great things. Alexander, you say, sustained great damage then when the Hellenes invaded and when they ravaged Troy, and when his brothers perished. By no means; for no man is damaged by an action which is not his own; but what happened at that time was only the destruction of stork's nests. Now the ruin of Alexander was when he lost the character of modesty, fidelity, regard to hospitality, and to decency. When was Achilles ruined? Was it when Patroclus died? Not so. But it happened when he began to be angry, when he wept for a girl, when he forgot that he was at Troy not to get mistresses, but to fight. These things are the ruin of men, this is being besieged, this is the destruction of cities, when right opinions are destroyed, when they are corrupted.

ON CONSTANCY (OR FIRMNESS).

The being (nature) of the good is a certain will; the being of the bad is a certain kind of will. What, then, are externals? Materials for the will, about which the will being conversant shall obtain its own good or evil. How shall it obtain the good? If it does not admire (over-value) the materials; for the opinions about the materials, if the opinions are right, make the will good: but perverse and distorted opinions make the will bad. God has fixed this law, and says, "If you would have anything good, receive it from yourself." You say, No, but I will have it from another. Do not so: but receive it from yourself. Therefore when the tyrant threatens and calls me, I say, Whom do you threaten? If he says, I will put you in chains, I say, You threaten my hands and my feet. If he says, I will cut off your head, I reply, You threaten my head. If he says, I will throw you into prison, I say, You threaten the whole of this poor body. If he threatens me with banishment, I say the same. Does he then not threaten you at all? If I feel that all these things do not concern me, he does not threaten me at all; but if I fear any of them, it is I whom he threatens. Whom then do I fear? the master of what? The master of things which are in my own power? There is no such master. Do I fear the master of things which are not in my power? And what are these things to me?

Do you philosophers then teach us to despise kings? I hope not. Who among us teaches to claim against them the power over things which they possess? Take my poor body, take my property, take my reputation, take those who are about me. If I advise any persons to claim these things, they may truly accuse me. Yes, but I intend to command your opinions also. And who has given you this power? How can you conquer the opinion of another man? By applying terror to it, he replies, I will conquer it. Do you not know that opinion conquers itself, and is not conquered by another? But nothing else can conquer will except the will itself. For this reason too the law of God is most powerful and most just, which is this: Let the stronger always be superior to the weaker. Ten are stronger than one. For what? For putting in chains, for killing, for dragging whither they choose, for taking away what a man has. The ten therefore conquer the one in this in which they are stronger. In what then are the ten weaker? If the one possesses right opinions and the others do not. Well then, can the ten conquer in this matter? How is it possible? If we were placed in the scales, must not the heavier draw down the scale in which it is.

How strange then that Socrates should have been so treated by the Athenians. Slave, why do you say Socrates? Speak of the thing as it is: how strange that the poor body of Socrates should have been carried off and dragged to prison by stronger men, and that anyone should have given hemlock to the poor body of Socrates, and that it should breathe out the life. Do these things seem strange, do they seem unjust, do you on account of these things blame God? Had Socrates then no equivalent for these things? Where then for him was the nature of good? Whom shall we listen to, you or him? And what does Socrates say? "Anytus and Melitus can kill me, but they cannot hurt me." And further, he says, "If it so pleases God, so let it be."

But show me that he who has the inferior principles overpowers him who is superior in principles. You will never show this, nor come near showing it; for this is the law of nature and of God that the superior shall always overpower the inferior. In what? In that in which it is superior. One body is stronger than another: many are stronger than one: the thief is stronger than he who is not a thief. This is the reason why I also lost my lamp, because in wakefulness the thief was superior to me. But the man bought the lamp at this price: for a lamp he became a thief, a faithless fellow, and like a wild beast. This seemed to him a good bargain. Be it so. But a man has seized me by the cloak, and is drawing me to the public place: then others bawl out, Philosopher, what has been the use of your opinions? see, you are dragged to prison, you are going to be beheaded. And what system of philosophy could I have made so that, if a stronger man should have laid hold of my cloak, I should not be dragged off; that if ten men should have laid hold of me and cast me into prison, I should not be cast in? Have I learned nothing else then? I have learned to see that everything which happens, if it be independent of my will, is nothing to me. I may ask, if you have not gained by this. Why then do you seek advantage in anything else than in that in which you have learned that advantage is?

Will you not leave the small arguments about these matters to others, to lazy fellows, that they may sit in a corner and receive their sorry pay, or grumble that no one gives them anything; and will you not come forward and make use of what you have learned? For it is not these small arguments that are wanted now; the writings of the Stoics are full of them. What then is the thing which is wanted? A man who shall apply them, one who by his acts shall bear testimony to his words. Assume, I intreat you, this character, that we may no longer use in the schools the examples of the ancients, but may have some example of our own.

To whom then does the contemplation of these matters (philosophical inquiries) belong? To him who has leisure, for man is an animal that loves contemplation. But it is shameful to contemplate these things as runaway slaves do; we should sit, as in a theatre, free from distraction, and listen at one time to the tragic actor, at another time to the lute-player; and not do as slaves do. As soon as the slave has taken his station he praises the actor and at the same time looks round; then if any one calls out his master's name, the slave is immediately frightened and disturbed. It is shameful for philosophers thus to contemplate the works of nature. For what is a master? Man is not the master of man; but death is, and life and pleasure and pain; for if he comes without these things, bring Cæsar to me and you will see how firm I am. But when he shall come with these things, thundering and lightning, and when I am afraid of them, what do I do then except to recognize my master like the runaway slave? But so long as I have any respite from these terrors, as a runaway slave stands in the theatre, so do I. I bathe, I drink, I sing; but all this I do with terror and uneasiness. But if I shall release myself from my masters, that is from those things by means of which masters are formidable, what further trouble have I, what master have I still?

What then, ought we to publish these things to all men? No, but we ought to accommodate ourselves to the ignorant and to say: "This man recommends to me that which he thinks good for himself. I excuse him." For Socrates also excused the jailer who had the charge of him in prison and was weeping when Socrates was going to drink the poison, and said, "How generously he laments over us." Does he then say to the jailer that for this reason we have sent away the women? No, but he says it to his friends who were able to hear (understand) it; and he treats the jailer as a child.

THAT CONFIDENCE (COURAGE) IS NOT INCONSISTENT WITH CAUTION.

The opinion of the philosophers perhaps seem to some to be a paradox; but still let us examine as well as we can, if it is true that it is possible to do everything both with caution and with confidence. For caution seems to be in a manner contrary to confidence, and contraries are in no way consistent. That which seems to many to be a paradox in the matter under consideration in my opinion is of this kind; if we asserted that we ought to employ caution and confidence in the same things, men might justly accuse us of bringing together things which cannot be united. But now where is the difficulty in what is said? for if these things are true, which have been often said and often proved, that the nature of good is in the use of appearances, and the nature of evil likewise, and that things independent of our will do not admit either the nature of evil or of good, what paradox do the philosophers assert if they say that where things are not dependent on the will, there you should employ confidence, but where they are dependent on the will, there you should employ caution? For if the bad consists in the bad exercise of the will, caution ought only to be used where things are dependent on the will. But if things independent of the will and not in our power are nothing to us, with respect to these we must employ confidence; and thus we shall both be cautious and confident, and indeed confident because of our caution. For by employing caution towards things which are really bad, it will result that we shall have confidence with respect to things which are not so.

We are then in the condition of deer; when they flee from the huntsmen's feathers in fright, whither do they turn and in what do they seek refuge as safe? They turn to the nets, and thus they perish by confounding things which are objects of fear with things that they ought not to fear. Thus we also act: in what cases do we fear? In things which are independent of the will. In what cases on the contrary do we behave with confidence, as if there were no danger? In things dependent on the will. To be deceived then, or to act rashly, or shamelessly, or with base desire to seek something, does not concern us at all, if we only hit the mark in things which are independent of our will. But where there is death or exile or pain or infamy, there we attempt to run away, there we are struck with terror. Therefore, as we may expect it to happen with those who err in the greatest matters, we convert natural confidence (that is, according to nature) into audacity, desperation, rashness, shamelessness; and we convert natural caution and modesty into cowardice and meanness, which are full of fear and confusion. For if a man should transfer caution to those things in which the will may be exercised and the acts of the will, he will immediately by willing to be cautious have also the power of avoiding what he chooses; but if he transfer it to the things which are not in his power and will, and attempt to avoid the things which are in the power of others, he will of necessity fear, he will be unstable, he will be disturbed; for death or pain is not formidable, but the fear of pain or death. For this reason we commend the poet, who said:

"Not death is evil, but a shameful death."

Confidence (courage) then ought to be employed against death, and caution against the fear of death. But now we do the contrary, and employ against death the attempt to escape; and to our opinion about it we employ carelessness, rashness, and indifference. These things Socrates properly used to call tragic masks; for as to children masks appear terrible and fearful from inexperience, we also are affected in like manner by events (the things which happen in life) for no other reason than children are by masks. For what is a child? Ignorance. What is a child? Want of knowledge. For when a child knows these things, he is in no way inferior to us. What is death? A tragic mask. Turn it and examine it. See, it does not bite. The poor body must be separated from the spirit either now or later as it was separated from it before. Why then are you troubled if it be separated now? for if it is not separated now, it will be separated afterwards. Why? That the period of the universe may be completed, for it has need of the present, and of the future, and of the past. What is pain? A mask. Turn it and examine it. The poor flesh is moved roughly, then on the contrary smoothly. If this does not satisfy (please) you, the door is open; if it does, bear (with things). For the door ought to be open for all occasions; and so we have no trouble.

What then is the fruit of these opinions? It is that which ought to be the most noble and the most becoming to those who are really educated, release from perturbation, release from fear. Freedom. For in these matters we must not believe the many, who say that free persons only ought to be educated, but we should rather believe the philosophers who say that the educated only are free. How is this? In this manner: Is freedom anything else than the power of living as we choose? Nothing else. Tell me then, ye men, do you wish to live in error? We do not. No one then who lives in error is free. Do you wish to live in fear? Do you wish to live in sorrow? Do you wish to live in perturbation? By no means. No one then who is in a state of fear or sorrow or perturbation is free; but whoever is delivered from sorrows and fears and perturbations, he is at the same time also delivered from servitude. How then can we continue to believe you, most dear legislators, when you say, We only allow free persons to be educated? For philosophers say we allow none to be free except the educated; that is, God does not allow it. When then a man has turned round before the prætor his own slave, has he done nothing? He has done something. What? He has turned round his own slave before the prætor. Has he done nothing more? Yes: he is also bound to pay for him the tax called the twentieth. Well then, is not the man who has gone through this ceremony become free? No more than he is become free from perturbations. Have you who are able to turn round (free) others no master? is not money your master, or a girl or a boy, or some tyrant or some friend of the tyrant? Why do you trouble then when you are going off to any trial (danger) of this kind? It is for this reason that I often say, study and hold in readiness these principles by which you may determine what those things are with reference to which you ought to be cautious, courageous in that which does not depend on your will, cautious in that which does depend on it.

OF TRANQUILLITY (FREEDOM FROM PERTURBATION).

Consider, you who are going into court, what you wish to maintain and what you wish to succeed in. For if you wish to maintain a will conformable to nature, you have every security, every facility, you have no troubles. For if you wish to maintain what is in your own power and is naturally free, and if you are content with these, what else do you care for? For who is the master of such things? Who can take them away? If you choose to be modest and faithful, who shall not allow you to be so? If you choose not to be restrained or compelled, who shall compel you to desire what you think that you ought not to desire? who shall compel you to avoid what you do not think fit to avoid? But what do you say? The judge will determine against you something that appears formidable; but that you should also suffer in trying to avoid it, how can he do that? When then the pursuit of objects and the avoiding of them are in your power, what else do you care for? Let this be your preface, this your narrative, this your confirmation, this your victory, this your peroration, this your applause (or the approbation which you will receive).

Therefore Socrates said to one who was reminding him to prepare for his trial, Do you not think then that I have been preparing for it all my life? By what kind of preparation? I have maintained that which was in my own power. How then? I have never done anything unjust either in my private or in my public life.

But if you wish to maintain externals also, your poor body, your little property, and your little estimation, I advise you to make from this moment all possible preparation, and then consider both the nature of your judge and your adversary. If it is necessary to embrace his knees, embrace his knees; if to weep, weep; if to groan, groan. For when you have subjected to externals what is your own, then be a slave and do not resist, and do not sometimes choose to be a slave, and sometimes not choose, but with all your mind be one or the other, either free or a slave, either instructed or uninstructed, either a well-bred cock or a mean one, either endure to be beaten until you die or yield at once; and let it not happen to you to receive many stripes and then to yield. But if these things are base, determine immediately. Where is the nature of evil and good? It is where truth is: where truth is and where nature is, there is caution: where truth is, there is courage where nature is.

For this reason also it is ridiculous to say, Suggest something to me (tell me what to do). What should I suggest to you? Well, form my mind so as to accommodate itself to any event. Why that is just the same as if a man who is ignorant of letters should say, Tell me what to write when any name is proposed to me. For if I should tell him to write Dion, and then another should come and propose to him not the name of Dion but that of Theon, what will be done? what will he write? But if you have practised writing, you are also prepared to write (or to do) anything that is required. If you are not, what can I now suggest? For if circumstances require something else, what will you say, or what will you do? Remember then this general precept and you will need no suggestion. But if you gape after externals, you must of necessity ramble up and down in obedience to the will of your master. And who is the master? He who has the power over the things which you seek to gain or try to avoid.

HOW MAGNANIMITY IS CONSISTENT WITH CARE.

Things themselves (materials) are indifferent; but the use of them is not indifferent. How then shall a man preserve firmness and tranquillity, and at the same time be careful and neither rash nor negligent? If he imitates those who play at dice. The counters are indifferent; the dice are indifferent. How do I know what the cast will be? But to use carefully and dexterously the cast of the dice, this is my business. Thus then in life also the chief business is this: distinguish and separate things, and say: Externals are not in my power: will is in my power. Where shall I seek the good and the bad? Within, in the things which are my own. But in what does not belong to you call nothing either good or bad, or profit or damage or anything of the kind.

What then? Should we use such things carelessly? In no way: for this on the other hand is bad for the faculty of the will, and consequently against nature; but we should act carefully because the use is not indifferent, and we should also act with firmness and freedom from perturbations because the material is indifferent. For where the material is not indifferent, there no man can hinder me or compel me. Where I can be hindered and compelled, the obtaining of those things is not in my power, nor is it good or bad; but the use is either bad or good, and the use is in my power. But it is difficult to mingle and to bring together these two things the carefulness of him who is affected by the matter (or things about him), and the firmness of him who has no regard for it; but it is not impossible: and if it is, happiness is impossible. But we should act as we do in the case of a voyage. What can I do? I can choose the master of the ship, the sailors, the day, the opportunity. Then comes a storm. What more have I to care for? for my part is done. The business belongs to another, the master. But the ship is sinking what then have I to do? I do the only thing that I can, not to be drowned full of fear, nor screaming nor blaming God, but knowing that what has been produced must also perish: for I am not an immortal being, but a man, a part of the whole, as an hour is a part of the day: I must be present like the hour, and past like the hour. What difference then does it make to me how I pass away, whether by being suffocated or by a fever, for I must pass through some such means.

How then is it said that some external things are according to nature and others contrary to nature? It is said as it might be said if we were separated from union (or society): for to the foot I shall say that it is according to nature for it to be clean; but if you take it as a foot and as a thing not detached (independent), it will befit it both to step into the mud and tread on thorns, and sometimes to be cut off for the good of the whole body; otherwise it is no longer a foot. We should think in some such way about ourselves also. What are you? A man. If you consider yourself as detached from other men, it is according to nature to live to old age, to be rich, to be healthy. But if you consider yourself as a man and a part of a certain whole, it is for the sake of that whole that at one time you should be sick, at another time take a voyage and run into danger, and at another time be in want, and in some cases die prematurely. Why then are you troubled? Do you not know, that as a foot is no longer a foot if it is detached from the body, so you are no longer a man if you are separated from other men. For what is a man? A part of a state, of that first which consists of gods and of men; then of that which is called next to it, which is a small image of the universal state. What then must I be brought to trial; must another have a fever, another sail on the sea, another die, and another be condemned? Yes, for it is impossible in such a universe of things, among so many living together, that such things should not happen, some to one and others to others. It is your duty then since you are come here, to say what you ought, to arrange these things as it is fit. Then some one says, "I shall charge you with doing me wrong." Much good may it do you: I have done my part; but whether you also have done yours, you must look to that; for there is some danger of this too, that it may escape your notice.

OF INDIFFERENCE.

The hypothetical proposition is indifferent: the judgment about it is not indifferent, but it is either knowledge or opinion or error. Thus life is indifferent: the use is not indifferent. When any man then tells you that these things also are indifferent, do not become negligent; and when a man invites you to be careful (about such things), do not become abject and struck with admiration of material things. And it is good for you to know your own preparation and power, that in those matters where you have not been prepared, you may keep quiet, and not be vexed, if others have the advantage over you. For you too in syllogisms will claim to have the advantage over them; and if others should be vexed at this, you will console them by saying, "I have learned them, and you have not." Thus also where there is need of any practice, seek not that which is acquired from the need (of such practice), but yield in that matter to those who have had practice, and be yourself content with firmness of mind.

Go and salute a certain person. How? Not meanly. But I have been shut out, for I have not learned to make my way through the window; and when I have found the door shut, I must either come back or enter through the window. But still speak to him. In what way? Not meanly. But suppose that you have not got what you wanted. Was this your business, and not his? Why then do you claim that which belongs to another? Always remember what is your own, and what belongs to another; and you will not be disturbed. Chrysippus therefore said well, So long as future things are uncertain, I always cling to those which are more adapted to the conservation of that which is according to nature; for God himself has given me the faculty of such choice. But if I knew that it was fated (in the order of things) for me to be sick, I would even move towards it; for the foot also, if it had intelligence, would move to go into the mud. For why are ears of corn produced? Is it not that they may become dry? And do they not become dry that they may be reaped? for they are not separated from communion with other things. If then they had perception, ought they to wish never to be reaped? But this is a curse upon ears of corn to be never reaped. So we must know that in the case of men too it is a curse not to die, just the same as not to be ripened and not to be reaped. But since we must be reaped, and we also know that we are reaped, we are vexed at it; for we neither know what we are nor have we studied what belongs to man, as those who have studied horses know what belongs to horses. But Chrysantas when he was going to strike the enemy checked himself when he heard the trumpet sounding a retreat: so it seemed better to him to obey the general's command than to follow his own inclination. But not one of us chooses, even when necessity summons, readily to obey it, but weeping and groaning we suffer what we do suffer, and we call them "circumstances." What kind of circumstances, man? If you give the name of circumstances to the things which are around you, all things are circumstances; but if you call hardships by this name, what hardship is there in the dying of that which has been produced? But that which destroys is either a sword, or a wheel, or the sea, or a tile, or a tyrant. Why do you care about the way of going down to Hades? All ways are equal. But if you will listen to the truth, the way which the tyrant sends you is shorter. A tyrant never killed a man in six months: but a fever is often a year about it. All these things are only sound and the noise of empty names.

HOW WE OUGHT TO USE DIVINATION.

Through an unreasonable regard to divination many of us omit many duties. For what more can the diviner see than death or danger or disease, or generally things of that kind? If then I must expose myself to danger for a friend, and if it is my duty even to die for him, what need have I then for divination? Have I not within me a diviner who has told me the nature of good and of evil, and has explained to me the signs (or marks) of both? What need have I then to consult the viscera of victims or the flight of birds, and why do I submit when he says, It is for your interest? For does he know what is for my interest, does he know what is good; and as he has learned the signs of the viscera, has he also learned the signs of good and evil? For if he knows the signs of these, he knows the signs both of the beautiful and of the ugly, and of the just and of the unjust. Do you tell me, man, what is the thing which is signified for me: is it life or death, poverty or wealth? But whether these things are for my interest or whether they are not, I do not intend to ask you. Why don't you give your opinion on matters of grammar, and why do you give it here about things on which we are all in error and disputing with one another?

What then leads us to frequent use of divination? Cowardice, the dread of what will happen. This is the reason why we flatter the diviners. Pray, master, shall I succeed to the property of my father? Let us see: let us sacrifice on the occasion. Yes, master, as fortune chooses. When he has said, You shall succeed to the inheritance, we thank him as if we received the inheritance from him. The consequence is that they play upon us.

Will you not then seek the nature of good in the rational animal? for if it is not there, you will not choose to say that it exists in any other thing (plant or animal). What then? are not plants and animals also the works of God? They are; but they are not superior things, nor yet parts of the gods. But you are a superior thing; you are a portion separated from the Deity; you have in yourself a certain portion of him. Why then are you ignorant of your own noble descent? Why do you not know whence you came? will you not remember when you are eating who you are who eat and whom you feed? When you are in social inter-course, when you are exercising yourself, when you are engaged in discussion, know you not that you are nourishing a god, that you are exercising a god? Wretch, you are carrying about a god with you, and you know it not. Do you think that I mean some god of silver or of gold, and external? You carry him within yourself, and you perceive not that you are polluting him by impure thoughts and dirty deeds. And if an image of God were present, you would not dare to do any of the things which you are doing; but when God himself is present within and sees all and hears all, you are not ashamed of thinking such things and doing such things, ignorant as you are of your own nature and subject to the anger of God. Then why do we fear when we are sending a young man from the school into active life, lest he should do anything improperly, eat im-properly, have improper intercourse with women; and lest the rags in which he is wrapped should debase him, lest fine garments should make him proud. This youth (if he acts thus) does not know his own God; he knows not with whom he sets out (into the world). But can we endure when he says, "I wish I had you (God) with me." Have you not God with you? and do you seek for any other when you have him? or will God tell you anything else than this? If you were a statue of Phidias, either Athena or Zeus, you would think both of yourself and of the artist, and if you had any understanding (power of perception) you would try to do nothing unworthy of him who made you or of yourself, and try not to appear in an unbecoming dress (attitude) to those who look upon you. But now because Zeus has made you, for this reason do you care not how you shall appear? And yet is the artist (in the one case) like the artist in the other? or the work in the one case like the other? And what work of an artist, for instance, has in itself the faculties, which the artist shows in making it? Is it not marble or bronze, or gold or ivory? and the Athena of Phidias, when she has once extended the hand and received in it the figure of Victory, stands in that attitude for ever. But the works of God have power of motion, they breathe, they have the faculty of using the appearances of things and the power of examining them. Being the work of such an artist do you dishonor him? And what shall I say, not only that he made you, but also entrusted you to yourself and made you a deposit to yourself? Will you not think of this too, but do you also dishonor your guardianship? But if God had entrusted an orphan to you, would you thus neglect him? He has delivered yourself to your own care, and says: "I had no one fitter to entrust him to than yourself; keep him for me such as he is by nature, modest, faithful, erect, unterrified, free from passion and perturbation." And then you do not keep him such.

But some will say, Whence has this fellow got the arrogance which he displays and these supercilious looks? I have not yet so much gravity as befits a philosopher; for I do not yet feel confidence in what I have learned and in what I have assented to. I still fear my own weakness. Let me get confidence and then you shall see a countenance such as I ought to have and an attitude such as I ought to have; then I will show to you the statue, when it is perfected, when it is polished. What do you expect? a supercilious countenance? Does the Zeus at Olympia lift up his brow? No, his look is fixed as becomes him who is ready to say:

Irrevocable is my word and shall not fail. Iliad, i., 526.

Such will I show myself to you, faithful, modest, noble, free from perturbation. What, and immortal, too, except from old age, and from sickness? No, but dying as becomes a god, sickening as becomes a god. This power I possess; this I can do. But the rest I do not possess, nor can I do. I will show the nerves (strength) of a philosopher. What nerves are these? A desire never disappointed, an aversion which never falls on that which it would avoid, a proper pursuit, a diligent purpose, an assent which is not rash. These you shall see.

THAT WHEN WE CANNOT FULFIL THAT WHICH THE CHARACTER OF A MAN PROMISES, WE ASSUME THE CHARACTER OF A PHILOSOPHER.

It is no common (easy) thing to do this only, to fulfil the promise of a man's nature. For what is a man? The answer is, A rational and mortal being. Then by the rational faculty from whom are we separated? From wild beasts. And from what others? From sheep and like animals. Take care then to do nothing like a wild beast; but if you do, you have lost the character of a man; you have not fulfilled your promise. See that you do nothing like a sheep; but if you do, in this case also the man is lost. What then do we do as sheep? When we act gluttonously, when we act lewdly, when we act rashly, filthily, inconsiderately, to what have we declined? To sheep. What have we lost? The rational faculty. When we act contentiously and harmfully and passionately and violently, to what have we declined? To wild beasts. Consequently some of us are great wild beasts, and others little beasts, of a bad disposition and small, whence we may say, Let me be eaten by a lion. But in all these ways the promise of a man acting as a man is destroyed. For when is a conjunctive (complex) proposition maintained? When it fulfils what its nature promises; so that the preservation of a complex proposition is when it is a conjunction of truths. When is a disjunctive maintained? When it fulfils what it promises. When are flutes, a lyre, a horse, a dog, preserved? (When they severally keep their promise.) What is the wonder then if man also in like manner is preserved, and in like manner is lost? Each man is improved and preserved by corresponding acts, the carpenter by acts of carpentry, the grammarian by acts of grammar. But if a man accustoms himself to write ungrammatically, of necessity his art will be corrupted and destroyed. Thus modest actions preserve the modest man, and immodest actions destroy him; and actions of fidelity preserve the faithful man, and the contrary actions destroy him. And on the other hand contrary actions strengthen contrary characters: shamelessness strengthens the shameless man, faithlessness the faithless man, abusive words the abusive man, anger the man of an angry temper, and unequal receiving and giving make the avaricious man more avaricious.

For this reason philosophers admonish us not to be satisfied with learning only, but also to add study, and then practice. For we have long been accustomed to do contrary things, and we put in practice opinions which are contrary to true opinions. If then we shall not also put in practice right opinions, we shall be nothing more than the expositors of the opinions of others. For now who among us is not able to discourse according to the rules of art about good and evil things (in this fashion)? That of things some are good, and some are bad, and some are indifferent: the good then are virtues, and the things which participate in virtues; and the bad are the contrary; and the indifferent are wealth, health, reputation. Then, if in the midst of our talk there should happen some greater noise than usual, or some of those who are present should laugh at us, we are disturbed. Philosopher, where are the things which you were talking about? Whence did you produce and utter them? From the lips, and thence only. Why then do you corrupt the aids provided by others? Why do you treat the weightiest matters as if you were playing a game of dice? For it is one thing to lay up bread and wine as in a storehouse, and another thing to eat. That which has been eaten, is digested, distributed, and is become sinews, flesh, bones, blood, healthy color, healthy breath. Whatever is stored up, when you choose you can readily take and show it; but you have no other advantage from it except so far as to appear to possess it. For what is the difference between explaining these doctrines and those of men who have different opinions? Sit down now and explain according to the rules of art the opinions of Epicurus, and perhaps you will explain his opinions in a more useful manner than Epicurus himself. Why then do you call yourself a Stoic? Why do you deceive the many? Why do you act the part of a Jew, when you are a Greek? Do you not see how (why) each is called a Jew, or a Syrian, or an Egyptian? and when we see a man inclining to two sides, we are accustomed to say, This man is not a Jew, but he acts as one. But when he has assumed the affects of one who has been imbued with Jewish doctrine and has adopted that sect, then he is in fact and he is named a Jew.

HOW WE MAY DISCOVER THE DUTIES OF LIFE FROM NAMES.

Consider who you are. In the first place, you are a man; and this is one who has nothing superior to the faculty of the will, but all other things subjected to it; and the faculty itself he possesses unenslaved and free from subjection. Consider then from what things you have been separated by reason. You have been separated from wild beasts; you have been separated from domestic animals. Further, you are a citizen of the world, and a part of it, not one of the subservient (serving), but one of the principal (ruling) parts, for you are capable of comprehending the divine administration and of considering the connection of things. What then does the character of a citizen promise (profess)? To hold nothing as profitable to himself; to deliberate about nothing as if he were detached from the community, but to act as the hand or foot would do, if they had reason and understood the constitution of nature, for they would never put themselves in motion nor desire anything otherwise than with reference to the whole. Therefore, the philosophers say well, that if the good man had foreknowledge of what would happen, he would co-operate towards his own sickness and death and mutilation, since he knows that these things are assigned to him according to the universal arrangement, and that the whole is superior to the part, and the state to the citizen. But now because we do not know the future, it is our duty to stick to the things which are in their nature more suitable for our choice, for we were made among other things for this.

After this, remember that you are a son. What does this character promise? To consider that everything which is the son's belongs to the father, to obey him in all things, never to blame him to another, nor to say or do anything which does him injury, to yield to him in all things and give way, co-operating with him as far as you can. After this know that you are a brother also, and that to this character it is due to make concessions; to be easily persuaded, to speak good of your brother, never to claim in opposition to him any of the things which are independent of the will, but readily to give them up, that you may have the larger share in what is dependent on the will. For see what a thing it is, in place of a lettuce, if it should so happen, or a seat, to gain for yourself goodness of disposition. How great is the advantage.

Next to this, if you are a senator of any state, remember that you are a senator; if a youth, that you are a youth; if an old man, that you are an old man; for each of such names, if it comes to be examined, marks out the proper duties. But if you go and blame your brother, I say to you, You have forgotten who you are and what is your name. In the next place, if you were a smith and made a wrong use of the hammer, you would have forgotten the smith; and if you have forgotten the brother and instead of a brother have become an enemy, would you appear not to have changed one thing for another in that case? And if instead of a man, who is a tame animal and social, you are become a mischievous wild beast, treacherous, and biting, have you lost nothing? But (I suppose) you must lose a bit of money that you may suffer damage? And does the loss of nothing else do a man damage? If you had lost the art of grammar or music, would you think the loss of it a damage? and if you shall lose modesty, moderation and gentleness, do you think the loss nothing? And yet the things first mentioned are lost by some cause external and independent of the will, and the second by our own fault; and as to the first neither to have them nor to lose them is shameful; but as to the second, not to have them and to lose them is shameful and matter of reproach and a misfortune.

What then? shall I not hurt him who has hurt me? In the first place consider what hurt is, and remember what you have heard from the philosophers. For if the good consists in the will (purpose, intention), and the evil also in the will, see if what you say is not this: What then, since that man has hurt himself by doing an unjust act to me, shall I not hurt myself by doing some unjust act to him? Why do we not imagine to ourselves (mentally think of) something of this kind? But where there is any detriment to the body or to our possession, there is harm there; and where the same thing happens to the faculty of the will, there is (you suppose) no harm; for he who has been deceived or he who has done an unjust act neither suffers in the head nor in the eye nor in the hip, nor does he lose his estate; and we wish for nothing else than (security to) these things. But whether we shall have the will modest and faithful or shameless and faithless, we care not the least, except only in the school so far as a few words are concerned. Therefore our proficiency is limited to these few words; but beyond them it does not exist even in the slightest degree.

WHAT THE BEGINNING OF PHILOSOPHY IS.

The beginning of philosophy, to him at least who enters on it in the right way and by the door is a consciousness of his own weakness and inability about necessary things; for we come into the world with no natural notion of a right-angled triangle, or of a diesis (a quarter tone), or of a half-tone; but we learn each of these things by a certain transmission according to art; and for this reason those who do not know them do not think that they know them. But as to good and evil, and beautiful and ugly, and becoming and unbecoming, and happiness and misfortune, and proper and improper, and what we ought to do and what we ought not to do, who ever came into the world without having an innate idea of them? Wherefore we all use these names, and we endeavor to fit the preconceptions to the several cases (things) thus: he has done well; he has not done well; he has done as he ought, not as he ought; he has been unfortunate, he has been fortunate; he is unjust, he is just; who does not use these names? who among us defers the use of them till he has learned them, as he defers the use of the words about lines (geometrical figures) or sounds? And the cause of this is that we come into the world already taught as it were by nature some things on this matter, and proceeding from these we have added to them self-conceit. For why, a man says, do I not know the beautiful and the ugly? Have I not the notion of it? You have. Do I not adapt it to particulars? You do. Do I not then adapt it properly? In that lies the whole question; and conceit is added here; for beginning from these things which are admitted men proceed to that which is matter of dispute by means of unsuitable adaptation; for if they possessed this power of adaptation in addition to those things, what would hinder them from being perfect? But now since you think that you properly adapt the preconceptions to the particulars, tell me whence you derive this (assume that you do so). Because I think so. But it does not seem so to another, and he thinks that he also makes a proper adaptation; or does he not think so? He does think so. Is it possible then that both of you can properly apply the preconceptions to things about which you have contrary opinions? It is not possible. Can you then show us anything better towards adapting the preconceptions beyond your thinking that you do? Does the madman do any other things than the things which seem to him right? Is then this criterion sufficient for him also? It is not sufficient. Come then to something which is superior to seeming. What is this?

Observe, this is the beginning of philosophy, a perception of the disagreement of men with one another, and an inquiry into the cause of the disagreement, and a condemnation and distrust of that which only "seems," and a certain investigation of that which "seems" whether it "seems" rightly, and a discovery of some rule, as we have discovered a balance in the determination of weights, and a carpenter's rule (or square) in the case of straight and crooked things. This is the beginning of philosophy. Must we say that all things are right which seem so to all? And how is it possible that contradictions can be right?Not all then, but all which seem to us to be right.How more to you than those which seem right to the Syrians? why more than what seem right to the Egyptians? why more than what seems right to me or to any other man? Not at all more. What then "seems" to every man is not sufficient for determining what "is"; for neither in the case of weights nor measures are we satisfied with the bare appearance, but in each case we have discovered a certain rule. In this matter then is there no rule superior to what "seems"? And how is it possible that the most necessary things among men should have no sign (mark), and be incapable of being discovered? There is then some rule. And why then do we not seek the rule and discover it, and afterwards use it without varying from it, not even stretching out the finger without it? For this, I think, is that which when it is discovered cures of their madness those who use mere "seeming" as a measure, and misuse it; so that for the future proceeding from certain things (principles) known and made clear we may use in the case of particular things the preconceptions which are distinctly fixed.

What is the matter presented to us about which we are inquiring? Pleasure (for example). Subject it to the rule, throw it into the balance. Ought the good to be such a thing that it is fit that we have confidence in it? Yes. And in which we ought to confide? It ought to be. Is it fit to trust to anything which is insecure? No. Is then pleasure anything secure? No. Take it then and throw it out of the scale, and drive it far away from the place of good things. But if you are not sharp-sighted, and one balance is not enough for you, bring another. Is it fit to be elated over what is good? Yes. Is it proper then to be elated over present pleasure? See that you do not say that it is proper; but if you do, I shall then not think you worthy even of the balance. Thus things are tested and weighed when the rules are ready. And to philosophize is this, to examine and confirm the rules; and then to use them when they are known is the act of a wise and good man.

OF DISPUTATION OR DISCUSSION.

What things a man must learn in order to be able to apply the art of disputation, has been accurately shown by our philosophers (the Stoics); but with respect to the proper use of the things, we are entirely without practice. Only give to any of us, whom you please, an illiterate man to discuss with, and he cannot discover how to deal with the man. But when he has moved the man a little, if he answers beside the purpose, he does not know how to treat him, but he then either abuses or ridicules him, and says, He is an illiterate man; it is not possible to do anything with him. Now a guide, when he has found a man out of the road, leads him into the right way; he does not ridicule or abuse him and then leave him. Do you also show the illiterate man the truth, and you will see that he follows. But so long as you do not show him the truth, do not ridicule him, but rather feel your own incapacity.

Now this was the first and chief peculiarity of Socrates, never to be irritated in argument, never to utter anything abusive, anything insulting, but to bear with abusive persons and to put an end to the quarrel. If you would know what great power he had in this way, read the Symposium of Xenophon, and you will see how many quarrels he put an end to. Hence with good reason in the poets also this power is most highly praised:

> Quickly with skill he settles great disputes.
> Hesiod, Theogony, v. 87.

ON ANXIETY (SOLICITUDE).

When I see a man anxious, I say, What does this man want? If he did not want something which is not in his power, how could he be anxious? For this reason a lute player when he is singing by himself has no anxiety, but when he enters the theatre, he is anxious, even if he has a good voice and plays well on the lute; for he not only wishes to sing well, but also to obtain applause: but this is not in his power. Accordingly, where he has skill, there he has confidence. Bring any single person who knows nothing of music, and the musician does not care for him. But in the matter where a man knows nothing and has not been practised, there he is anxious. What matter is this? He knows not what a crowd is or what the praise of a crowd is. However, he has learned to strike the lowest chord and the highest; but what the praise of the many is, and what power it has in life, he neither knows nor has he thought about it. Hence he must of necessity tremble and grow pale. Is any man then afraid about things which are not evils? No. Is he afraid about things which are evils, but still so far within his power that they may not happen? Certainly he is not. If then the things which are independent of the will are neither good nor bad, and all things which do depend on the will are within our power, and no man can either take them from us or give them to us, if we do not choose, where is room left for anxiety? But we are anxious about our poor body, our little property, about the will of Cæsar; but not anxious about things internal. Are we anxious about not forming a false opinion? No, for this is in my power. About not exerting our movements contrary to nature? No, not even about this. When then you see a man pale, as the physician says, judging from the complexion, this man's spleen is disordered, that man's liver; so also say, this man's desire and aversion are disordered, he is not in the right way, he is in a fever. For nothing else changes the color, or causes trembling or chattering of the teeth, or causes a man to

> Sink in his knees and shift from foot to foot.
> Iliad, xiii., 281.

For this reason, when Zeno was going to meet Antigonus, he was not anxious, for Antigonus had no power over any of the things which Zeno admired; and Zeno did not care for those things over which Antigonus had power. But Antigonus was anxious when he was going to meet Zeno, for he wished to please Zeno; but this was a thing external (out of his power). But Zeno did not want to please Antigonus; for no man who is skilled in any art wishes to please one who has no such skill.

Should I try to please you? Why? I suppose, you know the measure by which one man is estimated by another. Have you taken pains to learn what is a good man and what is a bad man, and how a man becomes one or the other? Why then are you not good yourself? How, he replies, am I not good? Because no good man laments or groans or weeps, no good man is pale and trembles, or says, How will he receive me, how will he listen to me? Slave, just as it pleases him. Why do you care about what belongs to others? Is it now his fault if he receives badly what proceeds from you? Certainly. And is it possible that a fault should be one man's, and the evil in another? No. Why then are you anxious about that which belongs to others? Your question is reasonable; but I am anxious how I shall speak to him. Cannot you then speak to him as you choose? But I fear that I may be disconcerted? If you are going to write the name of Dion, are you afraid that you would be disconcerted? By no means. Why? is it not because you have practised writing the name? Certainly. Well, if you were going to read the name, would you not feel the same? and why? Because every art has a certain strength and confidence in the things which belong to it. Have you then not practised speaking? and what else did you learn in the school? Syllogisms and sophistical propositions? For what purpose? was it not for the purpose of discoursing skilfully? and is not discoursing skilfully the same as discoursing seasonably and cautiously and with intelligence, and also without making mistakes and without hindrance, and besides all this with confidence? Yes. When then you are mounted on a horse and go into a plain, are you anxious at being matched against a man who is on foot, and anxious in a matter in which you are practised, and he is not? Yes, but that person (to whom I am going to speak) has power to kill me. Speak the truth, then, unhappy man, and do not brag, nor claim to be a philosopher, nor refuse to acknowledge your masters, but so long as you present this handle in your body, follow every man who is stronger than yourself. Socrates used to practice speaking, he who talked as he did to the tyrants, to the dicasts (judges), he who talked in his prison. Diogenes had practised speaking, he who spoke as he did to Alexander, to the pirates, to the person who bought him. These men were confident in the things which they practised. But do you walk off to your own affairs and never leave them: go and sit in a corner, and weave syllogisms, and propose them to another. There is not in you the man who can rule a state.

TO NASO.

When a certain Roman entered with his son and listened to one reading, Epictetus said, This is the method of instruction; and he stopped. When the Roman asked him to go on, Epictetus said, Every art when it is taught causes labor to him who is unacquainted with it and is unskilled in it, and indeed the things which proceed from the arts immediately show their use in the purpose for which they were made; and most of them contain something attractive and pleasing. For indeed to be present and to observe how a shoemaker learns is not a pleasant thing; but the shoe is useful and also not disagreeable to look at. And the discipline of a smith when he is learning is very disagreeable to one who chances to be present and is a stranger to the art: but the work shows the use of the art. But you will see this much more in music; for if you are present while a person is learning, the discipline will appear most disagreeable; and yet the results of music are pleasing and delightful to those who know nothing of music. And here we conceive the work of a philosopher to be something of this kind: he must adapt his wish to what is going on, so that neither any of the things which are taking place shall take place contrary to our wish, nor any of the things which do not take place shall not take place when we wish that they should. From this the result is to those who have so arranged the work of philosophy, not to fail in the desire, nor to fall in with that which they would avoid; without uneasiness, without fear, without perturbation to pass through life themselves, together with their associates maintaining the relations both natural and acquired, as the relation of son, of father, of brother, of citizen, of man, of wife, of neighbor, of fellow-traveller, of ruler, of ruled. The work of a philosopher we conceive to be something like this. It remains next to inquire how this must be accomplished.

We see then that the carpenter when he has learned certain things becomes a carpenter; the pilot by learning certain things becomes a pilot. May it not then in philosophy also not be sufficient to wish to be wise and good, and that there is also a necessity to learn certain things? We inquire then what these things are. The philosophers say that we ought first to learn that there is a God and that he provides for all things; also that it is not possible to conceal from him our acts, or even our intentions and thoughts. The next thing is to learn what is the nature of the gods; for such as they are discovered to be, he, who would please and obey them, must try with all his power to be like them. If the divine is faithful, man also must be faithful; if it is free, man also must be free; if beneficent, man also must be beneficent; if magnanimous, man also must be magnanimous; as being then an imitator of God he must do and say everything consistently with this fact.

TO OR AGAINST THOSE WHO OBSTINATELY PERSIST IN WHAT THEY HAVE DETERMINED.

When some persons have heard these words, that a man ought to be constant (firm), and that the will is naturally free and not subject to compulsion, but that all other things are subject to hindrance, to slavery, and are in the power of others, they suppose that they ought without deviation to abide by everything which they have determined. But in the first place that which has been determined ought to be sound (true). I require tone (sinews) in the body, but such as exists in a healthy body, in an athletic body; but if it is plain to me that you have the tone of a frenzied man and you boast of it, I shall say to you, Man, seek the physician; this is not tone, but atony (deficiency in right tone). In a different way something of the same kind is felt by those who listen to these discourses in a wrong manner; which was the case with one of my companions, who for no reason resolved to starve himself to death. I heard of it when it was the third day of his abstinence from food, and I went to inquire what had happened. "I have resolved," he said. "But still tell me what it was which induced you to resolve; for if you have resolved rightly, we shall sit with you and assist you to depart, but if you have made an unreasonable resolution, change your mind." "We ought to keep to our determinations." "What are you doing, man? We ought to keep not to all our determinations, but to those which are right; for if you are now persuaded that it is right, do not change your mind, if you think fit, but persist and say, We ought to abide by our determinations. Will you not make the beginning and lay the foundation in an inquiry whether the determination is sound or not sound, and so then build on it firmness and security? But if you lay a rotten and ruinous foundation, will not your miserable little building fall down the sooner, the more and the stronger are the materials which you shall lay on it? Without any reason would you withdraw from us out of life a man who is a friend and a companion, a citizen of the same city, both the great and the small city? Then while you are committing murder and destroying a man who has done no wrong, do you say that you ought to abide by your determinations? And if it ever in any way came into your head to kill me, ought you to abide by your determinations?"

Now this man was with difficulty persuaded to change his mind. But it is impossible to convince some persons at present; so that I seem now to know what I did not know before, the meaning of the common saying, that you can neither persuade nor break a fool. May it never be my lot to have a wise fool for my friend; nothing is more untractable. "I am determined," the man says. Madmen are also, but the more firmly they form a judgment on things which do not exist, the more hellebore they require. Will you not act like a sick man and call in the physician?I am sick, master, help me; consider what I must do: it is my duty to obey you. So it is here also: I know not what I ought to do, but I am come to learn.Not so; but speak to me about other things: upon this I have determined.What other things? for what is greater and more useful than for you to be persuaded that it is not sufficient to have made your determination and not to change it. This is the tone (energy) of madness, not of health.I will die, if you compel me to this.Why, man? What has happened?I have determinedI have had a lucky escape that you have not determined to kill meI take no money. Why?I have determinedBe assured that with the very tone (energy) which you now use in refusing to take, there is nothing to hinder you at some time from inclining without reason to take money, and then saying, I have determined. As in a distempered body, subject to defluxions, the humor inclines sometimes to these parts, and then to those, so too a sickly soul knows not which way to incline; but if to this inclination and movement there is added a tone (obstinate resolution), then the evil becomes past help and cure.

THAT WE DO NOT STRIVE TO USE OUR OPINIONS ABOUT GOOD AND EVIL.

Where is the good? In the will. Where is the evil? In the will. Where is neither of them? In those things which are independent of the will. Well then? Does any one among us think of these lessons out of the schools? Does any one meditate (strive) by himself to give an answer to things as in the case of questions?Is it day?Yes.Is it night?No.Well, is the number of stars even?I cannot say.When money is shown (offered) to you, have you studied to make the proper answer, that money is not a good thing? Have you practised yourself in these answers, or only against sophisms? Why do you wonder then if in the cases which you have studied, in those you have improved; but in those which you have not studied, in those you remain the same? When the rhetorician knows that he has written well, that he has committed to memory what he has written, and brings an agreeable voice, why is he still anxious? Because he is not satisfied with having studied. What then does he want? To be praised by the audience? For the purpose then of being able to practise declamation he has been disciplined; but with respect to praise and blame he has not been disciplined. For when did he hear from any one what praise is, what blame is, what the nature of each is, what kind of praise should be sought, or what kind of blame should be shunned? And when did he practise this discipline which follows these words (things)? Why then do you still wonder, if in the matters which a man has learned, there he surpasses others, and in those in which he has not been disciplined, there he is the same with the many. So the lute player knows how to play, sings well, and has a fine dress, and yet he trembles when he enters on the stage; for these matters he understands, but he does not know what a crowd is, nor the shouts of a crowd, nor what ridicule is. Neither does he know what anxiety is, whether it is our work or the work of another, whether it is possible to stop it or not. For this reason if he has been praised, he leaves the theatre puffed up, but if he has been ridiculed, the swollen bladder has been punctured and subsides.

This is the case also with ourselves. What do we admire? Externals. About what things are we busy? Externals. And have we any doubt then why we fear or why we are anxious? What then happens when we think the things, which are coming on us, to be evils? It is not in our power not to be afraid, it is not in our power not to be anxious. Then we say, Lord God, how shall I not be anxious? Fool, have you not hands, did not God make them for you? Sit down now and pray that your nose may not run. Wipe yourself rather and do not blame him. Well then, has he given to you nothing in the present case? Has he not given to you endurance? Has he not given to you magnanimity? Has he not given to you manliness? When you have such hands do you still look for one who shall wipe your nose? But we neither study these things nor care for them. Give me a man who cares how he shall do anything, not for the obtaining of a thing, but who cares about his own energy. What man, when he is walking about, cares for his own energy? Who, when he is deliberating, cares about his own deliberation, and not about obtaining that about which he deliberates? And if he succeeds, he is elated and says, How well we have deliberated; did I not tell you, brother, that it is impossible, when we have thought about anything, that it should not turn out thus? But if the thing should turn out otherwise, the wretched man is humbled; he knows not even what to say about what has taken place. Who among us for the sake of this matter has consulted a seer? Who among us as to his actions has not slept in indifference? Who? Give (name) to me one that I may see the man whom I have long been looking for, who is truly noble and ingenuous, whether young or old; name him.

What then are the things which are heavy on us and disturb us? What else than opinions? What else than opinions lies heavy upon him who goes away and leaves his companions and friends and places and habits of life? Now little children, for instance, when they cry on the nurse leaving them for a short time, forget their sorrow if they receive a small cake. Do you choose then that we should compare you to little children? No, by Zeus, for I do not wish to be pacified by a small cake, but by right opinions. And what are these? Such as a man ought to study all day, and not to be affected by anything that is not his own, neither by companion nor place nor gymnasia, and not even by his own body, but to remember the law and to have it before his eyes. And what is the divine law? To keep a man's own, not to claim that which belongs to others, but to use what is given, and when it is not given, not to desire it; and when a thing is taken away, to give it up readily and immediately, and to be thankful for the time that a man has had the use of it, if you would not cry for your nurse and mamma. For what matter does it make by what thing a man is subdued, and on what he depends? In what respect are you better than he who cries for a girl, if you grieve for a little gymnasium, and little porticos, and young men, and such places of amusement? Another comes and laments that he shall no longer drink the water of Dirce. Is the Marcian water worse than that of Dirce? But I was used to the water of Dirce. And you in turn will be used to the other. Then if you become attached to this also, cry for this too, and try to make a verse like the verse of Euripides,

> The hot baths of Nero and the Marcian water.

See how tragedy is made when common things happen to silly men.

When then shall I see Athens again and the Acropolis? Wretch, are you not content with what you see daily? Have you anything better or greater to see than the sun, the moon, the stars, the whole earth, the sea? But if indeed you comprehend Him who administers the whole, and carry him about in yourself, do you still desire small stones and a beautiful rock?

HOW WE MUST ADAPT PRECONCEPTIONS TO PARTICULAR CASES.

What is the first business of him who philosophizes? To throw away self-conceit. For it is impossible for a man to begin to learn that which he thinks that he knows. As to things then which ought to be done and ought not to be done, and good and bad, and beautiful and ugly, all of us talking of them at random go to the philosophers; and on these matters we praise, we censure, we accuse, we blame, we judge and determine about principles honorable and dishonorable. But why do we go to the philosophers? Because we wish to learn what we do not think that we know. And what is this? Theorems. For we wish to learn what philosophers say as being something elegant and acute; and some wish to learn that they may get profit from what they learn. It is ridiculous then to think that a person wishes to learn one thing, and will learn another; or further, that a man will make proficiency in that which he does not learn. But the many are deceived by this which deceived also the rhetorician Theopompus, when he blames even Plato for wishing everything to be defined. For what does he say? Did none of us before you use the words good or just, or do we utter the sounds in an unmeaning and empty way without understanding what they severally signify? Now who tells you, Theopompus, that we had not natural notions of each of these things and preconceptions? But it is not possible to adapt preconceptions to their correspondent objects if we have not distinguished (analyzed) them, and inquired what object must be subjected to each preconception. You may make the same charge against physicians also. For who among us did not use the words healthy and unhealthy before Hippocrates lived, or did we utter these words as empty sounds? For we have also a certain preconception of health, but we are not able to adapt it. For this reason one says, Abstain from food; another says, Give food; another says, Bleed; and another says, Use cupping. What is the reason? is it any other than that a man cannot properly adapt the preconceptions of health to particulars?

HOW WE SHOULD STRUGGLE AGAINST APPEARANCES.

Every habit and faculty is maintained and increased by the corresponding actions: the habit of walking by walking, the habit of running by running. If you would be a good reader, read; if a writer, write. But when you shall not have read for thirty days in succession, but have done something else, you will know the consequence. In the same way, if you shall have lain down ten days, get up and attempt to make a long walk, and you will see how your legs are weakened. Generally then if you would make anything a habit, do it; if you would not make it a habit, do not do it, but accustom yourself to do something else in place of it.

So it is with respect to the affections of the soul: when you have been angry, you must know that not only has this evil befallen you, but that you have also increased the habit, and in a manner thrown fuel upon fire.

In this manner certainly, as philosophers say, also diseases of the mind grow up. For when you have once desired money, if reason be applied to lead to a perception of the evil, the desire is stopped, and the ruling faculty of our mind is restored to the original authority. But if you apply no means of cure, it no longer returns to the same state, but being again excited by the corresponding appearance, it is inflamed to desire quicker than before: and when this takes place continually, it is henceforth hardened (made callous), and the disease of the mind confirms the love of money. For he who has had a fever, and has been relieved from it, is not in the same state that he was before, unless he has been completely cured. Something of the kind happens also in diseases of the soul. Certain traces and blisters are left in it, and unless a man shall completely efface them, when he is again lashed on the same places, the lash will produce not blisters (weals) but sores. If then you wish not to be of an angry temper, do not feed the habit: throw nothing on it which will increase it: at first keep quiet, and count the days on which you have not been angry. I used to be in passion every day; now every second day; then every third, then every fourth. But if you have intermitted thirty days, make a sacrifice to God. For the habit at first begins to be weakened, and then is completely destroyed. "I have not been vexed to-day, nor the day after, nor yet on any succeeding day during two or three months; but I took care when some exciting things happened." Be assured that you are in a good way.

How then shall this be done? Be willing at length to be approved by yourself, be willing to appear beautiful to God, desire to be in purity with your own pure self and with God. Then when any such appearance visits you, Plato says, Have recourse to expiations, go a suppliant to the temples of the averting deities. It is even sufficient if you resort to the society of noble and just men, and compare yourself with them, whether you find one who is living or dead.

But in the first place, be not hurried away by the rapidity of the appearance, but say, Appearances, wait for me a little; let me see who you are, and what you are about; let me put you to the test. And then do not allow the appearance to lead you on and draw lively pictures of the things which will follow; for if you do, it will carry you off wherever it pleases. But rather bring in to oppose it some other beautiful and noble appearance, and cast out this base appearance. And if you are accustomed to be exercised in this way, you will see what shoulders, what sinews, what strength you have. But now it is only trifling words, and nothing more.

This is the true athlete, the man who exercises himself against such appearances. Stay, wretch, do not be carried away. Great is the combat, divine is the work; it is for kingship, for freedom, for happiness, for freedom from perturbation. Remember God; call on him as a helper and protector, as men at sea call on the Dioscuri in a storm. For what is a greater storm than that which comes from appearances which are violent and drive away the reason? For the storm itself, what else is it but an appearance? For take away the fear of death, and suppose as many thunders and lightnings as you please, and you will know what calm and serenity there is in the ruling faculty. But if you have once been defeated and say that you will conquer hereafter, and then say the same again, be assured that you will at last be in so wretched a condition and so weak that you will not even know afterwards that you are doing wrong, but you will even begin to make apologies (defences) for your wrong-doing, and then you will confirm the saying of Hesiod to be true,

> With constant ills the dilatory strives.

OF INCONSISTENCY.

Some things men readily confess, and other things they do not. No one then will confess that he is a fool or without understanding; but quite the contrary you will hear all men saying, I wish that I had fortune equal to my understanding. But men readily confess that they are timid, and they say: I am rather timid, I confess; but as to other respects you will not find me to be foolish. A man will not readily confess that he is intemperate; and that he is unjust, he will not confess at all. He will by no means confess that he is envious or a busybody. Most men will confess that they are compassionate. What then is the reason?

The chief thing (the ruling thing) is inconsistency and confusion in the things which relate to good and evil. But different men have different reasons; and generally what they imagine to be base, they do not confess at all. But they suppose timidity to be a characteristic of a good disposition, and compassion also; but silliness to be the absolute characteristic of a slave. And they do not at all admit (confess) the things which are offences against society. But in the case of most errors for this reason chiefly they are induced to confess them, because they imagine that there is something involuntary in them as in timidity and compassion; and if a man confess that he is in any respect intemperate, he alleges love (or passion) as an excuse for what is involuntary. But men do not imagine injustice to be at all involuntary. There is also in jealousy, as they suppose, something involuntary; and for this reason they confess to jealousy also.

Living then among such men, who are so confused, so ignorant of what they say, and of the evils which they have or have not, and why they have them, or how they shall be relieved of them, I think it is worth the trouble for a man to watch constantly (and to ask) whether I also am one of them, what imagination I have about myself, how I conduct myself, whether I conduct myself as a prudent man, whether I conduct myself as a temperate man, whether I ever say this, that I have been taught to be prepared for everything that may happen. Have I the consciousness, which a man who knows nothing ought to have, that I know nothing? Do I go to my teacher as men go to oracles, prepared to obey? or do I like a snivelling boy go to my school to learn history and understand the books which I did not understand before, and, if it should happen so, to explain them also to others? Man, you have had a fight in the house with a poor slave, you have turned the family upside down, you have frightened the neighbors, and you come to me as if you were a wise man, and you take your seat and judge how I have explained some word, and how I have babbled whatever came into my head. You come full of envy, and humbled, because you bring nothing from home; and you sit during the discussion thinking of nothing else than how your father is disposed towards you and your brother. What are they saying about me there? now they think that I am improving, and are saying, He will return with all knowledge. I wish I could learn everything before I return; but much labor is necessary, and no one sends me anything, and the baths at Nicopolis are dirty; everything is bad at home, and bad here.

ON FRIENDSHIP.

What a man applies himself to earnestly, that he naturally loves. Do men then apply themselves earnestly to the things which are bad? By no means. Well, do they apply themselves to things which in no way concern themselves? Not to these either. It remains then that they employ themselves earnestly only about things which are good; and if they are earnestly employed about things, they love such things also. Whoever then understands what is good can also know how to love; but he who cannot distinguish good from bad, and things which are neither good nor bad from both, how can he possess the power of loving? To love, then, is only in the power of the wise.

For universally, be not deceived, every animal is attached to nothing so much as to its own interests. Whatever then appears to it an impediment to this interest, whether this be a brother, or a father, or a child, or beloved, or lover, it hates, spurns, curses; for its nature is to love nothing so much as its own interests: this is father, and brother, and kinsman, and country, and God. When then the gods appear to us to be an impediment to this, we abuse them and throw down their statues and burn their temples, as Alexander ordered the temples of Aesculapius to be burned when his dear friend died.

For this reason, if a man put in the same place his interest, sanctity, goodness, and country, and parents, and friends, all these are secured: but if he puts in one place his interest, in another his friends, and his country and his kinsmen and justice itself, all these give way, being borne down by the weight of interest. For where the I and the Mine are placed, to that place of necessity the animal inclines; if in the flesh, there is the ruling power; if in the will, it is there; and if it is in externals, it is there. If then I am there where my will is, then only shall I be a friend such as I ought to be, and son, and father; for this will be my interest, to maintain the character of fidelity, of modesty, of patience, of abstinence, of active co-operation, of observing my relations (towards all). But if I put myself in one place, and honesty in another, then the doctrine of Epicurus becomes strong, which asserts either that there is no honesty or it is that which opinion holds to be honest (virtuous).

It was through this ignorance that the Athenians and the Lacedaemonians quarrelled, and the Thebans with both; and the great king quarrelled with Hellas, and the Macedonians with both: and the Romans with the Getae. And still earlier the Trojan war happened for these reasons. Alexander was the guest of Menelaus, and if any man had seen their friendly disposition, he would not have believed any one who said that they were not friends. But there was cast between them (as between dogs) a bit of meat, a handsome woman, and about her war arose. And now when you see brothers to be friends appearing to have one mind, do not conclude from this anything about their friendship, not even if they swear it and say that it is impossible for them to be separated from one another. For the ruling principle of a bad man cannot be trusted; it is insecure, has no certain rule by which it is directed, and is overpowered at different times by different appearances. But examine, not what other men examine, if they are born of the same parents and brought up together, and under the same pedagogue; but examine this only, wherein they place their interest, whether in externals or in the will. If in externals, do not name them friends, no more than name them trustworthy or constant, or brave or free; do not name them even men, if you have any judgment. For that is not a principle of human nature which makes them bite one another, and abuse one another, and occupy deserted places or public places, as if they were mountains, and in the courts of justice display the acts of robbers; nor yet that which makes them intemperate and adulterers and corrupters, nor that which makes them do whatever else men do against one another through this one opinion only, that of placing themselves and their interests in the things which are not within the power of their will. But if you hear that in truth these men think the good to be only there, where will is, and where there is a right use of appearances, no longer trouble yourself whether they are father or son, or brothers, or have associated a long time and are companions, but when you have ascertained this only, confidently declare that they are friends, as you declare that they are faithful, that they are just. For where else is friendship than where there is fidelity, and modesty, where there is a communion of honest things and of nothing else.

But you may say, Such a one treated me with regard so long; and did he not love me? How do you know, slave, if he did not regard you in the same way as he wipes his shoes with a sponge, or as he takes care of his beast? How do you know, when you have ceased to be useful as a vessel, he will not throw you away like a broken platter? But this woman is my wife, and we have lived together so long. And how long did Eriphyle live with Amphiaraus, and was the mother of children and of many? But a necklace came between them: and what is a necklace? It is the opinion about such things. That was the bestial principle, that was the thing which broke asunder the friendship between husband and wife, that which did not allow the woman to be a wife nor the mother to be a mother. And let every man among you who has seriously resolved either to be a friend himself or to have another for his friend, cut out these opinions, hate them, drive them from his soul. And thus first of all he will not reproach himself, he will not be at variance with himself, he will not change his mind, he will not torture himself. In the next place, to another also, who is like himself, he will be altogether and completely a friend. But he will bear with the man who is unlike himself, he will be kind to him, gentle, ready to pardon on account of his ignorance, on account of his being mistaken in things of the greatest importance; but he will be harsh to no man, being well convinced of Plato's doctrine that every mind is deprived of truth unwillingly. If you cannot do this, yet you can do in all other respects as friends do, drink together, and lodge together, and sail together, and you may be born of the same parents, for snakes also are: but neither will they be friends, nor you, so long as you retain these bestial and cursed opinions.

ON THE POWER OF SPEAKING.

Every man will read a book with more pleasure or even with more ease, if it is written in fairer characters. Therefore every man will also listen more readily to what is spoken, if it is signified by appropriate and becoming words. We must not say then that there is no faculty of expression: for this affirmation is the characteristic of an impious and also of a timid man. Of an impious man, because he undervalues the gifts which come from God, just as if he would take away the commodity of the power of vision, or hearing, or of seeing. Has then God given you eyes to no purpose? and to no purpose has he infused into them a spirit so strong and of such skilful contrivance as to reach a long way and to fashion the forms of things which are seen? What messenger is so swift and vigilant? And to no purpose has he made the interjacent atmosphere so efficacious and elastic that the vision penetrates through the atmosphere which is in a manner moved? And to no purpose has he made light, without the presence of which there would be no use in any other thing?

Man, be neither ungrateful for these gifts nor yet forget the things which are superior to them. But indeed for the power of seeing and hearing, and indeed for life itself, and for the things which contribute to support it, for the fruits which are dry, and for wine and oil give thanks to God: but remember that he has given you something else better than all these, I mean the power of using them, proving them, and estimating the value of each. For what is that which gives information about each of these powers, what each of them is worth? Is it each faculty itself? Did you ever hear the faculty of vision saying anything about itself? or the faculty of hearing? or wheat, or barley, or a horse, or a dog? No; but they are appointed as ministers and slaves to serve the faculty which has the power of making use of the appearances of things. And if you inquire what is the value of each thing, of whom do you inquire? who answers you? How then can any other faculty be more powerful than this, which uses the rest as ministers and itself proves each and pronounces about them? for which of them knows what itself is, and what is its own value? which of them knows when it ought to employ itself and when not? what faculty is it which opens and closes the eyes, and turns them away from objects to which it ought not to apply them and does apply them to other objects? Is it the faculty of vision? No, but it is the faculty of the will. What is that faculty which closes and opens the ears? what is that by which they are curious and inquisitive, or on the contrary unmoved by what is said? is it the faculty of hearing? It is no other than the faculty of the will. Will this faculty then, seeing that it is amidst all the other faculties which are blind and dumb and unable to see anything else except the very acts for which they are appointed in order to minister to this (faculty) and serve it, but this faculty alone sees sharp and sees what is the value of each of the rest; will this faculty declare to us that anything else is the best, or that itself is? And what else does the eye do when it is opened than see? But whether we ought to look on the wife of a certain person, and in what manner, who tells us? The faculty of the will. And whether we ought to believe what is said or not to believe it, and if we do believe, whether we ought to be moved by it or not, who tells us? Is it not the faculty of the will?

But if you ask me what then is the most excellent of all things, what must I say? I cannot say the power of speaking, but the power of the will, when it is right. For it is this which uses the other (the power of speaking), and all the other faculties both small and great. For when this faculty of the will is set right, a man who is not good becomes good: but when it fails, a man becomes bad. It is through this that we are unfortunate, that we are fortunate, that we blame one another, are pleased with one another. In a word, it is this which if we neglect it makes unhappiness, and if we carefully look after it, makes happiness.

What then is usually done? Men generally act as a traveller would do on his way to his own country, when he enters a good inn, and being pleased with it should remain there. Man, you have forgotten your purpose: you were not travelling to this inn, but you were passing through it. But this is a pleasant inn. And how many other inns are pleasant? and how many meadows are pleasant? yet only for passing through. But your purpose is this, to return to your country, to relieve your kinsmen of anxiety, to discharge the duties of a citizen, to marry, to beget children, to fill the usual magistracies. For you are not come to select more pleasant places, but to live in these where you were born and of which you were made a citizen. Something of the kind takes place in the matter which we are considering. Since by the aid of speech and such communication as you receive here you must advance to perfection, and purge your will and correct the faculty which makes use of the appearances of things; and since it is necessary also for the teaching (delivery) of theorems to be effected by a certain mode of expression and with a certain variety and sharpness, some persons captivated by these very things abide in them, one captivated by the expression, another by syllogisms, another again by sophisms, and still another by some other inn of the kind; and there they stay and waste away as they were among sirens.

Man, your purpose (business) was to make yourself capable of using conformably to nature the appearances presented to you, in your desires not to be frustrated, in your aversion from things not to fall into that which you would avoid, never to have no luck (as one may say), nor ever to have bad luck, to be free, not hindered, not compelled, conforming yourself to the administration of Zeus, obeying it, well satisfied with this, blaming no one, charging no one with fault, able from your whole soul to utter these verses:

Lead me, O Zeus, and thou too Destiny.

TO (OR AGAINST) A PERSON WHO WAS ONE OF THOSE WHO WERE NOT VALUED (ESTEEMED) BY HIM.

A certain person said to him (Epictetus): Frequently I desired to hear you and came to you, and you never gave me any answer; and now, if it is possible, I entreat you to say something to me. Do you think, said Epictetus, that as there is an art in anything else, so there is also an art in speaking, and that he who has the art, will speak skilfully, and he who has not, will speak unskilfully? I do think so. He then who by speaking receives benefit himself, and is able to benefit others, will speak skilfully; but he who is rather damaged by speaking and does damage to others, will he be unskilled in this art of speaking? And you may find that some are damaged and others benefited by speaking. And are all who hear benefited by what they hear? Or will you find that among them also some are benefited and some damaged? There are both among these also, he said. In this case also then those who hear skilfully are benefited, and those who hear unskilfully are damaged? He admitted this. Is there then a skill in hearing also, as there is in speaking? It seems so. If you choose, consider the matter in this way also. The practice of music, to whom does it belong? To a musician. And the proper making of a statue, to whom do you think that it belongs? To a statuary. And the looking at a statue skilfully, does this appear to you to require the aid of no art? This also requires the aid of art. Then if speaking properly is the business of the skilful man, do you see that to hear also with benefit is the business of the skilful man? Now as to speaking and hearing perfectly, and usefully, let us for the present, if you please, say no more, for both of us are a long way from everything of the kind. But I think that every man will allow this, that he who is going to hear philosophers requires some amount of practice in hearing. Is it not so?

Why then do you say nothing to me? I can only say this to you, that he who knows not who he is, and for what purpose he exists, and what is this world, and with whom he is associated, and what things are the good and the bad, and the beautiful and the ugly, and who neither understands discourse nor demonstration, nor what is true nor what is false, and who is not able to distinguish them, will neither desire according to nature nor turn away nor move towards, nor intend (to act), nor assent, nor dissent, nor suspend his judgment: to say all in a few words, he will go about dumb and blind, thinking that he is somebody, but being nobody. Is this so now for the first time? Is it not the fact that ever since the human race existed, all errors and misfortunes have arisen through this ignorance?

This is all that I have to say to you; and I say even this not willingly. Why? Because you have not roused me. For what must I look to in order to be roused, as men who are expert in riding are roused by generous horses? Must I look to your body? You treat it disgracefully. To your dress? That is luxurious. To your behavior, to your look? That is the same as nothing. When you would listen to a philosopher, do not say to him, You tell me nothing; but only show yourself worthy of hearing or fit for hearing; and you will see how you will move the speaker.

THAT LOGIC IS NECESSARY.

When one of those who were present said, Persuade me that logic is necessary, he replied, Do you wish me to prove this to you? The answer was, Yes. Then I must use a demonstrative form of speech. This was granted. How then will you know if I am cheating you by my argument? The man was silent. Do you see, said Epictetus, that you yourself are admitting that logic is necessary, if without it you cannot know so much as this, whether logic is necessary or not necessary?

OF FINERY IN DRESS.

A certain young man, a rhetorician, came to see Epictetus, with his hair dressed more carefully than was usual and his attire in an ornamental style; whereupon Epictetus said, Tell me if you do not think that some dogs are beautiful and some horses, and so of all other animals. I do think so, the youth replied. Are not then some men also beautiful and others ugly? Certainly. Do we then for the same reason call each of them in the same kind beautiful, or each beautiful for something peculiar? And you will judge of this matter thus. Since we see a dog naturally formed for one thing, and a horse for another, and for another still, as an example, a nightingale, we may generally and not improperly declare each of them to be beautiful then when it is most excellent according to its nature; but since the nature of each is different, each of them seems to me to be beautiful in a different way. Is it not so? He admitted that it was. That then which makes a dog beautiful, makes a horse ugly; and that which makes a horse beautiful, makes a dog ugly, if it is true that their natures are different. It seems to be so. For I think that what makes a Pancratiast beautiful, makes a wrestler to be not good, and a runner to be most ridiculous; and he who is beautiful for the Pentathlon, is very ugly for wrestling. It is so, said he. What then makes a man beautiful? Is it that which in its kind makes both a dog and a horse beautiful? It is, he said. What then makes a dog beautiful? The possession of the excellence of a dog. And what makes a horse beautiful? The possession of the excellence of a horse. What then makes a man beautiful? Is it not the possession of the excellence of a man? And do you then, if you wish to be beautiful, young man, labor at this, the acquisition of human excellence? But what is this? Observe whom you yourself praise, when you praise many persons without partiality: do you praise the just or the unjust? The just. Whether do you praise the moderate or the immoderate? The moderate. And the temperate or the intemperate? The temperate. If then you make yourself such a person, you will know that you will make yourself beautiful; but so long as you neglect these things, you must be ugly, even though you contrive all you can to appear beautiful.

IN WHAT A MAN OUGHT TO BE EXERCISED WHO HAS MADE PROFICIENCY; AND THAT WE NEGLECT THE CHIEF THINGS.

There are three things (topics) in which a man ought to exercise himself who would be wise and good. The first concerns the desires and the aversions, that a man may not fail to get what he desires, and that he may not fall into that which he does not desire. The second concerns the movements towards an object and the movements from an object, and generally in doing what a man ought to do, that he may act according to order, to reason, and not carelessly. The third thing concerns freedom from deception and rashness in judgment, and generally it concerns the assents. Of these topics the chief and the most urgent is that which relates to the affects (perturbations); for an affect is produced in no other way than by a failing to obtain that which a man desires or falling into that which a man would wish to avoid. This is that which brings in perturbations, disorders, bad fortune, misfortunes, sorrows, lamentations, and envy; that which makes men envious and jealous; and by these causes we are unable even to listen to the precepts of reason. The second topic concerns the duties of a man; for I ought not to be free from affects like a statue, but I ought to maintain the relations natural and acquired, as a pious man, as a son, as a father, as a citizen.

The third topic is that which immediately concerns those who are making proficiency, that which concerns the security of the other two, so that not even in sleep any appearance unexamined may surprise us, nor in intoxication, nor in melancholy. This, it may be said, is above our power. But the present philosophers neglecting the first topic and the second (the affects and duties), employ themselves on the third, using sophistical arguments, making conclusions from questioning, employing hypotheses, lying. For a man must, it is said, when employed on these matters, take care that he is not deceived. Who must? The wise and good man. This then is all that is wanting to you. Have you successfully worked out the rest? Are you free from deception in the matter of money? If you see a beautiful girl do you resist the appearance? If your neighbor obtains an estate by will, are you not vexed? Now is there nothing else wanting to you except unchangeable firmness of mind? Wretch, you hear these very things with fear and anxiety that some person may despise you, and with inquiries about what any person may say about you. And if a man come and tell you that in a certain conversation in which the question was, Who is the best philosopher, a man who was present said that a certain person was the chief philosopher, your little soul which was only a finger's length stretches out to two cubits. But if another who is present says, You are mistaken; it is not worth while to listen to a certain person, for what does he know? he has only the first principles, and no more? then you are confounded, you grow pale, you cry out immediately, I will show him who I am, that I am a great philosopher. It is seen by these very things: why do you wish to show it by others? Do you not know that Diogenes pointed out one of the sophists in this way by stretching out his middle finger? And then when the man was wild with rage, This, he said, is the certain person: I have pointed him out to you. For a man is not shown by the finger, as a stone or a piece of wood; but when any person shows the man's principles, then he shows him as a man.

Let us look at your principles also. For is it not plain that you value not at all your own will, but you look externally to things which are independent of your will? For instance, what will a certain person say? and what will people think of you? Will you be considered a man of learning; have you read Chrysippus or Antipater? for if you have read Archedamus also, you have every thing (that you can desire). Why you are still uneasy lest you should not show us who you are? Would you let me tell you what manner of man you have shown us that you are? You have exhibited yourself to us as a mean fellow, querulous, passionate, cowardly, finding fault with everything, blaming everybody, never quiet, vain: this is what you have exhibited to us. Go away now and read Archedamus; then if a mouse should leap down and make a noise, you are a dead man. For such a death awaits you as it didwhat was the man's nameCrinis; and he too was proud, because he understood Archedamus. Wretch, will you not dismiss these things that do not concern you at all? These things are suitable to those who are able to learn them without perturbation, to those who can say: "I am not subject to anger, to grief, to envy: I am not hindered, I am not restrained. What remains for me? I have leisure, I am tranquil: let us see how we must deal with sophistical arguments; let us see how when a man has accepted an hypothesis he shall not be led away to any thing absurd." To them such things belong. To those who are happy it is appropriate to light a fire, to dine; if they choose, both to sing and to dance. But when the vessel is sinking, you come to me and hoist the sails.

WHAT IS THE MATTER ON WHICH A GOOD MAN SHOULD BE EMPLOYED, AND IN WHAT WE OUGHT CHIEFLY TO PRACTISE OURSELVES.

The material for the wise and good man is his own ruling faculty: and the body is the material for the physician and the aliptes (the man who oils persons); the land is the matter for the husbandman. The business of the wise and good man is to use appearances conformably to nature: and as it is the nature of every soul to assent to the truth, to dissent from the false, and to remain in suspense as to that which is uncertain; so it is its nature to be moved towards the desire for the good, and to aversion from the evil; and with respect to that which is neither good nor bad it feels indifferent. For as the money-changer (banker) is not allowed to reject Cæsar's coin, nor the seller of herbs, but if you show the coin, whether he chooses or not, he must give up what is sold for the coin; so it is also in the matter of the soul. When the good appears, it immediately attracts to itself; the evil repels from itself. But the soul will never reject the manifest appearance of the good, any more than persons will reject Cæsar's coin. On this principle depends every movement both of man and God.

Against (or with respect to) this kind of thing chiefly a man should exercise himself. As soon as you go out in the morning, examine every man whom you see, every man whom you hear; answer as to a question, What have you seen? A handsome man or woman? Apply the rule. Is this independent of the will, or dependent? Independent. Take it away. What have you seen? A man lamenting over the death of a child. Apply the rule. Death is a thing independent of the will. Take it away. Has the proconsul met you? Apply the rule. What kind of a thing is a proconsul's office? Independent of the will or dependent on it? Independent. Take this away also; it does not stand examination; cast it away; it is nothing to you.

If we practised this and exercised ourselves in it daily from morning to night, something indeed would be done. But now we are forthwith caught half asleep by every appearance, and it is only, if ever, that in the school we are roused a little. Then when we go out, if we see a man lamenting, we say, He is undone. If we see a consul, we say, He is happy. If we see an exiled man, we say, He is miserable. If we see a poor man, we say, He is wretched; he has nothing to eat.

We ought then to eradicate these bad opinions, and to this end we should direct all our efforts. For what is weeping and lamenting? Opinion. What is bad fortune? Opinion. What is civil sedition, what is divided opinion, what is blame, what is accusation, what is impiety, what is trifling? All these things are opinions, and nothing more, and opinions about things independent of the will, as if they were good and bad. Let a man transfer these opinions to things dependent on the will, and I engage for him that he will be firm and constant, whatever may be the state of things around him. Such as is a dish of water, such is the soul. Such as is the ray of light which falls on the water, such are the appearances. When the water is moved, the ray also seems to be moved, yet it is not moved. And when then a man is seized with giddiness, it is not the arts and the virtues which are confounded, but the spirit (the nervous power) on which they are impressed; but if the spirit be restored to its settled state, those things also are restored.

MISCELLANEOUS.

When some person asked him how it happened that since reason has been more cultivated by the men of the present age, the progress made in former times was greater. In what respect, he answered, has it been more cultivated now, and in what respect was the progress greater then? For in that in which it has now been more cultivated, in that also the progress will now be found. At present it has been cultivated for the purpose of resolving syllogisms, and progress is made. But in former times it was cultivated for the purpose of maintaining the governing faculty in a condition conformable to nature, and progress was made. Do not then mix things which are different, and do not expect, when you are laboring at one thing to make progress in another. But see if any man among us when he is intent upon this, the keeping himself in a state conformable to nature and living so always, does not make progress. For you will not find such a man.

It is not easy to exhort weak young men; for neither is it easy to hold (soft) cheese with a hook. But those who have a good natural disposition, even if you try to turn them aside, cling still more to reason.

TO THE ADMINISTRATOR OF THE FREE CITIES WHO WAS AN EPICUREAN.

When the administrator came to visit him, and the man was an Epicurean, Epictetus said, It is proper for us who are not philosophers to inquire of you who are philosophers, as those who come to a strange city inquire of the citizens and those who are acquainted with it, what is the best thing in the world, in order that we also after inquiry may go in quest of that which is best and look at it, as strangers do with the things in cities. For that there are three things which relate to man—soul, body, and things external, scarcely any man denies. It remains for you philosophers to answer what is the best. What shall we say to men? Is the flesh the best? and was it for this that Maximus sailed as far as Cassiope in winter (or bad weather) with his son, and accompanied him that he might be gratified in the flesh? When the man said that it was not, and added, Far be that from him. Is it not fit then, Epictetus said, to be actively employed about the best? It is certainly of all things the most fit. What then do we possess which is better than the flesh? The soul, he replied. And the good things of the best, are they better, or the good things of the worse? The good things of the best. And are the good things of the best within the power of the will or not within the power of the will? They are within the power of the will. Is then the pleasure of the soul a thing within the power of the will? It is, he replied. And on what shall this pleasure depend? On itself? But that cannot be conceived; for there must first exist a certain substance or nature of good, by obtaining which we shall have pleasure in the soul. He assented to this also. On what then shall we depend for this pleasure of the soul? for if it shall depend on things of the soul, the substance (nature) of the good is discovered; for good cannot be one thing, and that at which we are rationally delighted another thing; nor if that which precedes is not good, can that which comes after be good, for in order that the thing which comes after may be good, that which precedes must be good. But you would not affirm this, if you are in your right mind, for you would then say what is inconsistent both with Epicurus and the rest of your doctrines. It remains then that the pleasure of the soul is in the pleasure from things of the body; and again that those bodily things must be the things which precede and the substance (nature) of the good.

Seek for doctrines which are consistent with what I say, and by making them your guide you will with pleasure abstain from things which have such persuasive power to lead us and overpower us. But if to the persuasive power of these things, we also devise such a philosophy as this which helps to push us on towards them and strengthens us to this end, what will be the consequence? In a piece of toreutic art which is the best part? the silver or the workmanship? The substance of the hand is the flesh; but the work of the hand is the principal part (that which precedes and leads the rest). The duties then are also three: those which are directed towards the existence of a thing; those which are directed towards its existence in a particular kind; and third, the chief or leading things themselves. So also in man we ought not to value the material, the poor flesh, but the principal (leading things). What are these? Engaging in public business, marrying, begetting children, venerating God, taking care of parents, and generally, having desires, aversions, pursuits of things and avoidances, in the way in which we ought to do these things, and according to our nature. And how are we constituted by nature? Free, noble, modest; for what other animal blushes? what other is capable of receiving the appearance (the impression) of shame? and we are so constituted by nature as to subject pleasure to these things, as a minister, a servant, in order that it may call forth our activity, in order that it may keep us constant in acts which are conformable to nature.

HOW WE MUST EXERCISE OURSELVES AGAINST APPEARANCES.

As we exercise ourselves against sophistical questions, so we ought to exercise ourselves daily against appearances; for these appearances also propose questions to us. A certain person's son is dead. Answer; the thing is not within the power of the will: it is not an evil. A father has disinherited a certain son. What do you think of it? It is a thing beyond the power of the will, not an evil. Cæsar has condemned a person. It is a thing beyond the power of the will, not an evil. The man is afflicted at this. Affliction is a thing which depends on the will: it is an evil. He has borne the condemnation bravely. That is a thing within the power of the will: it is a good. If we train ourselves in this manner, we shall make progress; for we shall never assent to anything of which there is not an appearance capable of being comprehended. Your son is dead. What has happened? Your son is dead. Nothing more? Nothing. Your ship is lost. What has happened? Your ship is lost. A man has been led to prison. What has happened? He has been led to prison. But that herein he has fared badly, every man adds from his own opinion. But Zeus, you say, does not do right in these matters. Why? because he has made you capable of endurance? because he has made you magnanimous? because he has taken from that which befalls you the power of being evils? because it is in your power to be happy while you are suffering what you suffer? because he has opened the door to you, when things do not please you? Man, go out and do not complain!

Hear how the Romans feel towards philosophers, if you would like to know. Italicus, who was the most in repute of the philosophers, once when I was present, being vexed with his own friends and as if he was suffering something intolerable, said: "I cannot bear it, you are killing me; you will make me such as that man is," pointing to me.

TO A CERTAIN RHETORICIAN WHO WAS GOING UP TO ROME ON A SUIT.

When a certain person came to him, who was going up to Rome on account of a suit which had regard to his rank, Epictetus inquired the reason of his going to Rome, and the man then asked what he thought about the matter. Epictetus replied: If you ask me what you will do in Rome, whether you will succeed or fail, I have no rule about this. But if you ask me how you will fare, I can tell you: if you have right opinions, you will fare well; if they are false, you will fare ill. For to every man the cause of his acting is opinion. For what is the reason why you desired to be elected governor of the Cnossians? Your opinion. What is the reason that you are now going up to Rome? Your opinion. And going in winter, and with danger and expense? I must go. What tells you this? Your opinion. Then if opinions are the causes of all actions, and a man has bad opinions, such as the cause may be, such also is the effect! Have we then all sound opinions, both you and your adversary? And how do you differ? But have you sounder opinions than your adversary? Why? You think so. And so does he think that his opinions are better; and so do madmen. This is a bad criterion. But show to me that you have made some inquiry into your opinions and have taken some pains about them. And as now you are sailing to Rome in order to become governor of the Cnossians, and you are not content to stay at home with the honors which you had, but you desire something greater and more conspicuous, so when did you ever make a voyage for the purpose of examining your own opinions, and casting them out, if you have any that are bad? Whom have you approached for this purpose? What time have you fixed for it? What age? Go over the times of your life by yourself, if you are ashamed of me (knowing the fact) when you were a boy, did you examine your own opinions? and did you not then, as you do all things now, do as you did do? and when you were become a youth and attended the rhetoricians, and yourself practised rhetoric, what did you imagine that you were deficient in? And when you were a young man and engaged in public matters, and pleaded causes yourself, and were gaining reputation, who then seemed your equal? And when would you have submitted to any man examining and showing that your opinions are bad? What then do you wish me to say to you? Help me in this matter. I have no theorem (rule) for this. Nor have you, if you came to me for this purpose, come to me as a philosopher, but as to a seller of vegetables or a shoemaker. For what purpose then have philosophers theorems? For this purpose, that whatever may happen, our ruling faculty may be and continue to be conformable to nature. Does this seem to you a small thing? No; but the greatest. What then? does it need only a short time? and is it possible to seize it as you pass by? If you can, seize it.

Then you will say, I met with Epictetus as I should meet with a stone or a statue: for you saw me and nothing more. But he meets with a man as a man, who learns his opinions, and in his turn shows his own. Learn my opinions: show me yours; and then say that you have visited me. Let us examine one another: if I have any bad opinion, take it away; if you have any, show it. This is the meaning of meeting with a philosopher. Not so (you say): but this is only a passing visit, and while we are hiring the vessel, we can also see Epictetus. Let us see what he says. Then you go away and say: Epictetus was nothing; he used solecisms and spoke in a barbarous way. For of what else do you come as judges? Well, but a man may say to me, if I attend to such matters (as you do), I shall have no land as you have none; I shall have no silver cups as you have none, nor fine beasts as you have none. In answer to tins it is perhaps sufficient to say: I have no need of such things; but if you possess many things you have need of others: whether you choose or not, you are poorer than I am. What then have I need of? Of that which you have not? of firmness, of a mind which is conformable to nature, of being free from perturbation.

IN WHAT MANNER WE OUGHT TO BEAR SICKNESS.

When the need of each opinion comes, we ought to have it in readiness: on the occasion of breakfast, such opinions as relate to breakfast; in the bath, those that concern the bath; in bed, those that concern bed.

> Let sleep not come upon thy languid eyes
> Before each daily action thou hast scann'd;
> What's done amiss, what done, what left undone;
> From first to last examine all, and then
> Blame what is wrong, in what is right rejoice.

And we ought to retain these verses in such way that we may use them, not that we may utter them aloud, as when we exclaim, "Paean Apollo." Again in fever we should have ready such opinions as concern a fever; and we ought not, as soon as the fever begins, to lose and forget all. A man who has a fever may say: If I philosophize any longer, may I be hanged: wherever I go, I must take care of the poor body, that a fever may not come. But what is philosophizing? Is it not a preparation against events which may happen? Do you not understand that you are saying something of this kind? "If I shall still prepare myself to bear with patience what happens, may I be hanged." But this is just as if a man after receiving blows should give up the Pancratium. In the Pancratium it is in our power to desist and not to receive blows.

But in the other matter if we give up philosophy, what shall we gain? What then should a man say on the occasion of each painful thing? It was for this that I exercised myself, for this I disciplined myself. God says to you: Give me a proof that you have duly practised athletics, that you have eaten what you ought, that you have been exercised, that you have obeyed the aliptes (the oiler and rubber). Then do you show yourself weak when the time for action comes? Now is the time for the fever. Let it be borne well. Now is the time for thirst, bear it well. Now is the time for hunger, bear it well. Is it not in your power? Who shall hinder you? The physician will hinder you from drinking; but he cannot prevent you from bearing thirst well: and he will hinder you from eating; but he cannot prevent you from bearing hunger well.

But I cannot attend to my philosophical studies. And for what purpose do you follow them? Slave, is it not that you may be happy, that you may be constant, is it not that you may be in a state conformable to nature and live so? What hinders you when you have a fever from having your ruling faculty conformable to nature? Here is the proof of the thing, here is the test of the philosopher. For this also is a part of life, like walking, like sailing, like journeying by land, so also is fever. Do you read when you are walking? No. Nor do you when you have a fever. But if you walk about well, you have all that belongs to a man who walks. If you bear a fever well, you have all that belongs to a man in a fever. What is it to bear a fever well? Not to blame God or man; not to be afflicted at that which happens, to expect death well and nobly, to do what must be done: when the physician comes in, not to be frightened at what he says; nor if he says you are doing well, to be overjoyed. For what good has he told you? and when you were in health, what good was that to you? And even if he says you are in a bad way, do not despond. For what is it to be ill? is it that you are near the severance of the soul and the body? what harm is there in this? If you are not near now, will you not afterwards be near? Is the world going to be turned upside down when you are dead? Why then do you flatter the physician? Why do you say if you please, master, I shall be well? Why do you give him an opportunity of raising his eyebrows (being proud; or showing his importance)? Do you not value a physician, as you do a shoemaker when he is measuring your foot, or a carpenter when he is building your house, and so treat the physician as to the body which is not yours, but by nature dead? He who has a fever has an opportunity of doing this: if he does these things, he has what belongs to him. For it is not the business of a philosopher to look after these externals, neither his wine nor his oil nor his poor body, but his own ruling power. But as to externals how must he act? so far as not to be careless about them. Where then is there reason for fear? where is there then still reason for anger, and of fear about what belongs to others, about things which are of no value? For we ought to have these two principles in readiness, that except the will nothing is good nor bad; and that we ought not to lead events, but to follow them. My brother ought not to have behaved thus to me. No, but he will see to that; and, however he may behave,

I will conduct myself towards him as I ought. For this is my own business; that belongs to another: no man can prevent this, the other thing can be hindered.

ABOUT EXERCISE.

We ought not to make our exercises consist in means contrary to nature and adapted to cause admiration, for if we do so, we who call ourselves philosophers, shall not differ at all from jugglers. For it is difficult even to walk on a rope; and not only difficult, but it is also dangerous. Ought we for this reason to practice walking on a rope, or setting up a palm-tree, or embracing statues? By no means. Every thing which is difficult and dangerous is not suitable for practice; but that is suitable which conduces to the working out of that which is proposed to us. And what is that which is proposed to us as a thing to be worked out? To live with desire and aversion (avoidance of certain things) free from restraint. And what is this? Neither to be disappointed in that which you desire, nor to fall into anything which you would avoid. Towards this object then exercise (practice) ought to tend. For since it is not possible to have your desire not disappointed and your aversion free from falling into that which you would avoid, without great and constant practice, you must know that if you allow your desire and aversion to turn to things which are not within the power of the will, you will neither have your desire capable of attaining your object, nor your aversion free from the power of avoiding that which you would avoid. And since strong habit leads (prevails), and we are accustomed to employ desire and aversion only to things which are not within the power of our will, we ought to oppose to this habit a contrary habit, and where there is great slipperiness in the appearances, there to oppose the habit of exercise. Then at last, if occasion presents itself, for the purpose of trying yourself at a proper time you will descend into the arena to know if appearances overpower you as they did formerly. But at first fly far from that which is stronger than yourself; the contest is unequal between a charming young girl and a beginner in philosophy. The earthen pitcher, as the saying is, and the rock do not agree.

WHAT SOLITUDE IS, AND WHAT KIND OF PERSON A SOLITARY MAN IS.

Solitude is a certain condition of a helpless man. For because a man is alone, he is not for that reason also solitary; just as though a man is among numbers, he is not therefore not solitary. When then we have lost either a brother, or a son, or a friend on whom we were accustomed to repose, we say that we are left solitary, though we are often in Rome, though such a crowd meet us, though so many live in the same place, and sometimes we have a great number of slaves.

For the man who is solitary, as it is conceived, is considered to be a helpless person and exposed to those who wish to harm him. For this reason when we travel, then especially do we say that we are lonely when we fall among robbers, for it is not the sight of a human creature which removes us from solitude, but the sight of one who is faithful and modest and helpful to us. For if being alone is enough to make solitude, you may say that even Zeus is solitary in the conflagration and bewails himself saying, Unhappy that I am who have neither Hera, nor Athena, nor Apollo, nor brother, nor son, nor descendant, nor kinsman. This is what some say that he does when he is alone at the conflagration. For they do not understand how a man passes his life when he is alone, because they set out from a certain natural principle, from the natural desire of community and mutual love and from the pleasure of conversation among men. But none the less a man ought to be prepared in a manner for this also (being alone), to be able to be sufficient for himself and to be his own companion. For as Zeus dwells with himself, and is tranquil by himself, and thinks of his own administration and of its nature, and is employed in thoughts suitable to himself; so ought we also to be able to talk with ourselves, not to feel the want of others also, not to be unprovided with the means of passing our time; to observe the divine administration, and the relation of ourselves to everything else; to consider how we formerly were affected towards things that happened and how at present; what are still the things which give us pain; how these also can be cured and how removed; if any things require improvement, to improve them according to reason.

Well then, if some man should come upon me when I am alone and murder me? Fool, not murder You, but your poor body.

What kind of solitude then remains? what want? why do we make ourselves worse than children; and what do children do when they are left alone? They take up shells and ashes, and they build something, then pull it down, and build something else, and so they never want the means of passing the time. Shall I then, if you sail away, sit down and weep, because I have been left alone and solitary? Shall I then have no shells, no ashes? But children do what they do through want of thought (or deficiency in knowledge), and we through knowledge are unhappy.

Every great power (faculty) is dangerous to beginners. You must then bear such things as you are able, but conformably to nature: but not... Practise sometimes a way of living like a person out of health that you may at some time live like a man in health.

CERTAIN MISCELLANEOUS MATTERS.

As bad tragic actors cannot sing alone, but in company with many, so some persons cannot walk about alone. Man, if you are anything, both walk alone and talk to yourself, and do not hide yourself in the chorus. Examine a little at last, look around, stir yourself up, that you may know who you are.

You must root out of men these two things, arrogance (pride) and distrust. Arrogance then is the opinion that you want nothing (are deficient in nothing); but distrust is the opinion that you cannot be happy when so many circumstances surround you. Arrogance is removed by confutation; and Socrates was the first who practised this. And (to know) that the thing is not impossible inquire and seek. This search will do you no harm; and in a manner this is philosophizing, to seek how it is possible to employ desire and aversion without impediment.

I am superior to you, for my father is a man of consular rank. Another says, I have been a tribune, but you have not. If we were horses, would you say, My father was swifter? I have much barley and fodder, or elegant neck ornaments. If then you were saying this, I said, Be it so: let us run then. Well, is there nothing in a man such as running in a horse, by which it will be known which is superior and inferior? Is there not modesty, fidelity, justice? Show yourself superior in these, that you may be superior as a man. If you tell me that you can kick violently, I also will say to you, that you are proud of that which is the act of an ass.

THAT WE OUGHT TO PROCEED WITH CIRCUMSPECTION TO EVERYTHING.

In every act consider what precedes and what follows, and then proceed to the act. If you do not consider, you will at first begin with spirit, since you have not thought at all of the things which follow; but afterwards when some consequences have shown themselves, you will basely desist (from that which you have begun).I wish to conquer at the Olympic games.(And I too, by the gods; for it is a fine thing.) But consider here what precedes and what follows; and then, if it is for your good, undertake the thing. You must act according to rules, follow strict diet, abstain from delicacies, exercise yourself by compulsion at fixed times, in heat, in cold; drink no cold water, nor wine, when there is opportunity of drinking it. In a word, you must surrender yourself to the trainer, as you do to a physician. Next in the contest, you must be covered with sand, sometimes dislocate a hand, sprain an ankle, swallow a quantity of dust, be scourged with the whip; and after undergoing all this, you must sometimes be conquered. After reckoning all these things, if you have still an inclination, go to the athletic practice. If you do not reckon them, observe you will behave like children who at one time play as wrestlers, then as gladiators, then blow a trumpet, then act a tragedy, when they have seen and admired such things. So you also do: you are at one time a wrestler (athlete), then a gladiator, then a philosopher, then a rhetorician; but with your whole soul you are nothing: like the ape you imitate all that you see; and always one thing after another pleases you, but that which becomes familiar displeases you. For you have never undertaken anything after consideration, nor after having explored the whole matter and put it to a strict examination; but you have undertaken it at hazard and with a cold desire. Thus some persons having seen a philosopher and having heard one speak like Euphratesand yet who can speak like him?wish to be philosophers themselves.

Man, consider first what the matter is (which you propose to do), then your own nature also, what it is able to bear. If you are a wrestler, look at your shoulders, your thighs, your loins: for different men are naturally formed for different things. Do you think that, if you do (what you are doing daily), you can be a philosopher? Do you think that you can eat as you do now, drink as you do now, and in the same way be angry and out of humor? You must watch, labor, conquer certain desires, you must depart from your kinsmen, be despised by your slaves, laughed at by those who meet you, in everything you must be in an inferior condition, as to magisterial office, in honors, in courts of justice. When you have considered all these things completely, then, if you think proper, approach to philosophy, if you would gain in exchange for these things freedom from perturbations, liberty, tranquillity. If you have not considered these things, do not approach philosophy: do not act like children, at one time a philosopher, then a tax collector, then a rhetorician, then a procurator (officer) of Cæsar. These things are not consistent. You must be one man either good or bad; you must either labor at your own ruling faculty or at external things; you must either labor at things within or at external things; that is, you must either occupy the place of a philosopher or that of one of the vulgar.

A person said to Rufus when Galba was murdered: Is the world now governed by Providence? But Rufus replied: Did I ever incidentally form an argument from Galba that the world is governed by Providence?

THAT WE OUGHT WITH CAUTION TO ENTER INTO FAMILIAR INTERCOURSE WITH MEN.

If a man has frequent intercourse with others either for talk, or drinking together, or generally for social purposes, he must either become like them, or change them to his own fashion. For if a man places a piece of quenched charcoal close to a piece that is burning, either the quenched charcoal will quench the other, or the burning charcoal will light that which is quenched. Since then the danger is so great, we must cautiously enter into such intimacies with those of the common sort, and remember that it is impossible that a man can keep company with one who is covered with soot without being partaker of the soot himself. For what will you do if a man speaks about gladiators, about horses, about athletes, or what is worse about men? Such a person is bad, such a person is good; this was well done, this was done badly. Further, if he scoff, or ridicule, or show an ill-natured disposition? Is any man among us prepared like a lute-player when he takes a lute, so that as soon as he has touched the strings, he discovers which are discordant, and tunes the instrument? Such a power as Socrates had who in all his social intercourse could lead his companions to his own purpose? How should you have this power? It is therefore a necessary consequence that you are carried about by the common kind of people.

Why then are they more powerful than you? Because they utter these useless words from their real opinions; but you utter your elegant words only from your lips; for this reason they are without strength and dead, and it is nauseous to listen to your exhortations and your miserable virtue, which is talked of everywhere (up and down). In this way the vulgar have the advantage over you; for every opinion is strong and invincible. Until then the good sentiments are fixed in you, and you shall have acquired a certain power for your security, I advise you to be careful in your association with common persons; if you are not, every day like wax in the sun there will be melted away whatever you inscribe on your minds in the school. Withdraw then yourselves far from the sun so long as you have these waxen sentiments. For this reason also philosophers advise men to leave their native country, because ancient habits distract them and do not allow a beginning to be made of a different habit; nor can we tolerate those who meet us and say: See such a one is now a philosopher, who was once so and so. Thus also physicians send those who have lingering diseases to a different country and a different air; and they do right. Do you also introduce other habits than those which you have; fix you opinions and exercise yourselves in them. But you do not so; you go hence to a spectacle, to a show of gladiators, to a place of exercise, to a circus; then you come back hither, and again from this place you go to those places, and still the same persons. And there is no pleasing (good) habit, nor attention, nor care about self and observation of this kind. How shall I use the appearances presented to me? according to nature, or contrary to nature? how do I answer to them? as I ought, or as I ought not? Do I say to those things which are independent of the will, that they do not concern me? For if you are not yet in this state, fly from your former habits, fly from the common sort, if you intend ever to begin to be something.

ON PROVIDENCE.

When you make any charge against Providence, consider, and you will learn that the thing has happened according to reason. Yes, but the unjust man has the advantage. In what? In money. Yes, for he is superior to you in this, that he flatters, is free from shame, and is watchful. What is the wonder? But see if he has the advantage over you in being faithful, in being modest; for you will not find it to be so; but wherein you are superior, there you will find that you have the advantage. And I once said to a man who was vexed because Philostorgus was fortunate: Would you choose to lie with Sura? May it never happen, he replied, that this day should come? Why then are you vexed, if he receives something in return for that which he sells; or how can you consider him happy who acquires those things by such means as you abominate; or what wrong does Providence, if he gives the better things to the better men? Is it not better to be modest than to be rich? He admitted this. Why are you vexed then, man, when you possess the better thing? Remember then always and have in readiness the truth, that this is a law of nature, that the superior has an advantage over the inferior in that in which he is superior; and you will never be vexed.

But my wife treats me badly. Well, if any man asks you what this is, say, my wife treats me badly. Is there then nothing more? Nothing. My father gives me nothing. (What is this? my father gives me nothing. Is there nothing else then? Nothing); but to say that this is an evil is something which must be added to it externally, and falsely added. For this reason we must not get rid of poverty, but of the opinion about poverty, and then we shall be happy.

ABOUT CYNICISM.

When one of his pupils inquired of Epictetus, and he was a person who appeared to be inclined to Cynicism, what kind of person a Cynic ought to be, and what was the notion of the thing, we will inquire, said Epictetus, at leisure; but I have so much to say to you that he who without God attempts so great a matter, is hateful to God, and has no other purpose than to act indecently in public.

In the first place, in the things which relate to yourself, you must not be in any respect like what you do now; you must not blame God or man; you must take away desire altogether, you must transfer avoidance only to the things which are within the power of the will; you must not feel anger nor resentment or envy nor pity; a girl must not appear handsome to you, nor must you love a little reputation, nor be pleased with a boy or a cake. For you ought to know that the rest of men throw walls around them and houses and darkness when they do any such things, and they have many means of concealment. A man shuts the door, he sets somebody before the chamber; if a person comes, say that he is out, he is not at leisure. But the Cynic instead of all these things must use modesty as his protection; if he does not, he will be indecent in his nakedness and under the open sky. This is his house, his door; this is the slave before his bedchamber; this is his darkness. For he ought not to wish to hide anything that he does; and if he does, he is gone, he has lost the character of a Cynic, of a man who lives under the open sky, of a free man; he has begun to fear some external thing, he has begun to have need of concealment, nor can he get concealment when he chooses. For where shall he hide himself and how? And if by chance this public instructor shall be detected, this pædagogue, what kind of things will he be compelled to suffer? when then a man fears these things, is it possible for him to be bold with his whole soul to superintend men? It cannot be: it is impossible.

In the first place then you must make your ruling faculty pure, and this mode of life also. Now (you should say), to me the matter to work on is my understanding, as wood is to the carpenter, as hides to the shoemaker; and my business is the right use of appearances. But the body is nothing to me: the parts of it are nothing to me. Death? Let it come when it chooses, either death of the whole or of a part. Fly, you say. And whither; can any man eject me out of the world? He cannot. But wherever I go, there is the sun, there is the moon, there are the stars, dreams, omens, and the conversation with gods.

Then, if he is thus prepared, the true Cynic cannot be satisfied with this; but he must know that he is sent a messenger from Zeus to men about good and bad things, to show them that they have wandered and are seeking the substance of good and evil where it is not, but where it is, they never think; and that he is a spy, as Diogenes was carried off to Philip after the battle of Chaeroneia as a spy. For in fact a Cynic is a spy of the things which are good for men and which are evil, and it is his duty to examine carefully and to come and report truly, and not to be struck with terror so as to point out as enemies those who are not enemies, nor in any other way to be perturbed by appearances nor confounded.

It is his duty then to be able with a loud voice, if the occasion should arise, and appearing on the tragic stage to say like Socrates: Men, whither are you hurrying, what are you doing, wretches? like blind people you are wandering up and down; you are going by another road, and have left the true road; you seek for prosperity and happiness where they are not, and if another shows you where they are, you do not believe him. Why do you seek it without? In the body? It is not there. If you doubt, look at Myro, look at Ophellius. In possessions? It is not there. But if you do not believe me, look at Croesus: look at those who are now rich, with what lamentations their life is filled. In power? It is not there. If it is, those must be happy who have been twice and thrice consuls; but they are not. Whom shall we believe in these matters? You who from without see their affairs and are dazzled by an appearance, or the men themselves? What do they say? Hear them when they groan, when they grieve, when on account of these very consulships and glory and splendor they think that they are more wretched and in greater danger. Is it in royal power? It is not: if it were, Nero would have been happy, and Sardanapalus. But neither was Agamemnon happy, though he was a better man than Sardanapalus and Nero; but while others are snoring, what is he doing?

> Much from his head he tore his rooted hair:
> Iliad, x., 15.

and what does he say himself?

> "I am perplexed," he says, "and
> Disturb'd I am," and "my heart out of my bosom
> Is leaping."
> Iliad, x., 91.

Wretch, which of your affairs goes badly? Your possessions? No. Your body? No. But you are rich in gold and copper. What then is the matter with you? That part of you, whatever it is, has been neglected by you and is corrupted, the part with which we desire, with which we avoid, with which we move towards and move from things. How neglected? He knows not the nature of good for which he is made by nature and the nature of evil; and what is his own, and what belongs to another; and when anything that belongs to others goes badly, he says, Woe to me, for the Hellenes are in danger. Wretched is his ruling faculty, and alone neglected and uncared for. The Hellenes are going to die destroyed by the Trojans. And if the Trojans do not kill them, will they not die? Yes; but not all at once. What difference then does it make? For if death is an evil, whether men die altogether, or if they die singly, it is equally an evil. Is anything else then going to happen than the separation of the soul and the body? Nothing. And if the Hellenes perish, is the door closed, and is it not in your power to die? It is. Why then do you lament (and say), Oh, you are a king and have the sceptre of Zeus? An unhappy king does not exist more than an unhappy god. What then art thou? In truth a shepherd: for you weep as shepherds do, when a wolf has carried off one of their sheep: and these who are governed by you are sheep. And why did you come hither? Was your desire in any danger? was your aversion? was your movement (pursuits)? was your avoidance of things? He replies, No; but the wife of my brother was carried off. Was it not then a great gain to be deprived of an adulterous wife? Shall we be despised then by the Trojans? What kind of people are the Trojans, wise or foolish? If they are wise, why do you fight with them? If they are fools, why do you care about them?

Do you possess the body then free or is it in servile condition? We do not know. Do you not know that it is the slave of fever, of gout, ophthalmia, dysentery, of a tyrant, of fire, of iron, of everything which is stronger? Yes, it is a slave. How then is it possible that anything which belongs to the body can be free from hindrance? and how is a thing great or valuable which is naturally dead, or earth, or mud? Well then, do you possess nothing which is free? Perhaps nothing. And who is able to compel you to assent to that which appears false? No man. And who can compel you not to assent to that which appears true? No man. By this then you see that there is something in you naturally free. But to desire or to be averse from, or to move towards an object or to move from it, or to prepare yourself, or to propose to do anything, which of you can do this, unless he has received an impression of the appearance of that which is profitable or a duty? No man. You have then in these things also something which is not hindered and is free. Wretched men, work out this, take care of this, seek for good here.

THAT WE OUGHT NOT TO BE MOVED BY A DESIRE OF THOSE THINGS WHICH ARE NOT IN OUR POWER.

Let not that which in another is contrary to nature be an evil to you; for you are not formed by nature to be depressed with others nor to be unhappy with others, but to be happy with them. If a man is unhappy, remember that his unhappiness is his own fault; for God has made all men to be happy, to be free from perturbations. For this purpose he has given means to them, some things to each person as his own, and other things not as his own; some things subject to hindrance and compulsion and deprivation; and these things are not a man's own; but the things which are not subject to hindrances, are his own; and the nature of good and evil, as it was fit to be done by him who takes care of us and protects us like a father, he has made our own. But you say, I have parted from a certain person, and he is grieved. Why did he consider as his own that which belongs to another? why, when he looked on you and was rejoiced, did he not also reckon that you are a mortal, that it is natural for you to part from him for a foreign country? Therefore he suffers the consequences of his own folly. But why do you or for what purpose bewail yourself? Is it that you also have not thought of these things? but like poor women who are good for nothing, you have enjoyed all things in which you took pleasure, as if you would always enjoy them, both places and men and conversation; and now you sit and weep because you do not see the same persons and do not live in the same places. Indeed you deserve this, to be more wretched than crows and ravens who have the power of flying where they please and changing their nests for others, and crossing the seas without lamenting or regretting their former condition. Yes, but this happens to them because they are irrational creatures. Was reason then given to us by the gods for the purpose of unhappiness and misery, that we may pass our lives in wretchedness and lamentation? Must all persons be immortal and must no man go abroad, and must we ourselves not go abroad, but remain rooted like plants; and if any of our familiar friends goes abroad, must we sit and weep; and on the contrary, when he returns, must we dance and clap our hands like children?

But my mother laments when she does not see me. Why has she not learned these principles? and I do not say this, that we should not take care that she may not lament, but I say that we ought not to desire in every way what is not our own. And the sorrow of another is another's sorrow; but my sorrow is my own.

I then will stop my own sorrow by every means, for it is in my power; and the sorrow of another I will endeavor to stop as far as I can; but I will not attempt to do it by every means; for if I do, I shall be fighting against God, I shall be opposing Zeus and shall be placing myself against him in the administration of the universe; and the reward (the punishment) of this fighting against God and of this disobedience not only will the children of my children pay, but I also shall myself, both by day and by night, startled by dreams, perturbed, trembling at every piece of news, and having my tranquillity depending on the letters of others. Some person has arrived from Rome. I only hope there is no harm. But what harm can happen to you, where you are not? From Hellas (Greece) some one is come; I hope that there is no harm. In this way every place may be the cause of misfortune to you. Is it not enough for you to be unfortunate there where you are, and must you be so even beyond sea, and by the report of letters? Is this the way in which your affairs are in a state of security? Well then suppose that my friends have died in the places which are far from me. What else have they suffered than that which is the condition of mortals? Or how are you desirous at the same time to live to old age, and at the same time not to see the death of any person whom you love? Know you not that in the course of a long time many and various kinds of things must happen; that a fever shall overpower one, a robber another, and a third a tyrant? Such is the condition of things around us, such are those who live with us in the world; cold and heat, and unsuitable ways of living, and journeys by land, and voyages by sea, and winds, and various circumstances which surround us, destroy one man, and banish another, and throw one upon an embassy and another into an army. Sit down then in a flutter at all these things, lamenting, unhappy, unfortunate, dependent on another, and dependent not on one or two, but on ten thousands upon ten thousands.

Did you hear this when you were with the philosophers? did you learn this? do you not know that human life is a warfare? that one man must keep watch, another must go out as a spy, and a third must fight? and it is not possible that all should be in one place, nor is it better that it should be so. But you neglecting to do the commands of the general complain when anything more hard than usual is imposed on you, and you do not observe what you make the army become as far as it is in your power; that if all imitate you, no man will dig a trench, no man will put a rampart round, nor keep watch, nor expose himself to danger, but will appear to be useless for the purposes of an army. Again, in a vessel if you go as a sailor, keep to one place and stick to it. And if you are ordered to climb the mast, refuse; if to run to the head of the ship, refuse; and what master of a ship will endure you? and will he not pitch you overboard as a useless thing, an impediment only and bad example to the other sailors? And so it is here also: every man's life is a kind of warfare, and it is long and diversified. You must observe the duty of a soldier and do every thing at the nod of the general; if it is possible, divining what his wishes are; for there is no resemblance between that general and this, neither in strength nor in superiority of character. Know you not that a good man does nothing for the sake of appearance, but for the sake of doing right? What advantage is it then to him to have done right? And what advantage is it to a man who writes the name of Dion to write it as he ought? The advantage is to have written it. Is there no reward then? Do you seek a reward for a good man greater than doing what is good and just? At Olympia you wish for nothing more, but it seems to you enough to be crowned at the games. Does it seem to you so small and worthless a thing to be good and happy? For these purposes being introduced by the gods into this city (the world), and it being now your duty to undertake the work of a man, do you still want nurses also and a mamma, and do foolish women by their weeping move you and make you effeminate? Will you thus never cease to be a foolish child? know you not that he who does the acts of a child, the older he is, the more ridiculous he is?

So in this matter also: if you kiss your own child, or your brother or friend, never give full license to the appearance, and allow not your pleasure to go as far as it chooses; but check it, and curb it as those who stand behind men in their triumphs and remind them that they are mortal. Do you also remind yourself in like manner, that he whom you love is mortal, and that what you love is nothing of your own; it has been given to you for the present, not that it should not be taken from you, nor has it been given to you for all time, but as a fig is given to you or a bunch of grapes at the appointed season of the year. But if you wish for these things in winter, you are a fool. So if you wish for your son or friend when it is not allowed to you, you must know that you are wishing for a fig in winter. For such as winter is to a fig, such is every event which happens from the universe to the things which are taken away according to its nature. And further, at the times when you are delighted with a thing, place before yourself the contrary appearances. What harm is it while you are kissing your child to say with a lisping voice: To-morrow you will die; and to a friend also: To-morrow you will go away or I shall, and never shall we see one another again? But these are words of bad omenand some incantations also are of bad omen; but because they are useful, I don't care for this; only let them be useful. But do you call things to be of bad omen except those which are significant of some evil? Cowardice is a word of bad omen, and meanness of spirit, and sorrow, and grief, and shamelessness. These words are of bad omen; and yet we ought not to hesitate to utter them in order to protect ourselves against the things. Do you tell me that a name which is significant of any natural thing is of evil omen? say that even for the ears of corn to be reaped is of bad omen, for it signifies the destruction of the ears, but not of the world. Say that the falling of the leaves also is of bad omen, and for the dried fig to take the place of the green fig, and for raisins to be made from the grapes. For all these things are changes from a former state into other states; not a destruction, but a certain fixed economy and administration. Such is going away from home and a small change: such is death, a greater change, not from the state which now is to that which is not, but to that which is not now. Shall I then no longer exist? You will not exist, but you will be something else, of which the world now has need; for you also came into existence not when you chose, but when the world had need of you.

Let these thoughts be ready to hand by night and by day; these you should write, these you should read; about these you should talk to yourself and to others. Ask a man: Can you help me at all for this purpose? and further, go to another and to another. Then if anything that is said be contrary to your wish, this reflection first will immediately relieve you, that it is not unexpected. For it is a great thing in all cases to say: I knew that I begot a son who is mortal. For so you also will say: I knew that I am mortal, I knew that I may leave my home, I knew that I may be ejected from it, I knew that I may be led to prison. Then if you turn round and look to yourself, and seek the place from which comes that which has happened, you will forthwith recollect that it comes from the place of things which are out of the power of the will, and of things which are not my own. What then is it to me? Then, you will ask, and this is the chief thing: And who is it that sent it? The leader, or the general, the state, the law of the state. Give it me then, for I must always obey the law in everything. Then, when the appearance (of things) pains you, for it is not in your power to prevent this, contend against it by the aid of reason, conquer it: do not allow it to gain strength nor to lead you to the consequences by raising images such as it pleases and as it pleases. If you be in Gyara, do not imagine the mode of living at Rome, and how many pleasures there were for him who lived there and how many there would be for him who returned to Rome; but fix your mind on this matter, how a man who lives in Gyara ought to live in Gyara like a man of courage. And if you be in Rome, do not imagine what the life in Athens is, but think only of the life in Rome.

Then in the place of all other delights substitute this, that of being conscious that you are obeying God, that not in word, but in deed you are performing the acts of a wise and good man. For what a thing it is for a man to be able to say to himself: Now whatever the rest may say in solemn manner in the schools and may be judged to be saying in a way contrary to common opinion (or in a strange way), this I am doing; and they are sitting and are discoursing of my virtues and inquiring about me and praising me; and of this Zeus has willed that I shall receive from myself a demonstration, and shall myself know if he has a soldier such as he ought to have, a citizen such as he ought to have, and if he has chosen to produce me to the rest of mankind as a witness of the things which are independent of the will: See that you fear without reason, that you foolishly desire what you do desire; seek not the good in things external; seek it in yourselves: if you do not, you will not find it. For this purpose he leads me at one time hither, at another time sends me thither, shows me to men as poor, without authority, and sick; sends me to Gyara, leads me into prison, not because he hates me far from him be such a meaning, for who hates the best of his servants? nor yet because he cares not for me, for he does not neglect any even of the smallest things; but he does this for the purpose of exercising me and making use of me as a witness to others. Being appointed to such a service, do I still care about the place in which I am, or with whom I am, or what men say about me? and do I not entirely direct my thoughts to God and to his instructions and commands?

Having these things (or thoughts) always in hand, and exercising them by yourself, and keeping them in readiness, you will never be in want of one to comfort you and strengthen you. For it is not shameful to be without something to eat, but not to have reason sufficient for keeping away fear and sorrow. But if once you have gained exemption from sorrow and fear, will there any longer be a tyrant for you, or a tyrant's guard, or attendants on Cæsar? Or shall any appointment to offices at court cause you pain, or shall those who sacrifice in the Capitol on the occasion of being named to certain functions, cause pain to you who have received so great authority from Zeus? Only do not make a proud display of it, nor boast of it; but show it by your acts; and if no man perceives it, be satisfied that you are yourself in a healthy state and happy.

TO THOSE WHO FALL OFF (DESIST) FROM THEIR PURPOSE.

Consider as to the things which you proposed to yourself at first, which you have secured, and which you have not; and how you are pleased when you recall to memory the one, and are pained about the other; and if it is possible, recover the things wherein you failed. For we must not shrink when we are engaged in the greatest combat, but we must even take blows. For the combat before us is not in wrestling and the Pancration, in which both the successful and the unsuccessful may have the greatest merit, or may have little, and in truth may be very fortunate or very unfortunate; but the combat is for good fortune and happiness themselves. Well then, even if we have renounced the contest in this matter (for good fortune and happiness), no man hinders us from renewing the combat again, and we are not compelled to wait for another four years that the games at Olympia may come again; but as soon as you have recovered and restored yourself, and employ the same zeal, you may renew the combat again; and if again you renounce it, you may again renew it; and if you once gain the victory, you are like him who has never renounced the combat. Only do not through a habit of doing the same thing (renouncing the combat), begin to do it with pleasure, and then like a bad athlete go about after being conquered in all the circuit of the games like quails who have run away.

TO THOSE WHO FEAR WANT.

Are you not ashamed at being more cowardly and more mean than fugitive slaves? How do they when they run away leave their masters? on what estates do they depend, and what domestics do they rely on? Do they not after stealing a little, which is enough for the first days, then afterwards move on through land or through sea, contriving one method after another for maintaining their lives? And what fugitive slave ever died of hunger? But you are afraid lest necessary things should fail you, and are sleepless by night. Wretch, are you so blind, and don't you see the road to which the want of necessaries leads?Well, where does it lead?to the same place to which a fever leads, or a stone that falls on you, to death. Have you not often said this yourself to your companions? have you not read much of this kind, and written much? and how often have you boasted that you were easy as to death?

Learn then first what are the things which are shameful, and then tell us that you are a philosopher: but at present do not, even if any other man calls you so, allow it.

Is that shameful to you which is not your own act, that of which you are not the cause, that which has come to you by accident, as a headache, as a fever? If your parents were poor, and left their property to others, and if while they live, they do not help you at all, is this shameful to you? Is this what you learned with the philosophers? Did you never hear that the thing which is shameful ought to be blamed, and that which is blamable is worthy of blame? Whom do you blame for an act which is not his own, which he did not do himself? Did you then make your father such as he is, or is it in your power to improve him? Is this power given to you? Well then, ought you to wish the things which are not given to you, or to be ashamed if you do not obtain them? And have you also been accustomed while you were studying philosophy to look to others and to hope for nothing from yourself? Lament then and groan and eat with fear that you may not have food to-morrow. Tremble about your poor slaves lest they steal, lest they run away, lest they die. So live, and continue to live, you who in name only have approached philosophy, and have disgraced its theorems as far as you can by showing them to be useless and unprofitable to those who take them up; you, who have never sought constancy, freedom from perturbation, and from passions; you who have not sought any person for the sake of this object, but many for the sake of syllogisms; you who have never thoroughly examined any of these appearances by yourself, Am I able to bear, or am I not able to bear? What remains for me to do? But as if all your affairs were well and secure, you have been resting on the third topic, that of things being unchanged, in order that you may possess unchangedwhat? cowardice, mean spirit, the admiration of the rich, desire without attaining any end, and avoidance which fails in the attempt? About security in these things you have been anxious.

Ought you not to have gained something in addition from reason, and then to have protected this with security? And whom did you ever see building a battlement all around and encircling it with a wall? And what doorkeeper is placed with no door to watch? But you practise in order to be able to provewhat? You practise that you may not be tossed as on the sea through sophisms, and tossed about from what? Show me first what you hold, what you measure, or what you weigh; and show me the scales or the medimnus (the measure); or how long will you go on measuring the dust? Ought you not to demonstrate those things which make men happy, which make things go on for them in the way as they wish, and why we ought to blame no man, accuse no man, and acquiesce in the administration of the universe?

ABOUT FREEDOM.

He is free who lives as he wishes to live; who is neither subject to compulsion nor to hindrance, nor to force; whose movements to action are not impeded, whose desires attain their purpose, and who does not fall into that which he would avoid. Who then chooses to live in error? No man. Who chooses to live deceived, liable to mistake, unjust, unrestrained, discontented, mean? No man. Not one then of the bad lives as he wishes; nor is he then free. And who chooses to live in sorrow, fear, envy, pity, desiring and failing in his desires, attempting to avoid something and falling into it? Not one. Do we then find any of the bad free from sorrow, free from fear, who does not fall into that which he would avoid, and does not obtain that which he wishes? Not one; nor then do we find any bad man free.

Further, then, answer me this question, also: does freedom seem to you to be something great and noble and valuable? How should it not seem so? Is it possible then when a man obtains anything so great and valuable and noble to be mean? It is not possible. When then you see any man subject to another or flattering him contrary to his own opinion, confidently affirm that this man also is not free; and not only if he do this for a bit of supper, but also if he does it for a government (province) or a consulship; and call these men little slaves who for the sake of little matters do these things, and those who do so for the sake of great things call great slaves, as they deserve to be. This is admitted also. Do you think that freedom is a thing independent and self-governing? Certainly. Whomsoever then it is in the power of another to hinder and compel, declare that he is not free. And do not look, I entreat you, after his grandfathers and great-grandfathers, or inquire about his being bought or sold, but if you hear him saying from his heart and with feeling, "Master," even if the twelve fasces precede him (as consul), call him a slave. And if you hear him say, "Wretch that I am, how much I suffer," call him a slave. If, finally, you see him lamenting, complaining, unhappy, call him a slave, though he wears a praetexta. If, then, he is doing nothing of this kind do not yet say that he is free, but learn his opinions, whether they are subject to compulsion, or may produce hindrance, or to bad fortune, and if you find him such, call him a slave who has a holiday in the Saturnalia; say that his master is from home; he will return soon, and you will know what he suffers.

What then is that which makes a man free from hindrance and makes him his own master? For wealth does not do it, nor consulship, nor provincial government, nor royal power; but something else must be discovered. What then is that which when we write makes us free from hindrance and unimpeded? The knowledge of the art of writing. What then is it in playing the lute? The science of playing the lute. Therefore in life also it is the science of life. You have then heard in a general way; but examine the thing also in the several parts. Is it possible that he who desires any of the things which depend on others can be free from hindrance? No. Is it possible for him to be unimpeded? No. Therefore he cannot be free. Consider then, whether we have nothing which is in our own power only, or whether we have all things, or whether some things are in our own power, and others in the power of others. What do you mean? When you wish the body to be entire (sound) is it in your power or not? It is not in my power. When you wish it to be healthy? Neither is this in my power. When you wish it to be handsome? Nor is this. Life or death? Neither is this in my power. Your body then is another's, subject to every man who is stronger than yourself. It is. But your estate is it in your power to have it when you please, and as long as you please, and such as you please? No. And your slaves? No. And your clothes? No. And your house? No. And your horses? Not one of these things. And if you wish by all means your children to live, or your wife, or your brother, or your friends, is it in your power? This also is not in my power.

Whether then have you nothing which is in your own power, which depends on yourself only and cannot be taken from you, or have you anything of the kind? I know not. Look at the thing then thus, and examine it. Is any man able to make you assent to that which is false? No man. In the matter of assent then you are free from hindrance and obstruction. Granted. Well; and can a man force you to desire to move towards that to which you do not choose? He can, for when he threatens me with death or bonds he compels me to desire to move towards it. If then you despise death and bonds, do you still pay any regard to him? No. Is then the despising of death an act of your own or is it not yours? It is my act.

When you have made this preparation, and have practised this discipline, to distinguish that which belongs to another from that which is your own, the things which are subject to hindrance from those which are not, to consider the things free from hindrance to concern yourself, and those which are not free not to concern yourself, to keep your desire steadily fixed to the things which do concern yourself, and turned from the things which do not concern yourself; do you still fear any man? No one. For about what will you be afraid? About the things which are your own, in which consists the nature of good and evil? and who has power over these things? who can take them away? who can impede them? No man can, no more than he can impede God. But will you be afraid about your body and your possessions, about things which are not yours, about things which in no way concern you? and what else have you been studying from the beginning than to distinguish between your own and not your own, the things which are in your power and not in your power, the things subject to hindrance and not subject? and why have you come to the philosophers? was it that you may nevertheless be unfortunate and unhappy? You will then in this way, as I have supposed you to have done, be without fear and disturbance. And what is grief to you? for fear comes from what you expect, but grief from that which is present. But what further will you desire? For of the things which are within the power of the will, as being good and present, you have a proper and regulated desire; but of the things which are not in the power of the will you do not desire any one, and so you do not allow any place to that which is irrational, and impatient, and above measure hasty.

Then after receiving everything from another and even yourself, are you angry and do you blame the giver if he takes anything from you? Who are you, and for what purpose did you come into the world? Did not he (God) introduce you here, did he not show you the light, did he not give you fellow-workers, and perceptions and reason? and as whom did he introduce you here? did he not introduce you as subject to death, and as one to live on the earth with a little flesh, and to observe his administration, and to join with him in the spectacle and the festival for a short time? Will you not then, as long as you have been permitted, after seeing the spectacle and the solemnity, when he leads you out, go with adoration of him and thanks for what you have heard and seen? No; but I would still enjoy the feast. The initiated too would wish to be longer in the initiation; and perhaps also those at Olympia to see other athletes. But the solemnity is ended; go away like a grateful and modest man; make room for others; others also must be born, as you were, and, being born, they must have a place, and houses, and necessary things. And if the first do not retire, what remains? Why are you insatiable? Why are you not content? why do you contract the world? Yes, but I would have my little children with me and my wife. What, are they yours? do they not belong to the giver, and to him who made you? then will you not give up what belongs to others? will you not give way to him who is superior? Why then did he introduce me into the world on these conditions? And if the conditions do not suit you, depart. He has no need of a spectator who is not satisfied. He wants those who join in the festival, those who take part in the chorus, that they may rather applaud, admire, and celebrate with hymns the solemnity. But those who can bear no trouble, and the cowardly, he will not unwillingly see absent from the great assembly for they did not when they were present behave as they ought to do at a festival nor fill up their place properly, but they lamented, found fault with the deity, fortune, their companions; not seeing both what they had, and their own powers, which they received for contrary purposes, the powers of magnanimity, of a generous mind, manly spirit, and what we are now inquiring about, freedom. For what purpose then have I received these things? To use them. How long? So long as he who has lent them chooses. What if they are necessary to me? Do not attach yourself to them and they will not be necessary; do not say to yourself that they are necessary, and then they are not necessary.

You then, a man may say, are you free? I wish, by the gods, and pray to be free; but I am not yet able to face my masters, I still value my poor body, I value greatly the preservation of it entire, though I do not possess it entire. But I can point out to you a free man, that you may no longer seek an example. Diogenes was free. How was he free? Not because he was born of free parents, but because he was himself free, because he had cast off all the handles of slavery, and it was not possible for any man to approach him, nor had any man the means of laying hold of him to enslave him. He had everything easily loosed, everything only hanging to him. If you laid hold of his property, he would have rather let it go and be yours, than he would have followed you for it; if you had laid hold of his leg, he would have let go his leg; if of all his body, all his poor body; his intimates, friends, country, just the same. For he knew from whence he had them, and from whom, and on what conditions. His true parents indeed, the gods, and his real country he would never have deserted, nor would he have yielded to any man in obedience to them and to their orders, nor would any man have died for his country more readily. For he was not used to inquire when he should be considered to have done anything on behalf of the whole of things (the universe, or all the world), but he remembered that everything which is done comes from thence and is done on behalf of that country and is commanded by him who administers it. Therefore see what Diogenes himself says and writes: "For this reason," he says, "Diogenes, it is in your power to speak both with the King of the Persians and with Archidamus the King of the Lacedaemonians, as you please." Was it because he was born of free parents? I suppose all the Athenians and all the Lacedaemonians, because they were born of slaves, could not talk with them (these kings) as they wished, but feared and paid court to them. Why then does he say that it is in his power? Because I do not consider the poor body to be my own, because I want nothing, because law is everything to me, and nothing else is. These were the things which permitted him to be free.

Think of these things, these opinions, these words; look to these examples, if you would be free, if you desire the thing according to its worth. And what is the wonder if you buy so great a thing at the price of things so many and so great? For the sake of this which is called liberty, some hang themselves, others throw themselves down precipices, and sometimes even whole cities have perished; and will you not for the sake of the true and unassailable and secure liberty give back to God when he demands them the things which he has given? Will you not, as Plato says, study not to die only, but also to endure torture, and exile, and scourging, and, in a word, to give up all which is not your own? If you will not, you will be a slave among slaves, even if you be ten thousand times a consul; and if you make your way up to the palace (Cæsar's residence), you will no less be a slave; and you will feel that perhaps philosophers utter words which are contrary to common opinion (paradoxes), as Cleanthes also said, but not words contrary to reason. For you will know by experience that the words are true, and that there is no profit from the things which are valued and eagerly sought to those who have obtained them; and to those who have not yet obtained them there is an imagination, that when these things are come, all that is good will come with them; then, when they are come, the feverish feeling is the same, the tossing to and fro is the same, the satiety, the desire of things, which are not present; for freedom is acquired not by the full possession of the things which are desired, but by removing the desire. And that you may know that this is true, as you have labored for those things, so transfer your labor to these: be vigilant for the purpose of acquiring an opinion which will make you free; pay court to a philosopher instead of to a rich old man; be seen about a philosopher's doors; you will not disgrace yourself by being seen; you will not go away empty nor without profit, if you go to the philosopher as you ought, and if not (if you do not succeed), try at least; the trial (attempt) is not disgraceful.

ON FAMILIAR INTIMACY.

To this matter before all you must attend, that you be never so closely connected with any of your former intimates or friends as to come down to the same acts as he does. If you do not observe this rule, you will ruin yourself. But if the thought arises in your mind, "I shall seem disobliging to him and he will not have the same feeling towards me," remember that nothing is done without cost, nor is it possible for a man if he does not do the same things to be the same man that he was. Choose then which of the two you will have, to be equally loved by those by whom you were formerly loved, being the same with your former self; or, being superior, not to obtain from your friends the same that you did before.

WHAT THINGS WE SHOULD EXCHANGE FOR OTHER THINGS.

Keep this thought in readiness, when you lose anything external, what you acquire in place of it; and if it be worth more, never say, I have had a loss; neither if you have got a horse in place of an ass, or an ox in place of a sheep, nor a good action in place of a bit of money, nor in place of idle talk such tranquillity as befits a man, nor in place of lewd talk if you have acquired modesty. If you remember this, you will always maintain your character such as it ought to be. But if you do not, consider that the times of opportunity are perishing, and that whatever pains you take about yourself, you are going to waste them all and overturn them. And it needs only a few things for the loss and overturning of allnamely, a small deviation from reason. For the steerer of a ship to upset it, he has no need of the same means as he has need of for saving it; but if he turns it a little to the wind, it is lost; and if he does not do this purposely, but has been neglecting his duty a little, the ship is lost. Something of the kind happens in this case also; if you only fall a nodding a little, all that you have up to this time collected is gone. Attend therefore to the appearances of things, and watch over them; for that which you have to preserve is no small matter, but it is modesty and fidelity and constancy, freedom from the affects, a state of mind undisturbed, freedom from fear, tranquillity, in a word liberty. For what will you sell these things? See what is the value of the things which you will obtain in exchange for these.But shall I not obtain any such thing for it?See, and if you do in return get that, see what you receive in place of it. I possess decency, he possesses a tribuneship: he possesses a prætorship, I possess modesty. But I do not make acclamations where it is not becoming: I will not stand up where I ought not; for I am free, and a friend of God. and so I obey him willingly. But I must not claim (seek) anything else, neither body nor possession, nor magistracy, nor good report, nor in fact anything. For he (God) does not allow me to claim (seek) them, for if he had chosen, he would have made them good for me; but he has not done so, and for this reason I cannot transgress his commands. Preserve that which is your own good in everything; and as to every other thing, as it is permitted, and so far as to behave consistently with reason in respect to them, content with this only. If you do not, you will be unfortunate, you will fail in all things, you will be hindered, you will be impeded. These are the laws which have been sent from thence (from God); these are the orders. Of these laws a man ought to be an expositor, to these he ought to submit, not to those of Masurius and Cassius.

TO THOSE WHO ARE DESIROUS OF PASSING LIFE IN TRANQUILLITY.

Remember that not only the desire of power and of riches makes us mean and subject to others, but even the desire of tranquillity, and of leisure, and of travelling abroad, and of learning. For, to speak plainly, whatever the external thing may be, the value which we set upon it places us in subjection to others. What then is the difference between desiring to be a senator or not desiring to be one; what is the difference between desiring power or being content with a private station; what is the difference between saying, I am unhappy, I have nothing to do, but I am bound to my books as a corpse; or saying, I am unhappy, I have no leisure for reading? For as salutations and power are things external and independent of the will, so is a book. For what purpose do you choose to read? Tell me. For if you only direct your purpose to being amused or learning something, you are a silly fellow and incapable of enduring labor. But if you refer reading to the proper end, what else is this than a tranquil and happy life? But if reading does not secure for you a happy and tranquil life, what is the use of it? But it does secure this, the man replies, and for this reason I am vexed that I am deprived of it.And what is this tranquil and happy life, which any man can impede, I do not say Cæsar or Cæsar's friend, but a crow, a piper, a fever, and thirty thousand other things? But a tranquil and happy life contains nothing so sure as continuity and freedom from obstacle. Now I am called to do something: I will go then with the purpose of observing the measures (rules) which I must keep, of acting with modesty, steadiness, without desire and aversion to things external; and then that I may attend to men, what they say, how they are moved; and this not with any bad disposition, or that I may have something to blame or to ridicule; but I turn to myself, and ask if I also commit the same faults. How then shall I cease to commit them? Formerly I also acted wrong, but now I do not: thanks to God.

What then is the reason of this? The reason is that we have never read for this purpose, we have never written for this purpose, so that we may in our actions use in a way conformable to nature the appearances presented to us; but we terminate in this, in learning what is said, and in being able to expound it to another, in resolving a syllogism, and in handling the hypothetical syllogism. For this reason where our study (purpose) is, there alone is the impediment. Would you have by all means the things which are not in your power? Be prevented then, be hindered, fail in your purpose. But if we read what is written about action (efforts), not that we may see what is said about action, but that we may act well; if we read what is said about desire and aversion (avoiding things), in order that we may neither fail in our desires, nor fall into that which we try to avoid; if we read what is said about duty (officium), in order that remembering the relations (of things to one another) we may do nothing irrationally nor contrary to these relations; we should not be vexed, in being hindered as to our readings, but we should be satisfied with doing the acts which are conformable (to the relations), and we should be reckoning not what so far we have been accustomed to reckon: To-day I have read so many verses, I have written so many; but (we should say), To-day I have employed my action as it is taught by the philosophers; I have not employed my desire; I have used avoidance only with respect to things which are within the power of my will; I have not been afraid of such a person, I have not been prevailed upon by the entreaties of another; I have exercised my patience, my abstinence, my co-operation with others; and so we should thank God for what we ought to thank him.

There is only one way to happiness, and let this rule be ready both in the morning and during the day and by night: the rule is not to look towards things which are out of the power of our will, to think that nothing is our own, to give up all things to the Divinity, to Fortune; to make them the superintendents of these things, whom Zeus also has made so; for a man to observe that only which is his own, that which cannot be hindered; and when we read, to refer our reading to this only, and our writing and our listening. For this reason I cannot call the man industrious, if I hear this only, that he reads and writes; and even if a man adds that he reads all night, I cannot say so, if he knows not to what he should refer his reading. For neither do you say that a man is industrious if he keeps awake for a girl, nor do I. But if he does it (reads and writes) for reputation, I say that he is a lover of reputation. And if he does it for money, I say that he is a lover of money, not a lover of labor; and if he does it through love of learning, I say that he is a lover of learning. But if he refers his labor to his own ruling power that he may keep it in a state conformable to nature and pass his life in that state, then only do I say that he is industrious. For never commend a man on account of these things which are common to all, but on account of his opinions (principles); for these are the things which belong to each man, which make his actions bad or good. Remembering these rules, rejoice in that which is present, and be content with the things which come in season. If you see anything which you have learned and inquired about occurring to you in your course of life (or opportunely applied by you to the acts of life), be delighted at it. If you have laid aside or have lessened bad disposition and a habit of reviling; if you have done so with rash temper, obscene words, hastiness, sluggishness; if you are not moved by what you formerly were, and not in the same way as you once were, you can celebrate a festival daily, to-day because you have behaved well in one act, and to-morrow because you have behaved well in another. How much greater is this a reason for making sacrifices than a consulship or the government of a province? These things come to you from yourself and from the gods. Remember this, who gives these things and to whom, and for what purpose. If you cherish yourself in these thoughts, do you still think that it makes any difference where you shall be happy, where you shall please God? Are not the gods equally distant from all places? Do they not see from all places alike that which is going on?

AGAINST THE QUARRELSOME AND FEROCIOUS.

The wise and good man neither himself fights with any person, nor does he allow another, so far as he can prevent it. And an example of this as well as of all other things is proposed to us in the life of Socrates, who not only himself on all occasions avoided fights (quarrels), but would not allow even others to quarrel. See in Xenophon's Symposium how many quarrels he settled, how further he endured Thrasymachus and Polus and Callicles; how he tolerated his wife, and how he tolerated his son who attempted to confute him and to cavil with him. For he remembered well that no man has in his power another man's ruling principle. He wished therefore for nothing else than that which was his own. And what is this? Not that this or that man may act according to nature, for that is a thing which belongs to another; but that while others are doing their own acts, as they choose, he may nevertheless be in a condition conformable to nature and live in it, only doing what is his own to the end that others also may be in a state conformable to nature. For this is the object always set before him by the wise and good man. Is it to be commander (a prætor) of an army? No; but if it is permitted him, his object is in this matter to maintain his own ruling principle. Is it to marry? No; but if marriage is allowed to him, in this matter his object is to maintain himself in a condition conformable to nature. But if he would have his son not to do wrong or his wife, he would have what belongs to another not to belong to another: and to be instructed is this, to learn what things are a man's own and what belongs to another.

How then is there left any place for fighting (quarrelling) to a man who has this opinion (which he ought to have)? Is he surprised at any thing which happens, and does it appear new to him? Does he not expect that which comes from the bad to be worse and more grievous than that what actually befalls him? And does he not reckon as pure gain whatever they (the bad) may do which falls short of extreme wickedness? Such a person has reviled you. Great thanks to him for not having struck you. But he has struck me also. Great thanks that he did not wound you. But he wounded me also. Great thanks that he did not kill you. For when did he learn or in what school that man is a tame animal, that men love one another, that an act of injustice is a great harm to him who does it. Since then he has not learned this and is not convinced of it, why shall he not follow that which seems to be for his own interest? Your neighbor has thrown stones. Have you then done anything wrong? But the things in the house have been broken. Are you then a utensil? No; but a free power of will. What then is given to you (to do) in answer to this? If you are like a wolf, you must bite in return, and throw more stones. But, if you consider what is proper for a man, examine your storehouse, see with what faculties you came into the world. Have you the disposition of a wild beast, have you the disposition of revenge for an injury? When is a horse wretched? When he is deprived of his natural faculties, not when he cannot crow like a cock, but when he cannot run. When is a dog wretched? Not when he cannot fly, but when he cannot track his game. Is then a man also unhappy in this way, not because he cannot strangle lions or embrace statues, for he did not come into the world in the possession of certain powers from nature for this purpose, but because he has lost his probity and his fidelity? People ought to meet and lament such a man for the misfortunes into which he has fallen; not indeed to lament because a man has been born or has died, but because it has happened to him in his lifetime to have lost the things which are his own, not that which he received from his father, not his land and house, and his inn, and his slaves; for not one of these things is a man's own, but all belong to others, are servile, and subject to account, at different times given to different persons by those who have them in their power: but I mean the things which belong to him as a man, the marks (stamps) in his mind with which he came into the world, such as we seek also on coins, and if we find them we approve of the coins, and if we do not find the marks we reject them. What is the stamp on this sestertius? The stamp of Trajan. Present it. It is the stamp of Nero. Throw it away; it cannot be accepted, it is counterfeit. So also in this case: What is the stamp of his opinions? It is gentleness, a sociable disposition, a tolerant temper, a disposition to mutual affections. Produce these qualities. I accept them: I consider this man a citizen, I accept him as a neighbor, a companion in my voyages. Only see that he has not Nero's stamp. Is he passionate, is he full of resentment, is he fault-finding? If the whim seizes him, does he break the heads of those who come in his way? (If so), why then did you say that he is a man? Is everything judged (determined) by the bare form? If that is so, say that the form in wax is an apple and has the smell and the taste of an apple. But the external figure is not enough: neither then is the nose enough and the eyes to make the man, but he must have the opinions of a man. Here is a man who does not listen to reason, who does not know when he is refuted: he is an ass; in another man the sense of shame is become dead: he is good for nothing, he is anything rather than a man. This man seeks whom he may meet and kick or bite, so that he is not even a sheep or an ass, but a kind of wild beast.

What then? would you have me to be despised?By whom? by those who know you? and how shall those who know you despise a man who is gentle and modest? Perhaps you mean by those who do not know you? What is that to you? For no other artisan cares for the opinion of those who know not his art. But they will be more hostile to me for this reason. Why do you say "me"? Can any man injure your will, or prevent you from using in a natural way the appearances which are presented to you? In no way can he. Why then are you still disturbed and why do you choose to show yourself afraid? And why do you not come forth and proclaim that you are at peace with all men whatever they may do, and laugh at those chiefly who think that they can harm you? These slaves, you can say, know not either who I am, nor where lies my good or my evil, because they have no access to the things which are mine.

In this way also those who occupy a strong city mock the besiegers (and say): What trouble these men are now taking for nothing; our wall is secure, we have food for a very long time, and all other resources. These are the things which make a city strong and impregnable; but nothing else than his opinions makes a man's soul impregnable. For what wall is so strong, or what body is so hard, or what possession is so safe, or what honor (rank, character) so free from assault (as a man's opinions)? All (other) things everywhere are perishable, easily taken by assault, and if any man in any way is attached to them, he must be disturbed, except what is bad, he must fear, lament, find his desires disappointed, and fall into things which he would avoid. Then do we not choose to make secure the only means of safety which are offered to us, and do we not choose to withdraw ourselves from that which is perishable and servile and to labor at the things which are imperishable and by nature free; and do we not remember that no man either hurts another or does good to another, but that a man's opinions about each thing, is that which hurts him, is that which overturns him; this is fighting, this is civil discord, this is war? That which made Eteocles and Polynices enemies was nothing else than this opinion which they had about royal power, their opinion about exile, that the one is the extreme of evils, the other the greatest good. Now this is the nature of every man to seek the good, to avoid the bad; to consider him who deprives us of the one and involves us in the other an enemy and treacherous, even if he be a brother, or a son, or a father. For nothing is more akin to us than the good; therefore, if these things (externals) are good and evil, neither is a father a friend to sons, nor a brother to a brother, but all the world is everywhere full of enemies, treacherous men, and sycophants. But if the will, the purpose, the intention) being what it ought to be, is the only good; and if the will being such as it ought not to be, is the only evil, where is there any strife, where is there reviling? about what? about the things which do not concern us? and strife with whom? with the ignorant, the unhappy, with those who are deceived about the chief things?

Remembering this Socrates managed his own house and endured a very ill-tempered wife and a foolish (ungrateful?) son.

AGAINST THOSE WHO LAMENT OVER BEING PITIED.

I am grieved, a man says, at being pitied. Whether then is the fact of your being pitied a thing which concerns you or those who pity you? Well, is it in your power to stop this pity? It is in my power, if I show them that I do not require pity. And whether then are you in the condition of not deserving (requiring) pity, or are you not in that condition? I think that I am not; but these persons do not pity me, for the things for which, if they ought to pity me, it would be proper, I mean, for my faults; but they pity me for my poverty, for not possessing honorable offices, for diseases and deaths and other such things. Whether then are you prepared to convince the many, that not one of these things is an evil, but that it is possible for a man who is poor and has no office and enjoys no honor to be happy; or to show yourself to them as rich and in power? For the second of these things belong to a man who is boastful, silly, and good for nothing. And consider by what means the pretence must be supported. It will be necessary for you to hire slaves and to possess a few silver vessels, and to exhibit them in public, if it is possible, though they are often the same, and to attempt to conceal the fact that they are the same, and to have splendid garments, and all other things for display, and to show that you are a man honored by the great, and to try to sup at their houses, or to be supposed to sup there, and as to your person to employ some mean arts, that you may appear to be more handsome and nobler than you are. These things you must contrive, if you choose to go by the second path in order not to be pitied. But the first way is both impracticable and long, to attempt the very thing which Zeus has not been able to do, to convince all men what things are good and bad. Is this power given to you? This only is given to you, to convince yourself; and you have not convinced yourself. Then I ask you, do you attempt to persuade other men? and who has lived so long with you as you with yourself? and who has so much power of convincing you as you have of convincing yourself; and who is better disposed and nearer to you than you are to yourself? How then have you not yet convinced yourself in order to learn? At present are not things upside down? Is this what you have been earnest about doing, to learn to be free from grief and free from disturbance, and not to be humbled (abject), and to be free? Have you not heard then that there is only one way which leads to this end, to give up (dismiss) the things which do not depend on the will, to withdraw from them, and to admit that they belong to others? For another man then to have an opinion about you, of what kind is it? It is a thing independent of the willThen is it nothing to you? It is nothing. When then you are still vexed at this and disturbed, do you think that you are convinced about good and evil?

ON FREEDOM FROM FEAR.

What makes the tyrant formidable? The guards, you say, and their swords, and the men of the bedchamber, and those who exclude them who would enter. Why then if you bring a boy (child) to the tyrant when he is with his guards, is he not afraid; or is it because the child does not understand these things? If then any man does understand what guards are and that they have swords, and comes to the tyrant for this very purpose because he wishes to die on account of some circumstance and seeks to die easily by the hand of another, is he afraid of the guards? No, for he wishes for the thing which makes the guards formidable. If then any man neither wishing to die nor to live by all means, but only as it may be permitted, approaches the tyrant what hinders him from approaching the tyrant without fear? Nothing. If then a man has the same opinion about his property as the man whom I have instanced has about his body; and also about his children and his wife, and in a word is so affected by some madness or despair that he cares not whether he possesses them or not, but like children who are playing with shells (quarrel) about the play, but do not trouble themselves about the shells, so he too has set no value on the materials (things), but values the pleasure that he has with them and the occupation, what tyrant is then formidable to him, or what guards or what swords?

What hinders a man, who has clearly separated (comprehended) these things, from living with a light heart and bearing easily the reins, quietly expecting everything which can happen, and enduring that which has already happened? Would you have me to bear poverty? Come and you will know what poverty is when it has found one who can act well the part of a poor man. Would you have me to possess power? Let me have power, and also the trouble of it. Well, banishment? Wherever I shall go, there it will be well with me; for here also where I am, it was not because of the place that it was well with me, but because of my opinions which I shall carry off with me, for neither can any man deprive me of them; but my opinions alone are mine and they cannot be taken from me, and I am satisfied while I have them, wherever I may be and whatever I am doing. But now it is time to die. Why do you say to die? Make no tragedy show of the thing, but speak of it as it is. It is now time for the matter (of the body) to be resolved into the things out of which it was composed. And what is the formidable thing here? what is going to perish of the things which are in the universe? what new thing or wondrous is going to happen? Is it for this reason that a tyrant is formidable? Is it for this reason that the guards appear to have swords which are large and sharp? Say this to others; but I have considered about all these things; no man has power over me. I have been made free; I know his commands, no man can now lead me as a slave. I have a proper person to assert my freedom; I have proper judges. (I say) are you not the master of my body? What then is that to me? Are you not the master of my property? What then is that to me? Are you not the master of my exile or of my chains? Well, from all these things and all the poor body itself I depart at your bidding, when you please. Make trial of your power, and you will know how far it reaches.

Whom then can I still fear? Those who are over the bedchamber? Lest they should do, what? Shut me out? If they find that I wish to enter, let them shut me out. Why then do you go to the doors? Because I think it befits me, while the play (sport) lasts, to join in it. How then are you not shut out? Because unless some one allows me to go in, I do not choose to go in, but am always content with that which happens; for I think that what God chooses is better than what I choose. I will attach myself as a minister and follower to him; I have the same movements (pursuits) as he has, I have the same desires; in a word, I have the same will. There is no shutting out for me, but for those who would force their way in. Why then do not I force my way in? Because I know that nothing good is distributed within to those who enter. But when I hear any man called fortunate because he is honored by Cæsar, I say what does he happen to get? A province (the government of a province). Does he also obtain an opinion such as he ought? The office of a Prefect. Does he also obtain the power of using his office well? Why do I still strive to enter (Cæsar's chamber)? A man scatters dried figs and nuts: the children seize them, and fight with one another; men do not, for they think them to be a small matter. But if a man should throw about shells, even the children do not seize them. Provinces are distributed: let children look to that. Money is distributed; let children look to that. Prætorships, consulships, are distributed; let children scramble for them, let them be shut out, beaten, kiss the hands of the giver, of the slaves: but to me these are only dried figs and nuts. What then? If you fail to get them, while Cæsar is scattering them about, do not be troubled; if a dried fig come into your lap, take it and eat it; for so far you may value even a fig. But if I shall stoop down and turn another over, or be turned over by another, and shall flatter those who have got into (Cæsar's) chamber, neither is a dried fig worth the trouble, nor anything else of the things which are not good, which the philosophers have persuaded me not to think good.

TO A PERSON WHO HAD BEEN CHANGED TO A CHARACTER OF SHAMELESSNESS.

When you see another man in the possession of power (magistracy), set against this the fact that you have not the want (desire) of power; when you see another rich, see what you possess in place of riches: for if you possess nothing in place of them, you are miserable; but if you have not the want of riches, know that you possess more than this man possesses and what is worth much more.

WHAT THINGS WE OUGHT TO DESPISE AND WHAT THINGS WE OUGHT TO VALUE.

The difficulties of all men are about external things, their helplessness is about external. What shall I do? how will it be? how will it turn out? will this happen? will that? All these are the words of those who are turning themselves to things which are not within the power of the will. For who says, How shall I not assent to that which is false? how shall I not turn away from the truth? If a man be of such a good disposition as to be anxious about these things I will remind him of this: Why are you anxious? The thing is in your own power, be assured; do not be precipitate in assenting before you apply the natural rule. On the other side, if a man is anxious (uneasy) about desire, lest it fail in its purpose and miss its end, and with respect to the avoidance of things, lest he should fall into that which he would avoid, I will first kiss (love) him, because he throws away the things about which others are in a flutter (others desire) and their fears, and employs his thoughts about his own affairs and his own condition. Then I shall say to him: If you do not choose to desire that which you will fail to obtain nor to attempt to avoid that into which you will fall, desire nothing which belongs to (which is in the power of) others, nor try to avoid any of the things which are not in your power. If you do not observe this rule, you must of necessity fail in your desires and fall into that which you would avoid. What is the difficulty here? where is there room for the words How will it be? and How will it turn out? and Will this happen or that?

Now is not that which will happen independent of the will? Yes. And the nature of good and of evil, is it not in the things which are within the power of the will? Yes. Is it in your power then to treat according to nature everything which happens? Can any person hinder you? No man. No longer then say to me, How will it be? For, however it may be, you will dispose of it well, and the result to you will be a fortunate one. What would Hercules have been if he said: How shall a great lion not appear to me, or a great boar, or savage men? And what do you care for that? If a great boar appear, you will fight a greater fight; if bad men appear, you will relieve the earth of the bad. Suppose then that I lose my life in this way. You will die a good man, doing a noble act. For since he must certainly die, of necessity a man must be found doing something, either following the employment of a husbandman, or digging, or trading, or serving in a consulship, or suffering from indigestion or from diarrhoea. What then do you wish to be doing when you are found by death? I, for my part, would wish to be found doing something which belongs to a man, beneficent, suitable to the general interest, noble. But if I cannot be found doing things so great, I would be found doing at least that which I cannot be hindered from doing, that which is permitted me to do, correcting myself, cultivating the faculty which makes use of appearances, laboring at freedom from the affects (laboring at tranquillity of mind); rendering to the relations of life their due. If I succeed so far, also (I would be found) touching on (advancing to) the third topic (or head) safety in forming judgments about things. If death surprises me when I am busy about these things, it is enough for me if I can stretch out my hands to God and say: The means which I have received from thee for seeing thy administration (of the world) and following it I have not neglected; I have not dishonored thee by my acts; see how I have used my perceptions, see how I have used my preconceptions; have I ever blamed thee? have I been discontented with anything that happens, or wished it to be otherwise? have I wished to transgress the (established) relations (of things)? That thou hast given me life, I thank thee for what thou hast given. So long as I have used the things which are thine I am content. Take them back and place them wherever thou mayest choose, for thine were all things, thou gavest them to me. Is it not enough to depart in this state of mind? and what life is better and more becoming than that of a man who is in this state of mind? and what end is more happy?

ABOUT PURITY (CLEANLINESS).

Some persons raise a question whether the social feeling is contained in the nature of man; and yet I think that these same persons would have no doubt that love of purity is certainly contained in it, and that if man is distinguished from other animals by anything, he is distinguished by this. When then we see any other animal cleaning itself, we are accustomed to speak of the act with surprise, and to add that the animal is acting like a man; and on the other hand, if a man blames an animal for being dirty, straightway, as if we were making an excuse for it, we say that of course the animal is not a human creature. So we suppose that there is something superior in man, and that we first receive it from the gods. For since the gods by their nature are pure and free from corruption, so far as men approach them by reason, so far do they cling to purity and to a love (habit) of purity. But since it is impossible that man's nature can be altogether pure, being mixed (composed) of such materials, reason is applied, as far as it is possible, and reason endeavors to make human nature love purity.

The first then and highest purity is that which is in the soul; and we say the same of impurity. Now you could not discover the impurity of the soul as you could discover that of the body; but as to the soul, what else could you find in it than that which makes it filthy in respect to the acts which are her own? Now the acts of the soul are movement towards an object or movement from it, desire, aversion, preparation, design (purpose), assent. What then is it which in these acts makes the soul filthy and impure? Nothing else than her own bad judgments. Consequently the impurity of the soul is the soul's bad opinions; and the purification of the soul is the planting in it of proper opinions; and the soul is pure which has proper opinions, for the soul alone in her own acts is free from perturbation and pollution.

For we ought not even by the appearance of the body to deter the multitude from philosophy; but as in other things, a philosopher should show himself cheerful and tranquil, so also he should in the things that relate to the body. See, ye men, that I have nothing, that I want nothing; see how I am without a house, and without a city, and an exile, if it happens to be so, and without a hearth I live more free from trouble and more happily than all of noble birth and than the rich. But look at my poor body also and observe that it is not injured by my hard way of living. But if a man says this to me, who has the appearance (dress) and face of a condemned man, what god shall persuade me to approach philosophy, if it makes men such persons? Far from it; I would not choose to do so, even if I were going to become a wise man. I indeed would rather that a young man, who is making his first movements towards philosophy, should come to me with his hair carefully trimmed than with it dirty and rough, for there is seen in him a certain notion (appearance) of beauty and a desire of (attempt at) that which is becoming; and where he supposes it to be, there also he strives that it shall be. It is only necessary to show him (what it is), and to say: Young man, you seek beauty, and you do well; you must know then that it (is produced) grows in that part of you where you have the rational faculty; seek it there where you have the movements towards and movements from things, where you have the desires towards and the aversion from things; for this is what you have in yourself of a superior kind; but the poor body is naturally only earth; why do you labor about it to no purpose? if you shall learn nothing else, you will learn from time that the body is nothing. But if a man comes to me daubed with filth, dirty, with a moustache down to his knees, what can I say to him, by what kind of resemblance can I lead him on? For about what has he busied himself which resembles beauty, that I may be able to change him and say, Beauty is not in this, but in that? Would you have me to tell him, that beauty consists not in being daubed with muck, but that it lies in the rational part? Has he any desire of beauty? has he any form of it in his mind? Go and talk to a hog, and tell him not to roll in the mud.

ON ATTENTION.

When you have remitted your attention for a short time, do not imagine this, that you will recover it when you choose; but let this thought be present to you, that in consequence of the fault committed today your affairs must be in a worse condition for all that follows. For first, and what causes most trouble, a habit of not attending is formed in you; then a habit of deferring your attention. And continually from time to time you drive away by deferring it the happiness of life, proper behavior, the being and living conformably to nature. If then the procrastination of attention is profitable, the complete omission of attention is more profitable; but if it is not profitable, why do you not maintain your attention constant? Today I choose to play. Well then, ought you not to play with attention? I choose to sing. What then hinders you from doing so with attention? Is there any part of life excepted, to which attention does not extend? For will you do it (anything in life) worse by using attention, and better by not attending at all? And what else of the things in life is done better by those who do not use attention? Does he who works in wood work better by not attending to it? Does the captain of a ship manage it better by not attending? and are any of the smaller acts done better by inattention? Do you not see that when you have let your mind loose, it is no longer in your power to recall it, either to propriety, or to modesty, or to moderation; but you do everything that comes into your mind in obedience to your inclinations.

First then we ought to have these (rules) in readiness, and to do nothing without them, and we ought to keep the soul directed to this mark, to pursue nothing external, and nothing which belongs to others (or is in the power of others), but to do as he has appointed who has the power; we ought to pursue altogether the things which are in the power of the will, and all other things as it is permitted. Next to this we ought to remember who we are, and what is our name, and to endeavor to direct our duties towards the character (nature) of our several relations (in life) in this manner: what is the season for singing, what is the season for play, and in whose presence; what will be the consequence of the act; whether our associates will despise us, whether we shall despise them; when to jeer, and whom to ridicule; and on what occasion to comply and with whom; and finally, in complying how to maintain our own character. But wherever you have deviated from any of these rules, there is damage immediately, not from anything external, but from the action itself.

What then? is it possible to be free from faults (if you do all this)? It is not possible; but this is possible, to direct your efforts incessantly to being faultless. For we must be content if by never remitting this attention we shall escape at least a few errors. But now when you have said, Tomorrow I will begin to attend, you must be told that you are saying this, Today I will be shameless, disregardful of time and place, mean; it will be in the power of others to give me pain; today I will be passionate and envious. See how many evil things you are permitting yourself to do. If it is good to use attention tomorrow, how much better is it to do so today? if tomorrow it is in your interest to attend, much more is it today, that you may be able to do so tomorrow also, and may not defer it again to the third day.

AGAINST OR TO THOSE WHO READILY TELL THEIR OWN AFFAIRS.

When a man has seemed to us to have talked with simplicity (candor) about his own affairs, how is it that at last we are ourselves also induced to discover to him our own secrets and we think this to be candid behavior? In the first place, because it seems unfair for a man to have listened to the affairs of his neighbor, and not to communicate to him also in turn our own affairs; next, because we think that we shall not present to them the appearance of candid men when we are silent about our own affairs. Indeed, men are often accustomed to say, I have told you all my affairs, will you tell me nothing of your own? where is this done? Besides, we have also this opinion that we can safely trust him who has already told us his own affairs; for the notion rises in our mind that this man could never divulge our affairs because he would be cautious that we also should not divulge his. In this way also the incautious are caught by the soldiers at Rome. A soldier sits by you in a common dress and begins to speak ill of Cæsar; then you, as if you had received a pledge of his fidelity by his having begun the abuse, utter yourself also what you think, and then you are carried off in chains.

Something of this kind happens to us also generally. Now as this man has confidently intrusted his affairs to me, shall I also do so to any man whom I meet? (No), for when I have heard, I keep silence, if I am of such a disposition; but he goes forth and tells all men what he has heard. Then, if I hear what has been done, if I be a man like him, I resolve to be revenged, I divulge what he has told me; I both disturb others, and am disturbed myself. But if I remember that one man does not injure another, and that every man's acts injure and profit him, I secure this, that I do not anything like him, but still I suffer what I do suffer through my own silly talk.

True, but it is unfair when you have heard the secrets of your neighbor for you in your turn to communicate nothing to him. Did I ask you for your secrets, my man? did you communicate your affairs on certain terms, that you should in return hear mine also? If you are a babbler and think that all who meet you are friends, do you wish me also to be like you? But why, if you did well in intrusting your affairs to me, and it is not well for me to intrust mine to you, do you wish me to be so rash? It is just the same as if I had a cask which is water-tight, and you one with a hole in it, and you should come and deposit with me your wine that I might put it into my cask, and then should complain that I also did not intrust my wine to you, for you have a cask with a hole in it. How then is there any equality here? You intrusted your affairs to a man who is faithful and modest, to a man who thinks that his own actions alone are injurious and (or) useful, and that nothing external is. Would you have me intrust mine to you, a man who has dishonored his own faculty of will, and who wishes to gain some small bit of money or some office or promotion in the court (emperor's palace), even if you should be going to murder your own children, like Medea? Where (in what) is this equality (fairness)? But show yourself to me to be faithful, modest, and steady; show me that you have friendly opinions; show that your cask has no hole in it; and you will see how I shall not wait for you to trust me with your own affairs, but I myself shall come to you and ask you to hear mine. For who does not choose to make use of a good vessel? Who does not value a benevolent and faithful adviser? Who will not willingly receive a man who is ready to bear a share, as we may say, of the difficulty of his circumstances, and by this very act to ease the burden, by taking a part of it.

Also from Benediction Books ...
Wandering Between Two Worlds: Essays on Faith and Art
Anita Mathias
Benediction Books, 2007
152 pages
ISBN: 0955373700

In these wide-ranging lyrical essays, Anita Mathias writes, in lush, lovely prose, of her naughty Catholic childhood in Jamshedpur, India; her large, eccentric family in Mangalore, a sea-coast town converted by the Portuguese in the sixteenth century; her rebellion and atheism as a teenager in her Himalayan boarding school, run by German missionary nuns, St. Mary's Convent, Nainital; and her abrupt religious conversion after which she entered Mother Teresa's convent in Calcutta as a novice. Later rich, elegant essays explore the dualities of her life as a writer, mother, and Christian in the United States-- Domesticity and Art, Writing and Prayer, and the experience of being "an alien and stranger" as an immigrant in America, sensing the need for roots.

The Story of Dirk Willems: The Man who Died to Save his Enemy
Anita Mathias
Benediction Classics, 2019
18 pages, Full colour.
ISBN: 9781789430448

The religious wars of the Reformation had heroes and villains. There were giants like Luther and Calvin, and quieter unsung heroes. Five hundred years later, one of these stands out: the Dutch Anabaptist, Dirk Willems, who sacrificed his life to save his enemy.

The Meek Shall Inherit The Earth
Anita Mathias
Benediction Books, 2013
38 pages
ISBN: 9781781393956

"Blessed are the meek, for they shall inherit the earth," Jesus says in his most puzzling Beatitude. Puzzling, because, if we are honest, it does not feel true to our experience. So do the meek inherit the earth? Is this true? Or isn't it? In The Meek Shall Inherit the Earth, an extended meditation on the power of gentleness, Anita Mathias grapples with this mystifying Beatitude.

Francesco, Artist of Florence: The Man Who Gave Too Much
Anita Mathias
Benediction Books, 2014
52 pages (full colour)
ISBN: 978-1781394175

In this lavishly illustrated book by Anita Mathias, Francesco, artist of Florence, creates magic in pietre dure, inlaying precious stones in marble in life-like "paintings." While he works, placing lapis lazuli birds on clocks, and jade dragonflies on vases, he is purely happy. However, he must sell his art to support his family. Francesco, who is incorrigibly soft-hearted, cannot stand up to his haggling customers. He ends up almost giving away an exquisite jewellery box to Signora Farnese's bambina, who stands, captivated, gazing at a jade parrot nibbling a cherry. Signora Stallardi uses her daughter's wedding to cajole him into discounting his rainbowed marriage chest. His old friend Girolamo bullies him into letting him have the opulent table he hoped to sell to the Medici almost at cost. Carrara is raising the price of marble; the price of gems keeps rising. His wife is in despair. Francesco fears ruin.

* * *

Sitting in the church of Santa Maria Novella at Mass, very worried, Francesco hears the words of Christ. The lilies of the field and the birds of the air do not worry, yet their Heavenly Father looks after them. As He will look after us. He resolves not to worry. And as he repeats the prayer the Saviour taught us, Francesco resolves to forgive the friends and neighbours who repeatedly put their own interests above his. But can he forgive himself for his own weakness, as he waits for the eternal city of gold whose walls are made of jasper, whose gates are made of pearls, and whose foundations are sapphire, emerald, ruby and amethyst? There time and money shall be no more, the lion shall live with the lamb, and we shall dwell trustfully together. Francesco leaves Santa Maria Novella, resolving to trust the One who told him to live like the lilies and the birds, deciding to forgive those who haggled him into bad bargains--while making a little resolution for the future.

About the Author

Anita Mathias is the author of *Wandering Between Two Worlds: Essays on Faith and Art*. She has a B.A. and M.A. in English from Somerville College, Oxford University, and an M.A. in Creative Writing from the Ohio State University, USA. Anita won a National Endowment of the Arts fellowship in Creative Nonfiction in 1997. She lives in Oxford, England with her husband, Roy, and her daughters, Zoe and Irene.

Visit Anita at http://www.anitamathias.com.

www.ingramcontent.com/pod-product-compliance
Lightning Source LLC
Chambersburg PA
CBHW030103070426
42448CB00037B/900